The International Politics of
Sport in the Twentieth Century

The International Politics of Sport in the Twentieth Century

Edited by
James Riordan and Arnd Krüger

E & FN SPON
ALERE FLAMMAM
Taylor & Francis Group

London and New York

This edition published 1999
by E & FN Spon, an imprint of the Taylor & Francis Group
11 New Fetter Lane, London EC4P 4EE

Simultaneously published in the USA and Canada
by Routledge
29 West 35th Street, New York, NY 10001

Typeset in TimesTen by The Florence Group, Stoodleigh, Devon, UK

Printed and bound in Great Britain by
MPG Books Ltd, Bodmin

British Library Cataloguing in Publication Data
A catalogue record for this book is available from the British Library

Library of Congress Cataloguing in Publication Data
The international politics of sport in the 20th century / [edited by]
  Jim Riordan and Arnd Krüger.
       p.   cm.
  Includes bibliographical references and index.
  ISBN 0–419–21160–8
    1. Sports – Political aspects – History – 20th century. 2. Sport and
state – History – 20th century. 3. Sports – Social aspects –
– History – 20th century. I. Riordan, James, 1936–   . II. Krüger,
Arnd.
GV706.35.I57   1999
796'.09'04–dc21   98–41234
                                                                   CIP

ISBN 0 419 21160 8

Contents

List of illustrations

Tables

Figure

Contributors

Gudrun Doll-Tepper is Professor of Sport for the Handicapped at the Institut für Sportwissenschaften, Free University of Berlin, Schwendenstrasse, 8, 14195 Berlin, Germany.

Othello Harris is Associate Professor in Black World Studies in the Department of Physical Education, Health and Sport Studies, Miama University, Oxford, Ohio 45056, USA.

Grant Jarvie is Chair of Sports Studies at the University of Stirling, Stirling FK9 4LA, Scotland.

Arnd Krüger is Head of the Institut für Sportwissenschaften, the Georg-August University, 3400 Göttingen, Germany.

Annette Müller is a doctoral student at the above Institute.

Bill Murray is Professor of History in the Faculty of Humanities, La Trobe University, Bundoora, Victoria, Australia 3083.

Irene Reid is Lecturer in Sports Studies at the University of Stirling, Stirling FK9 4LA, Scotland.

James Riordan is Chair of Russian Studies in the School of Language and International Studies, University of Surrey, Guildford GU2 5XH, England.

Swantje Scharenberg is Assistant Professor at the Institut für Sportwissenschaften, Georg-August University, 3400 Göttingen, Germany.

Bernd Wedemeyer is Professor of Sports History at the Lower Saxony Institute for the History of Sport, Hoya, Germany.

Introduction

Modern sport entered the twentieth century largely as the private fiefdom of the new social strata born of industrialization and urbanization. It was a social innovation, confined to national boundaries, that had its roots in the emergence of new forms of sociability. Engendered thus by private initiative, the new sports associations and clubs pursued goals that were essentially commercial and hedonistic. What is more, for the most part they excluded women, labourers and certain ethnic minorities.

What was interesting about these early sports developments is that in all European countries and the USA, the state displayed a total lack of interest in the new movement. Modern sport in its institutionalized and competitive forms (the setting up of national and international federations, the organization of international competition between national teams, the re-invention of the Olympic Games) barely permits one to envisage its immediate utilization for political ends.

The defenders and promoters of sport could hardly have imagined, at the turn of the century, that sports competition would have an impact on public opinion and become an instrument of international policy. Sport, *sportsmen*, sports associations and clubs were never seen as potential actors in social and cultural life, in politics and economics.

That was not the case with gymnastics, physical and military training. Gymnastics societies, for example, were the pedagogical and political instruments for building a national identity. To learn to put one's body at the service of one's country stems from a strategy of acculturation of the common people in the same way as was the learning of language and national culture.

After World War I, however, all this began to change. Particularly in Europe, there was an extraordinary upsurge in the sports phenomenon and, more especially, a constant rise in the number of international tournaments. Universalization of sport is the remarkable feature of the post-1918 world. This was a new situation in its sheer magnitude and in its impact on the public. Sport and sporting spectacle became a near-universal phenomenon to which the press, both general and specialized, contributed powerfully to expand.

What happened next was to change the face of sport: the coming to power of authoritarian regimes (communism from 1917, fascism from 1922, Nazism from 1933, Francoism from 1936) that put the role of sport near the top of the political agenda; it also put the international sports movement on the horns of a dilemma: to play or not to play with such regimes.

While from the 1920s sport was winning a national and international audience, the relationship between sports and geopolitical events was posing an autonomy problem for the national and international sports movement, for its capacity to override petty prejudices and divergent ideologies.

This growing internationalization and politicization of sport inevitably drew in broader issues, like religion, social class, women and race. Sometimes this engendered a split in the movement, with various groups playing among themselves and developing new sporting values – and sometimes modes of playing suited to themselves (British games exported to the colonies, like cricket in the West Indies; worker non-competitive sports; specifically female sports and competitions).

As the century progressed, there was also a growing tension, especially in Europe, between amateur-élitist sport for rich, privileged males and commercial spectator sport for the mainly middle classes, with the latter finally winning out.

After World War II, sport took an increasingly political stance, not only with the Cold War rivalry between capitalist and communist states, using sporting victories as evidence of political superiority, but also with previously underprivileged and persecuted groups gaining support for attention and even integration – blacks, women, the disabled, the gay community.

This book puts these processes into their historical context, thereby providing an extensive description and analysis of sport in the twentieth century. The contributors are ten sports scholars, four women and six men, from five countries of Europe, the USA and Australia. They each examine an important element of contemporary sport.

Part I deals with global issues, starting with two of the century's major sports institutions: the Olympic Games and the International Football Federation. There follow two more chapters on the impact on sport of totalitarian philosophies which dominated much of the century: communism (1971–91) and fascism (1922–45). The final two chapters of Part I focus mainly on the first part of the century when the role of religion and the worker sports movement had significant effects on sport.

Part II covers more specific issues in regard to sport: the struggle of black athletes for recognition in the USA and the part played by sport in the racist apartheid regime of South Africa; the rise of women's sport against considerable male prejudice and the debate within the women's movement; the fight for rights by the handicapped and gay athletes in sport; and the often little-known relationship between sport and terrorism.

The book aims to provide as full a picture as possible of the major issues and institutions shaping sport in the twentieth century.

Part I

1 The unfinished symphony

A history of the Olympic Games from Coubertin to Samaranch

Arnd Krüger

Introduction

The story begins with Charles Darwin (1809–82) whose *Origin of the Species* led to the idea that a nation's vitality depends on its physical characteristics and that these can be improved through training or breeding, as with horses. After the Franco-German War of 1870–1 in which France had lost its eastern provinces to Germany and which had brought German unification as an empire under a Prussian Kaiser, France fell back on its culture, its technical ingenuity, and – if men like Coubertin had their way – ultimately its physical training.

French culture was blooming. Artists like Auguste Renoir, Edgar Degas, Edouard Manet, Paul Cézanne, Claude Monet and others were dominating the salons of Paris and attracted devotees from all over the world. French ingenuity was at its best. Architects like Alexandre-Gustave Eiffel (1832–1923) created gigantic monuments such as the Eiffel Tower in Paris. While England still had the red flag law (until 1896) prohibiting a motor car from going any faster than a man could walk ahead with a red flag by day, or a red lantern at night to warn pedestrians and horseback riders, France had the first real automobile race (1894), the largest automobile production and the fastest racing cars anywhere in the world by the turn of the century, and was dreaming of technical domination of the world.

In this spirit of French domination of the technical, artistic and intellectual worlds, while at the same time being humiliated in the physical and sporting world, young Pierre de Coubertin (1860–1937) was sent to England to study English physical education to see what could be transferred to France, so that *la grande nation* could catch up with the British, have a share in the world yet to be conquered, and eventually get Alsace-Lorraine back from Germany. Coubertin returned from England a fan of the British public school and its sports and henceforth started to work to *rebronzer la France.*

The Olympic Games of antiquity (776 BC–AD 393) were a motor for Greek physical education; they strengthened the cultural bond among Greeks and symbolized the unity of the civilized world – in spite of all the political differences. Ever since the Olympic Games had been outlawed by the Christian Roman Emperor Theodosius because of the underlying pagan cult, there had been over forty known attempts to revive them (Lennartz 1974). Coubertin knew of three and soon would learn of a fourth. The 'Olympick' Games of Robert Dover, a contemporary of William Shakespeare, were well remembered for their strength in combining nobility and ordinary people in open competition in Worcestershire (Rühl 1975). Penny Brookes in Much Wenlock (Shropshire) had staged Olympic Games on a regional scale since 1866 (Rühl 1991). In 1891 the Australian John Astley Cooper asked to have sports competitions included in the Empire Exhibitions to demonstrate the unity of the British Empire (Krüger 1986; Moore 1991). The idea was much discussed in the press. The Oxford historian Anthony Froude recommended in a letter to *The Times* that this should not just be a periodic Pan-Britannic Festival, but the Pan-Britannic Olympic Games held every four years. Now the idea took off. There were John Astley Cooper committees in Australia, New Zealand and South Africa, all desiring to take part in these games. But Astley Cooper was no sportsman and the sports associations were reluctant to have such an enterprise that left many questions open.

Not so the young enthusiastic Coubertin. As secretary of the French Athletics Federation and manager of a Paris sports club he had realized how difficult it was to compete in England under English rules. He had been to Henley to have his French amateurs compete in the famous regatta and the amateur status of many of his French athletes had been questioned – although they were amateurs under French rules – and they had been sent home. In the case of Olympic Games around Henley, as had been proposed by Astley Cooper, his French athletes could never compete in these games, although the French considered themselves as much heirs to the classical Greek culture as anybody else.

In November 1892, Coubertin therefore started a test to see whether a proposal to have international Olympic Games, instead of just British, would be accepted – and there was much enthusiasm for the idea in general. In June of 1894 he called for an international conference at the Sorbonne in Paris to define internationally the amateur rules and start the Olympic Games. Coubertin had planned to begin with them in the year 1900 in Paris as part of the World Fair – the one for which the Eiffel Tower was built. But the energetic Frenchman learned that there were other Olympic traditions he had ignored. Evangelis Zappas had staged national Olympic Games in Athens since 1859. The Greeks had come to Paris to claim the international Olympic Games as theirs. These international games should come to Athens and stay there. A compromise was reached: the first Olympic Games should be in Athens in 1896 and the second in Paris in 1900, respecting the four year cycle, but giving the Greeks relatively little time to prepare. It was also agreed that the Greek literary historian Vikelas should be the first president of the International

Olympic Committee (IOC) and Coubertin the secretary-general (Krüger 1980). The presidents of the IOC are shown in Table 1.1.

Coubertin and the formative years of the IOC

For Coubertin the Olympic Games were a part of his educational efforts to *rebronzer la France*. He was therefore trying to make the Olympic Games as attractive as possible, so that many young men would be interested in taking part in them. Borrowing heavily from John Ruskin and the British Arts and Crafts movement, Coubertin assumed that the beautification of the games and the attempt to imbue them with the solemn spirit of the ancient Greeks would instill in them a spirit that young people would readily accept. For this he developed flags, hymns and an Olympic oath; he was thinking about fireworks for the opening ceremony to give the games a uniqueness that would set them apart from mere world championships that were being started for several amateur and professional sports at that time (Krüger 1996a). He summarized his idea in the paradigm:

> For one hundred people to take part in physical education there have to be fifty going in for sport, and for fifty to go in for sport, there have to be twenty specializing in sport: in order to have twenty specializing in sport there have to be five who are able to achieve the highest level of performance.
>
> (Coubertin 1935)

Coubertin later used the words over the door of the school of his friend Father Pierre Didon *citius altius fortius* as the Olympic motto, and summarized the sermon preached by the Anglican bishop of Philadelphia, E. Talbot, at the 1912 Olympics as yet another sign of Olympism: it is not important to win, it is important to take part and put up an honourable fight to win (Boulogne 1975).

Table 1.1 Presidents of the IOC

Name	Country	Lifespan	In office
Demetrius Vikelas	Greece	1835–1908	1894–6
Pierre de Coubertin	France	1860–1937	1896–1925
Henri de Baillet-Latour	Belgium	1876–1942	1925–42
Sigfried Edström	Sweden	1870–1964	1942*–52
Avery Brundage	US	1887–1975	1952–72
Lord Killanin	Ireland	1914–	1972–80
Juan Antonio de Samaranch	Spain	1920–	1980–

*Acting Vice President from 1942–6.

The rise of the Olympic Games is closely connected with the rise of international amateur sports. Very often England (sometimes Great Britain) was the first country to organize a sport, but then international federations were founded. The more that were being formed (Table 1.2), the easier it was to organize international competitions.

As Coubertin invited his friends into his International Olympic Committee (IOC), it stayed aloof at first from the federations. The IOC, which until today has continued to be a self-recruiting body in which not even all participating nations are represented, was the only international organization in which people interested in more than one sport would co-operate on questions of common concern. Coubertin realized this function and therefore organized International Olympic Congresses to make sure that the unity of the sports movement could be achieved (Table 1.3). These congresses at first also served the function of convincing the Greeks that they had given the Olympic Games and the Olympic spirit to the world, but that only international games which move from country to country would have a chance in the twentieth century.

The Olympic Games of 1896 are best remembered for the fact that they took place. Three hundred and eleven athletes (males only) from thirteen nations were present, but very few of them were of any representative calibre. International competitions were already taking place regularly, for example between athletes of American and British colleges, and world championships in figure and speed skating had already combined the best of the world since 1892. The results in Athens were relatively poor by international standards. Some of the installations of the former Zappas Olympic Games could still be used. The new Olympic stadium was fascinating but slow because of its extremely short bends. It was important that the Greek Crown Prince had taken over the patronage of the Olympic Games and thus showed the ennoblement that Coubertin was talking about all the time. For the founder of the Olympic movement it was also important to show that athletes from countries that normally did not

Table 1.2 Foundation years of international amateur sports federations

Sport	British Federation	Year	International Federation	Year
Athletics	AAA	1880	IAAF	1912
Boxing	ABA	1880	IBU (professionals)	1911
			FIBA (amateurs)	1920
Fencing	AFA	1902	FIE	1913
Football	FA	1863	FIFA	1904
Gymnastics	AGA	1890	FIG	1897
Ice skating	NSAGB	1879	ISU	1892
Lawn tennis	LTA	1888	ILTF	1913
Rowing	ARA	1882	FISA	1892
Swimming	ASA	1886	FINA	1908

Table 1.3 Olympic Congresses

Year	Site	Main theme
1894	Paris	Study and promotion of the principles of amateurism
1897	Le Havre	Hygiene, education, history relating to physical exercise
1905	Brussels	Issues of sport and physical education
1906	Paris	Integration of fine arts in the Olympic Games
1913	Lausanne	Psychology and physiology of sport
1914	Paris	Unification of Olympic sports, conditions of participation
1921	Lausanne	Modification of Olympic sports, conditions of participation
1925	Prague	Pedagogical problems, Olympic regulations and programme
1930	Berlin	Modifications of Olympic rules
1973	Varna	Future of the Olympic movement
1981	Baden-Baden	International co-operation and future of the Olympic Games
1994	Paris	Olympic movement's contribution to modern society

compete much against each other could meet on friendly terms on the field of sport.

In Paris, Coubertin had his way and combined the games of 1900 with the World Fair. As much as he thought that this would work, sport had started to gain such importance that the athletes did not really like games that were spread out over a five-month period and were more like a series of separate meets than a unified Olympic Games – 1,319 male participants (plus 11 females) from 22 countries. It showed that Coubertin had relatively little experience of the organization of the new big-time sports and that he resented bringing in too many federation people. But the Paris games demonstrated the viability of the Olympics, respect for the four-year cycle and the steady growth of the Olympic idea.

Coubertin did not even attend the Olympic Games in 1904. What had happened? The IOC had given the Olympic Games to Chicago. As the big Louisiana Purchase Exhibition in St. Louis was postponed from 1903 for one year, Chicago transferred the games unilaterally to St. Louis without even asking the IOC. This reduced the function of the IOC and Coubertin took measures to avoid such setbacks in the future. The games were again stretched out, this time over 146 days, involving 617 male participants (plus 8 women) from 12 countries. The local organizer was the St. Louis Turnverein, a German club that provided good facilities for the athletes that had come, but only 92 were not Americans (Table 1.4).

In the world show anything was being compared. No wonder that the organizer also staged Anthropological Days in which natives of various African and North and South American tribes showed their skills. In the

Table 1.4 Participants in the Olympic Summer Games

Year	City	Countries	Female participants	Male participants
1896	Athens	13	—	311
1900	Paris	22	11	1319
1904	St. Louis	12	8	617
1906	Athens	20	7	877
1908	London	22	36	1,999
1912	Stockholm	28	57	2,490
1920	Antwerp	29	64	2,543
1924	Paris	44	136	2,956
1928	Amsterdam	46	290	2,724
1932	Los Angeles	37	127	1,281
1936	Berlin	49	328	3,738
1948	London	59	385	3,714
1952	Helsinki	69	518	4,407
1956	Melbourne/	67	371	2,813
	Stockholm	29	13	145
1960	Rome	83	610	4,738
1964	Tokyo	93	683	4,457
1968	Mexico City	112	781	4,750
1972	Munich	122	1,299	5,848
1976	Montreal	94	1,247	4,781
1980	Moscow	81	1,125	4,092
1984	Los Angeles	141	1,567	6,797
1988	Seoul	159	2,476	7,105
1992	Barcelona	169	2,708	6,659
1996	Atlanta	197	3,779	6,582

true Olympic spirit these young men also had to try their luck at western sports and did, of course, do relatively poorly, thus underlining the theory of white superiority: the best breed the human species can produce (Goksoyr 1991).

Athens staged an Intermediate Olympics as an Olympic ten-year revival show in 1906. This meet was quite important for the development of the IOC. After a decline in interest because of the connection with the World Fairs, these games can be considered the first major media event. This was a time when sport was becoming more and more important. Special sports newspapers were formed and started to create an excitement for sport. They started to organize sports meets like the Tour de France and the Giro d'Italia to fill the pages over the summer with exclusive information, and jumped on the bandwagon of the Olympic Games. Ordinary newspapers started to carry more sports pages and even sent special correspondents to Athens.

Athens also saw a development that would later become far more prominent in the Olympic Games: the first public demonstration. From the beginning Coubertin had cherished his own 'Olympic geography', granting an independent team to whomever he pleased. Bohemia, although part of the Austro-Hungarian Empire had as much a separate team as Hungary. Finland, a Grand Duchy within the Russian Empire, had its own team. When a Finnish team won, the Russian and the Finnish flag were hoisted jointly. Peter O'Connor of Ireland placed second in the long jump in Athens for Great Britain. As a proud Irishman he asked that the Irish flag be raised for him, but the anglophile Coubertin refused. A team-mate climbed the flag pole at the victory stand and put up the Irish flag. Later Coubertin also rejected separate teams from Catalonia and the Pays Basques, in spite of their autonomous status within Spain (Varela 1992, 135ff.).

The first modern Olympics in our sense of the word are the ones of 1908 in London. The English Amateur Athletics Association stood behind them and showed what a sports meeting could be like when it was organized by experienced people in the true amateur spirit. The sports press of many countries was full of reports of the games and the quarrels surrounding them, particularly between the British and the Americans because both assumed that their rules should be the right ones. Eventually even the American President Theodore Roosevelt stepped in as he thought that his American 'boys' were being cheated (Lucas 1982/3).

National fervour was even greater four years later in Stockholm. Coubertin had been reluctant to give the games to the Swedish capital as for him Swedish Gymnastics stood for health and the equilibrium of strength and not for the joyous, boundless overflow of manly vigour. Because of this defiance against exercise and the medically oriented Swedish Gymnastics which Coubertin struggled for a lifetime against, he had replaced the *mens sana in corpore sano* spirit of the medical profession by his own *mens fervida in corpore lacertoso* (an oveflowing mind in a muscular body). In view of the difficulties in London and the peculiar Swedish rules, the programme for the Olympic competitions and their rules were no longer left to the organizer, but the IOC and the sports federations stepped in and assured a unification of standards, rules and by-laws. They could not stop the Swedes, however, from prohibiting the Olympic boxing tournament, as this sport had been outlawed in Sweden for health reasons (Krüger 1979). In many cases one agreed simply that the rules of the London games should also apply. This is, for instance, why the marathon race today is 42.195 km long. In 1896 the race was on the original road a little over 36 km, in Paris it was exactly 25 miles (= 40.260 km). In St. Louis it was 40 km and in London the little distance was added so that the start could be just in front of the centre balcony of Windsor Castle, to assure the best seats for the royal household. In London a tradition was invented and in Paris 1924 finally codified and treated as if it were the proper distance that had been run in antiquity.

The Swedes were desperate to win in 1912 not just because their king was in the stadium all the time, or because they wanted to demonstrate the superiority of their scientific system, but also because they had received money from a special lottery to build the stadium and to prepare the athletes (Lindroth 1974). The Swedes can be considered the ones who invented the state amateurs. By definition, you were not a professional while you were serving in the armed forces, so the Swedes called up their best athletes for national service to prepare for the games – and won ahead of the United States and Great Britain.

This was considered such a humiliation in England that serious steps were undertaken to do much better in 1916 – in Berlin of all places. It should not be overlooked that this was the period of the highest nationalistic fervour, which led to many international crises and eventually to the outbreak of the Great War (1914–18). *The Times* published leading articles to collect money for the preparation of a strong Olympic force – Sir Arthur Conan Doyle, the author of the Sherlock Holmes stories, became the head of a finance committee that attempted to collect £100,000 to bring glory to Britain. Their effort was supported by the king himself and *The Times* printed the list of all the donations (Krüger 1995).

The discussion was taken up in all major countries, building up their athletic prowess for 1916. Every country reacted somewhat differently according to its own national character: in Britain it was thought that 'buying victories is positively degrading'. The Amateur Rowing Association decided that any athlete that was thus sponsored would lose his amateur status. But the Amateur Athletics Association (AAA) decided that it was time to hire the first full time professional coach for the benefit of athletes – a Canadian was chosen who had experience with the American system that had been so successful previously and could still be considered British. Walter R. Knox received a three-year contract in 1914. As the next British national coaches in athletics were hired almost fifty years later, this fact has been more or less forgotten.

In Sweden the national lottery for the stadium of 1912 simply continued and the athletes had enough money to train well. The Swedes also hired a professional former American college coach. In Germany where everything was organized by the government, the national parliament discussed the feasibility of financing Olympic sports, not just for staging the games, but to pay for selecting and coaching the athletes. While in England this was discussed from the viewpoint of the amateur rules, in Germany it was discussed as a matter of state rights, as sport from the German viewpoint was considered part of culture. This was a field where central government had no say; the matter that was left to the 35 separate states that formed the German Empire. Eventually 200,000 marks were paid by the Reich and another 100,000 marks by Prussia, the largest of the German states. The money had been directly earmarked by the German Kaiser himself. The children of the imperial household were ardent sprinters and the emperor came to watch many sports meets. Germany organized a fact-finding tour to the United States and came back with a full-time American national coach – and also hired the first professional administrator for athletics. In France it was industrial sponsorship that benefited the athletes: Pommery, the largest champagne manufacturer, sponsored a Collège des Athlètes, a place where athletes could stay in Reims free of charge and be coached by experts (from France). Full-time American coaches were also hired in most other European countries and even in Australia and New Zealand (Krüger 1994a).

As everything centred on the Darwinistic definition of the vitality of a nation – or its degeneration – the medal tables that were to point to who was number one were officially discussed at IOC meetings. In June 1914, just ten weeks before the outbreak of the war, the IOC decided at its annual session in Paris the question whether a woman's medal should have the same weight as a man's or whether women's medals should simply not be counted, inasmuch as the Olympic Games in the tradition of antiquity (and from the Darwinist breeding perspective) were men's events. Coubertin fought against women's equal rights and lost – only the United States, Turkey and Japan voted with France against equality for women. The compromise was, however, that there should not be too many women's events.

In 1914 yet another ancient Olympic tradition was broken and a new one invented: in 1916 the first winter Olympics were to take place in the Black Forest in Germany (Krüger 1996b). As the games of 1916 were cancelled because of the war, it took until 1924 before the first winter Olympics were staged, but the roots were there already prior to the Great War. If the Olympic Games showed in a social Darwinist way which was the strongest nation that had least to worry about in the struggle of the fittest, the Great War soon took over and replaced mere games by deadly reality.

During the war, Coubertin moved his domicile from Paris to Lausanne in neutral Switzerland to assure that the Olympics would not be drawn into the struggle of the warring parties. It should not be overlooked that from the very beginning people from the international peace movement had been actively involved with the Olympic movement and that Coubertin – although not a pacifist – thought that sport would make a good ersatz war, this not requiring the real one any more (Quanz 1993).

It was difficult to stage the Olympic Games of 1920 as the situation in most countries had been quite desperate. If there had not been successful Inter Allied Games in Paris in 1919 under the American General Pershing, the IOC would not have dared stage the Olympic Games so shortly after the war. But the IOC went to Antwerp, where the American team could stay on its ship and could also assure the food supply of some of the other teams. The games produced good results and showed the vitality of the Olympic movement. Although Germany, Austria and its allies were excluded from the games, since the wounds of the destruction of nearby Flanders had been too deep to warrant a sporting competition with the former enemy, the games were a complete success. The main organizer of the games, Henri de Baillet-Latour, also made such an impression that Coubertin started to build him up as his successor (Boulogne 1994).

Coubertin had planned his retirement from the Olympic movement ever since the Russian October 1917 Revolution. He had invested heavily in tsarist Bonds that paid the highest interest – and lost. After the Revolution they had no value at all. As Coubertin had paid most of the expenses for the IOC Bureau and his travel from his own pocket, he simply could not afford to be the president of the IOC any more.

His IOC paid him their respects by granting the Olympic Games of 1924 a final time to Paris, but the French had been somewhat out of step with the development of sport world-wide. The games were dominated by the American team. Only the Germans were still excluded, while the other warring parties of the Great War took part. Soon afterwards Coubertin retired and Baillet-Latour was elected his successor. Coubertin had sent him on a goodwill tour through South America where Baillet-Latour helped to form national Olympic Committees and received the right to select one future IOC member from each.

The Baillet-Latour years

The IOC had traditionally two blocks, the anglophone and the francophone. Baillet-Latour was the last of the francophone presidents before Samaranch. In 1926 the IOC also readmitted Germany, which had been very active in the workers' sports movement where it was not banned (Krüger and Riordan 1996). While Coubertin had been an autocratic visionary who tried to mould the IOC according to his will and formed the Olympic movement according to his vision, Baillet-Latour was a committee man. Just as he had run the Antwerp Games by leaving enough space for experts to do what they could do best, he transformed the IOC into a three-layer organization, introducing an executive committee as the main decision-making body. His own management style could best be described as management by moderation. While for Coubertin the functionaries from the sports federations had been the 'leprosy of sport' whom he resented and he tried to make the IOC something better, Baillet-Latour accepted that without these functionaries there would not be any decent sport. Baillet-Latour had to deal with the rise of fascism in Europe. By avoiding too many strong decisions himself, he succeeded in keeping the IOC together (Lennartz 1994). The rise of fascism in sport will be dealt with elsewhere in this book.

In the Amsterdam Olympics Germany was back for the first time and placed a surprising second behind the United States. Amsterdam saw a first in games marketing: not only were the photo rights for the games sold exclusively, but the games organizers also made some money by selling the concessions. Among others Coca-Cola started to be present and be a sponsor at the Olympic Games as of 1928 (Krüger, 1996c). The Amsterdam Olympics are best known for the inclusion of women's events in such sports as track and field athletics. As of 1921 an International Women's Sports Federation (FSFI) had staged world championships. They had become very popular and thus threatened the universality of the Olympics. Baillet-Latour made sure that they were included into the Olympic movement (Quercetani 1990).

With the worker sports movement he was not as successful. The first International Workers' Olympics were staged in Frankfurt, Germany, and were a tremendous success with 60,000 participants (there had been some mass demonstration events) from ten nations. Coubertin had already approached the workers, but the sports federations which now started to dominate the IOC refused to follow this idea up. For them the mono-polistic principle of mutual help was self-evident: just one federation per country or per sport could be members of the IOC. The social-democratic-oriented workers staged their alternative Olympics in Vienna (1931) and Antwerp (1937).

Coubertin's desire, 'all games – all nations', became a reality under Baillet-Latour. By trying to include everyone, he accepted any political creed that a particular country might cherish, whether democracy, mili-tary dictatorships, just as long as they would underwrite the notion that sport and politics were separate and that they would not try to force their beliefs on any of the other members. The number of events also increased under him, and finally he ensured that the winter Olympics continued to be staged, even if there were difficulties concerning the amateur rules between the Scandinavian and the central European ski federations.

Life for Baillet-Latour was not all that easy as IOC president, as Coubertin was still around throughout most of his presidency and the old man grumbled that a lot of things in the IOC did not go his way. Baillet-Latour stayed in Belgium most of the time, and let the Lausanne headquarters be run by friends of Coubertin. The annual subscription of IOC members was barely sufficient to pay for a part-time secretary to do the correspondence. An honorary secretary ran the office for the honour and the fun of it. For Baillet-Latour's notion of the limited function of the IOC this was enough. Coubertin, however, had set up yet another international organization, his thirty-fifth, the International Bureau of Sport Pedagogy as he did not just want a machine to run a big interna-tional sports meet, but wanted athletic education to prepare for a better human race. The Olympic Games for Coubertin were like an unfinished symphony as they lacked educational input (Coubertin 1936).

The 1932 Olympic Games in Los Angeles came in the midst of the Depression. The foreign teams that travelled to America were few and small, as they could not afford it. Financially the Olympic Games were, however, a gigantic success. As all the facilities were already there, the athletes could stay in university dormitories and come at their own expense, the games produced a net gain of over $1,000,000. Avery Brundage, then president of the American Olympic Committee (AOC), started to negotiate on whether either the AOC or the IOC could get some of the financial gain. IOC member William M. Garland (1866–1948), the president of the Organizing Committee (OC) for the games, refused. It was he who had had the idea that brought, for the first time in Olympic history more than one million spectators into the stadium: as everybody was poor at the time of the Depression, he simply cut the planned ticket price by half – and had a full stadium throughout all of the games. The AOC eventually sued the OC and lost. A Los Angeles court ruled that the organization that had carried all the risks should also get all the profits. Neither the AOC, nor the IOC had yet secured property rights on the Olympic trademarks (Guttmann 1984).

The Los Angeles Olympics were already broadcast live by radio and the American radio stations even paid for the exclusive rights. Brundage had sold the exclusive radio rights for the American track and field championships, and the courts had upheld such exclusive property rights on sports spectacles if these rights were printed on the tickets.

The Olympic Games of 1936 outdid many of the previous games and were the first games on yet another stage of hyper-reality. The struggle and the arguments to have a boycott or not, to avoid bending Olympic rules to go along with the Nazis will be dealt with elsewhere. Here we will just look at what the IOC got for its willingness to provide the Nazis with a stage that permitted them to break the cultural isolation of the Reich after the Nazis started to boycott, beat, disinherit and eventually kill its Jewish fellow citizens.

The OC for the 1936 Olympics could enlist the most efficient propaganda machine in the world for its services. Goebbels' Ministry of Public Enlightenment and Propaganda, which was brainwashing the Germans, had the chance to test its skills on the Olympic Games. But as of October 1933, the balance of power shifted: Theodor Lewald, president of the German OC, had to sign a declaration that henceforth he would only appear to be independent – in accordance with international rules – but in reality as a subsidiary of the German Olympic Committee, he would do as he was told (Krüger 1975a). Many of the inventions that came out of the joint committee of the Ministry and the OC have become Olympic standards. The lighting of the torch and the torch relay from Olympia to the site of the games was invented by one of Goebbels' men. The purpose of Herr Haeggart's invention was to heighten last-minute interest in the games and set the stage for them. It also helped to put the Nazis in line with the Greeks, seeing themselves as the legitimate heirs of Sparta (Krüger and Ramba 1991). The security measures in the stadium were unrivalled; the corporate identity of the games was brought to such a point that only selected photos received clearance and were permitted to be published about the games. The legal basis for this – which was challenged immediately by international press agencies – had been laid down in Amsterdam 1928: as the exclusive photo rights had been sold there, the use of exclusive rights by the Reich's minister of propaganda could not be stopped (Alkemeyer 1996; Rürup 1996).

Germany had also had its National Olympia (Krüger 1994b), and so Olympic winners did not only get the obligatory Olympic gold medal, but also a little potted oak tree, an ancient Germanic tradition that was not followed by any of the other games. Baillet-Latour and the IOC made sure that their strong bargaining position with the Germans was used to have as normal Olympic Games as possible. They were gigantic. The opening ceremony of the winter Olympics in Garmisch-Partenkirchen alone had more spectators than all of the events in Lake Placid in 1932 combined. New spectator records were set with more than one million in winter and more than three million in summer. Germany won the summer games ahead of the United States.

The Nazi Olympics are best remembered for their hero Jesse Owens who won four Olympic gold medals and for Hitler not shaking his hand. Hitler was an ardent sports fan who spent all day in the stadium rooting for his German team. He was quite upset when he had to witness the German football team losing to Norway. He would have preferred to see a German team win. On the first day in the Olympic stadium he invited all the medal winners up to his special box to congratulate them in public, which was against all Olympic protocol. The last event of the first day had been the men's high jump in which two Afro-Americans placed one and two. Hitler, who had already stayed longer in the stadium than the original time schedule of the event, left immediately after the final jumps and did not congratulate the high jumpers. Baillet-Latour complained to Hitler the next day and told him that he should congratulate in public all or none, to avoid discrimination. So from then onward Hitler welcomed only the German medal winners in the VIP room underneath the grandstand of the stadium. That way the two persons these games are best known for, Jesse Owens and Adolf Hitler, did not meet.

The 1936 Olympics were termed a gigantic Nazi propaganda show. Coubertin, who had given a radio message for the games exactly one year before (Coubertin 1935), was enthusiastic about them, but did not go to Berlin, just as he had refrained from attending any of the previous games after his retirement from the presidency. But in an interview with Jack Lang, which was published in much of the French press after the games, he was asked what he thought about them. The father of the Olympic movement was quite candid. He had always wanted a nation to be fully committed to the Olympic effort, and that was the case with Germany. And, Coubertin concluded, what is the difference whether you use the games to advertise southern Californian weather for the sake of tourism, or a political regime? The most important thing is that the games are celebrated in a decent manner. Coubertin died in 1937 and was buried in Lausanne, but his heart was later buried at Olympia.

Baillet-Latour's aim to bring the games to all corners of the world can best be seen by the Olympics of 1940. The winter games were to be held in Sapporo and the summer games in Tokyo. Baillet-Latour visited the sites to make sure they were satisfactory. Japan had participated in the Olympic Games since 1912 and had often sent as many experts to accompany the team as athletes to make sure that the educational impetus, the training and the running of a big international meet could be copied. Because of the Sino-Japanese War Japan returned the games to the IOC in 1938. At the IOC meeting in Cairo the same year the games were moved to Helsinki, which had applied for them at short notice. But Baillet-Latour, the committee man, also had his committee take another decision: the role of the IOC in the event of war had to be defined.

It had never been a problem for the IOC for any of its participating nations to be at war at the time the games were staged. Great Britain did not stop the Boer War for the 1900 Paris Olympics. The Olympic Truce of antiquity had been nothing but a memory. But so far the Olympic Games had not been staged in a country at war. In 1938, however, the IOC decided that the organizer could be involved in a war, as long as the games themselves would not be in a war zone and athletes would not be in danger on their way to the games, at the games, or on their way back. This decision soon became of importance, as the winter Olympics of 1940 did not find as easy a home as had the summer Olympics. Oslo and St. Moritz were both trying to persuade the IOC with their controversial amateur definitions. In June 1939, Germany was granted the games in appreciation of the fine games of 1936. Garmisch-Partenkirchen still had all the facilities and offered to step in at short notice. For the IOC it did not matter that Hitler had already broken the Munich Accord of 1938 and occupied all of Czechoslovakia, marching directly into the Second World War. What mattered to Baillet-Latour, just as it had been crucial to Coubertin, was that the games could be celebrated.

As the war lasted longer than anticipated by Hitler or the IOC, Germany gave them back in early 1940. In so far as Germany was victorious in the first part of the war on most fronts, there were soon more international sporting competitions in Europe than before. In 1941 and 1942 Baillet-Latour, who lived reasonably well in German occupied Belgium, had to deal with German plans to organize European sports federations for all Olympic sports and, since these federations ranked below the international ones, thereby gain access to the running of international sport. As most of central Europe was either pro-fascist or occupied by Germany, and the neutral powers enjoyed good terms with Germany, this looked quite a prospect. These federations staged European Boxing Championships in 1942 (Teichler 1991). Baillet-Latour resented, however, having anything changed in the statutes of the IOC. He had to accept a German secret agent as IOC secretary-general, the IOC journal, *Olympische Rundschau,* was printed in Germany and could be filled with material that did not reflect the opinion of all of the IOC members. But at least there was an IOC bureau and a journal, in spite of the financial difficulties of the IOC (Krüger 1982).

As Baillet-Latour realized that he was not much more than a hostage of the Germans, towards whom he had mixed feelings, and as he felt that he was getting frail, he appointed Sigfried Edström as vice-president. This way he made sure that somebody from neutral Sweden would follow him, who in spite of being pro-German was sufficiently independent. Edström also served as president of the IAAF (1912–46), the most prominent of the Olympic sports.

The Edström years

In two respects Edström was completely different from his two prede-cessors. He was involved in the international sports federations as president of the IAAF, thus part of what Coubertin had termed the 'leprosy of sport' and he was one of the English-speaking group. He had been the president of the OC at the 1912 Olympics, and thus was not a young man either when he became president. He therefore immediately appointed Avery Brundage as his own vice-president to assure the continuity of the IOC that depended to some extent on having a legitimate person there to convene the committee (Lennartz 1995).

At first Edström could not do much, as the war lingered on. He had avoided, as IAAF president, a German-dominated European Athletics Championship of 1942. The Olympic Games of 1944 could not take place, although it was discussed having them in the United States as they would be reasonably safe there. Edström's big moment as president came as soon as the war was over. The question then was, should there be two world sports movements (or even three) as there had been between the wars with the bourgeois Olympics, the social-democratic worker sports, and the communist worker sports? Or should they be combined? The IAAF staged the European Athletics Championships in 1946 in Oslo, including the Soviet Union, which reached a respectable second place. Norway had old socialist ties to the Soviet worker sports and simply invited its big neighbour against all IAAF rules that forbade competition with non-members (Krüger and Riordan 1996). Edström, a stout capitalist in the monopolistic electricity industry, saw the chance to bring all of the sports movement together and he worked hard at it. The other members of the executive board were somewhat more reluctant. In the Olympic Games in St. Moritz and in London in 1948 the Soviet Union did not take part. But the other eastern European countries that were either already in the Soviet-dominated eastern bloc or in the process of being drawn into it, all sent teams.

The question then was, would the Soviet Union take part in the next games? Would it prohibit its allies from taking part? Edström kept all lines of communication open to draw the Soviet Union into bourgeois world sport. The Soviet Union asked as one of the conditions that Franco Spain be excluded from the Olympic movement. Spain was generally considered pro-fascist (see Chapter 4) and had not only been responsible for the slaughter of many socialists at the time of the Spanish Civil War, but had also entered the war against the USSR – but not against the western allies. The IOC refused, stating that only members could demand the exclusion of other members. The Soviet Union demanded that Russian be accepted as a third IOC language – the IOC refused, but it accepted that the Soviet delegates could bring their own interpreter. Brundage demanded as a condition for the Soviet Union to go in the IOC that his friend and fellow IOC member Karl von Halt, Hitler's last *Reichssportführer* (1942–5), who was considered a war criminal by the Americans, be released from a Soviet detention camp where he had been from 1945 to 1949. Eventually, the Soviet Union gave in on all areas. It wanted to end the communist sports movement and find its way into the bourgeois sports world. The demands to exclude Spain were dropped, von Halt was released, the Soviet amateur rules were brought into line with international standards – at least on paper.

The 1952 Helsinki Olympics still saw two separate Olympic villages, one for athletes of the eastern bloc and one for athletes of the West, but all the eastern bloc took part with the Soviet Union which placed a close second to the United States. Edström and Brundage had also achieved another aim: Germany had been readmitted to the Olympic Games ten years after the end of World War I, now it was back seven years after World War II. But the problems of the three divided countries, Germany, Korea and China, would continue to plague the IOC for years to come.

The Brundage years

The towering figure of Avery Brundage, participant in the 1912 Olympic decathlon, long time president of the American Olympic Committee, vice-president of the IAAF, brought American pragmatism to the solution of a lot of Olympic problems over the next twenty years (Guttmann 1984). When the two Germanies could not decide who should represent the country that in theory was still one, he ruled against the fears of his West German friends that there should be a united German team, for which one would qualify in the American way: one qualification meet, and may the best man win and be in the team. Whichever side had more people in the team would have the spokesperson for the team. Germany had never had such selection competitions, but a national selector had selected the potentially best team. Even when, after the ending of any inner German travel and competition with the building of the Berlin Wall and the other border fortifications in 1961, neither side wanted to have a united team any more, Brundage insisted. So the selection meets took place in Czechoslovakia and in Sweden as both sides refused to compete on the terrain of the other (Krüger 1975b). Only after the East German side had more athletes in the team and started to run the show in 1964, did Brundage give in. In 1968 there were already two teams but under one united flag and anthem, and in 1972 there were finally two teams. In the case of China and Korea, Brundage and the IOC reflected American policy and simply demanded that their ally be accepted as the representative of the country. Eventually two Chinas were accepted, but now mainland China tried to have Taiwan excluded (Espy 1981).

Brundage, although a federation man himself, ignored the demands of the federations to be better represented in the IOC and have more of a say in IOC matters. With the decolonialization of the countries, particularly in Africa, the IOC willingly let all in to participate, but the IOC refused them equal voting rights. While the traditional IOC member countries had two or even three members, many of the young African nations had none. Brundage did not want to have equal representation as in the United Nations, but insisted that the IOC should be run in a traditional way. He had been used to this from the IAAF, which had a voting system that gave countries votes according to the number of due-paying members.

With his pragmatic approach he simply ignored the Suez crisis and the Soviet invasion of Hungary that threatened the 1956 Olympics in Melbourne. Purist countries like Switzerland and the Netherlands refused to compete under such conditions, but even the Hungarians went, converting the water-polo final between those two countries into an ersatz war, and using the opportunity to defect afterwards. When the Olympic Games had been given for the first time to Australia, some logistical problems had to be taken care of. For the first time a major portion of the games had to take place not just in a different country, but on a different continent, as the riders could not get their horses to the fifth continent. The Equestrian Games therefore took place in Stockholm.

The Olympic Games of 1960 in Rome and 1964 in Tokyo saw Brundage at the height of his power. Neither the problems with 'black' Africa, nor with rising professionalism were yet so strong that he could not handle them. Brundage himself had been in favour of regional games, helping in staging the Pan-American Games, the Caribbean and Central American Games, and the Mediterranean Games. He was glad to have African Games, but the Games of the Newly Emergent Forces (GANEFO) he resented, as these were no longer on a regional basis, but combined those countries that felt left out by the First and Second World, and defined themselves not as regional but as rising nations of the Third World.

American racism also showed its face to the world. When the AOC had protested at German racism in 1936, it had to acknowledge that in the American South competitions between white and Afro-American athletes were not possible, even a Jesse Owens could only qualify because he competed for Ohio State University in the North. Often the world record holder could not compete for his college, as in competitions in the South he had to stay home. Although the situation had improved after the Second World War, there were still many areas in American sport that were segregated or had just one 'token Negro' to demonstrate an integration that did not exist. The prominent New York Athletic Club, which had provided American sport with most of its presidents, did not admit Jews and Afro-Americans until as late as 1968. The black power movement threatened to boycott the American team. Eventually it did not, but Tommie Smith and John Carlos showed their disdain for the American flag by raising their fist in the black power salute on the victory stand (Edwards 1969).

In 1972 the situation was getting even more out of hand. Brundage was making a last stand against the hypocrisy of the 'shamateurism' and disqualified the best downhill skier, Karl Schranz of Austria. Schranz was not disqualified for professionalism, he did not make more money than many of the other top skiers who all could buy mountain hotels after their retirement, but he refused to pay lip-service as all of the others had done when asked about their income. Brundage preferred to live with hypocrisy and double standards than to change anything in the rules (Schantz 1995).

The Olympic Summer Games of Munich 1972 were supposed to be the friendly games in which Germany tried to show to the world that it, too, could stage non-militaristic joyful games that were to make people forget the Nazi Olympics of 1936. The contrast was supposed to be even greater as the Mexican government had dealt with a student revolt just prior to the games with tanks and a massive military presence, so that the opening ceremony of the 1968 Olympics had taken place under the protection of tanks and with a massive military presence.

Unfortunately, the new Germany mistook friendliness for lack of security measures. Anybody could walk in and out of the Olympic village at random. So, it was not much of a surprise that a Palestinian terror organization used the opportunity to take members of the Israeli team hostage in the Olympic village. The Israelis were not surprised either, and there- fore only a small select group of them, all with a military rank, had stayed in the Olympic village, while most of the team preferred to stay in Munich with friends – spread out all over town for security reasons to avoid being a ready target. As the Israeli government refused to trade the hostages for Palestinian prisoners – it never did with its military – a shoot-out resulted in which all eleven captured Israelis, five Palestinians, and a German policeman died. The games were interrupted for twenty-four hours, a memorial service was performed in the Olympic stadium, and Brundage concluded, as all of his predecessors would have done: 'The Games must go on!'

The Killanin years

Lord Killanin had the shortest reign of all IOC presidents. While Brundage had taken most decisions himself with just a small group of advisors, that often had little to do with the actual structure of the IOC, Killanin was the first to attempt a democratization of the IOC. If in his leadership style Brundage was close to Coubertin, Killanin can be compared with Baillet-Latour. While Brundage had maintained a certain degree of unity in the IOC by an iron fist, Killanin was less firm. The African nations that had succeeded in excluding Rhodesia from the Munich games, tried to persuade the IOC in 1976 to exclude not only racist regimes but also those countries that continued to stage sports contests on a national level with them. As New Zealand had had an international rugby match against South Africa, the African nations demanded the exclusion of New Zealand. It is questionable whether they would have tried the same with Brundage, as the American was known for his strength of character. Killanin showed some understanding for the African position and then took it to a vote by the full IOC. The IOC did not exclude New Zealand and 35 African nations were left to boycott the Montreal Olympics. In a similar unclear decision, Taiwan was eventually excluded by the Canadian government against all Olympic rules, with the IOC not doing anything about it.

The Montreal Olympics are also known for the financial deficit they brought to the citizens of that city and for the unfinished stadium. It is doubtful whether this was really the highest deficit of all Olympics, but under the Canadian fiscal system the expenses stayed clearly with the city, while in 1972 the deficit was split between the city, the Bavarian state government, and the Federal government. Eventually the city of Munich gained tremendously by the games, as it could not have attracted federal money to such an extent for the improvement of the infrastructure had it not been for the Olympic Games. The Montreal Games are less known for the amount of sponsorship that went into them: a record 628 sponsors were enlisted. The Americans were quite embarrassed, as the tiny GDR placed second to the USSR and ahead of the US, demonstrating, with the help of prime-time television, that the American sporting scene had deteriorated to such an extent that a country the size of Tennessee and with a population of less than New York State could outdo the mighty United States.

The IOC was also relatively helpless in 1980. After the Soviet Union had invaded Afghanistan, American President Carter demanded that the Olympic Games be transferred to another country, or be postponed, or at least that the American team and its allies should boycott the games. According to the 1938 vote of the IOC there was no basis for this. In blatant disrespect for the autonomy of the IOC, American Secretary of State Baker tried to threaten the IOC. This resulted in an even stronger reaction from IOC members. Killanin was touring from capital to capital, disregarding his health problems, to maintain the unity of the Olympic movement (Kanin 1981; Hulme 1990). Eventually only eighty-one nations participated in Moscow, some not showing their national flag, some not marching into the stadium at the opening ceremony. Thirty teams boycotted the games, while another thirty-three did not respond to the invitation. In some countries, the sending of a team to the 1980 Olympics was a test for the actual independence of the national Olympic committees. While the American NOC, which had always spoken of its independence, was financially dependent on the Amateur Sports Act of 1978 and, through this, on government coercion, France, which had always been thought of as a government agency, was able to demonstrate its independence. While the British, who respected the desire of individual federations not to go, went to Moscow, the Germans showed that they were financially so dependent on the government that they did not dare take independent action.

The Samaranch years

Avery Brundage had already built up Juan Antonio Samaranch as his legitimate heir. What made the Catalan businessman such a logical choice for the IOC that he could modernize the organization without objections? Samaranch had shown several skills which other IOC members were lacking. Already in 1946 he had invested in the staging of the roller-hockey world championship (a popular sport in Spain) in his home town and had emerged as a hero: Spain had won its first world title ever with 'Kid' Samaranch as coach and he made a profit on the gate receipts which he reinvested in the sport. He also converted the moribund Mediterranean Games into a spectacular success. In his political life Samaranch also showed a high degree of flexibility: his political career was closely connected with the Franco regime – eventually he became head of the Catalonia parliament for Franco's Falange. He was so identified with this regime that at the time of Franco's death a mob ran wild through Barcelona, trying to find and lynch him. Yet, he had already ingratiated himself with the new government which sent him to Moscow as the new Spanish Ambassador, his first ever diplomatic appointment. This brought him into a position where all IOC members who travelled to Moscow prior to the 1980 Olympics would see him and be wined and dined by him (Boix and Espada 1991).

Samaranch brought the Francophone and the Eastern Blocs behind him so as to be the new president. It has been speculated that Horst Dassler, a close friend of his, used his and his company's (Adidas) influence throughout the East to have him elected (Miller 1992). Samaranch made some drastic changes in the IOC in a democratic way: in 1981 the Olympic Congress reduced the amateur rules to a formality. If in sport you had a professional and an amateur international federation, only the one that was already a member of the IOC could continue to send athletes. Therefore, tennis could readily become an Olympic sport and send its top people as it had only one international federation, while in boxing it was still the amateur rules and the amateur federation. As a logical consequence, those athletes who had been stripped of their glory because of difficulties with the amateur rules, such as Jim Thorpe, Paovo Nurmi or Karl Schranz, were all reinstated.

The Olympic Games could be sponsored on a much greater scale as well. This was largely the idea of Peter Ueberroth, the general secretary of the 1984 Los Angeles Olympics, who made big changes. While the 1976 Olympics had 628 sponsors, he reduced them to 30 exclusive ones, each paying more than all the previous sponsors together. Exclusivity was the key word, that provided the 1984 Olympics with a big surplus which was invested into the improvement of amateur sport in southern California (Reich 1986). Samaranch learned a lot faster than Brundage had in 1932. With the help of Adidas he started to market the Olympic emblem between the games. This, named the Olympic programme (TOP), provided the IOC with an enormous amount of money which was partially distributed among the federations, the National Olympic Committees, but it was also put into the Olympic solidarity programme with which the IOC tried to raise the standard of sport in young and developing countries – one of the major results of the 1981 Baden-Baden Olympic Congress. The Los Angeles organizers did not mind that the Eastern bloc (with the exception of Romania and Yugoslavia) boycotted the games as a reprisal for the American boycott of 1980. This way Americans could win more medals, for many spectators a good reason to buy a ticket.

The first 'normal' Olympics for a long time took place in Seoul. When South Korea had obtained the games, there was a worry that these would also be games torn between the political power blocs, so visible in the divided country, with a military dictatorship on the one side and a strong communist government on the other. But the opposite was the case. International interest in Korea forced the military dictatorship to speed up the democratization process, and even the communist North started to open up channels of negotiations with the South (Pound 1994). Athletically, the games will probably best be remembered for the stunning 100-metre sprint victory of Ben Johnson (Canada) and his disqualification soon afterwards for taking anabolic steroids. This had been the drugs case with the highest profile, demonstrating to all sponsors that they had better not invest too much in individual athletes, but that they should stick with sports meetings, since the image of an athlete may change from one moment to the next, while the image of the Olympic Games even improved after the disqualification of the Canadian sprinter.

Samaranch had worked very hard to have the Olympic Games in his home town of Barcelona. Here he could come back to the city a hero after he had almost been lynched fourteen years before. Barcelona, a city of old sport traditions that had just barely lost out to Berlin for the 1936 Olympics and could not stage the Workers' Olympics the same year because of the outbreak of the Civil War, saw the biggest Olympics yet. The country was proudly united behind the Olympic idea, including the *Olimpiada Cultural*, put into the programme not by force, but out of conviction. Barcelona was the first and only city that filled the stadium for the Paralympics after the actual games almost as much as for the real games, showing a warmth of character and an understanding of sport.

Samaranch made yet another strategic move to manage the Olympic product better. Traditionally, the Olympic Games take place every four years. The dates of the Olympics 1896, 1900, etc. is an invented tradition. To have winter games at all is yet another invented tradition unheard of in Greek or Roman antiquity. Technically speaking, every four years the IOC had an excessive supply situation of Olympic moments of glory, and marketing and sponsorship opportunities, while it had nothing to offer in between. The overflow was balanced by disconnecting the summer games from the winter games. Lillehammer 1994 showed that the public did not mind the two-year interval, as the Norwegians produced an impressive show (Krüger 1996b).

Atlanta 1996 has been criticized, as many had thought that the centennial Olympic Games would return to Greece. But why should they? Athens in summer is pure chaos and smog even without the games. The Greeks were upset, assuming that Coca-Cola money (Atlanta is the seat of the Coca-Cola Company) had paved the way for Atlanta, overlooking the fact that the preparation of the games in Athens was also mainly paid for by Coca-Cola Greece. The Olympic Games in Nagano 1998 and Sidney 2000 will show that the IOC has a strong brand that is well managed.

Conclusion

The Olympic Games have adapted well to the postmodern world. If the games are such an attractive commodity, have they ever been something different? Coubertin wanted to have them beautiful, unique and with a logo that is now part of the corporate identity that can be sold so well. Brundage helped to maintain the notion that the Olympics are something exclusive and special. Being an Olympian meant being in line with the heroes and demi-gods of antiquity. Yet for Coubertin that was only half the story (Krüger 1996a). 'Winning is all' was not his credo. He wanted an Olympic education comprising an absolute will to win, but coupled with an understanding of losing; the Darwinist conviction of the superiority of the victor, but with complete tolerance for the loser – who had tried just as hard to win. For Coubertin the Olympic Games, therefore, were but an unfinished symphony, as he had provided the perfect goal to strive for, but the games had become no longer striving to win to become a better human being, but wanting to sell one's glory to the highest bidder.

It is part of the postmodern absurdity that the opportunity for an Olympic revival lies exactly in its core. For a company it is not worth investing in athletes who are corrupt and hollow, nor in a sports meet that is just a circus. An extensive international fair play campaign has tried to improve the image of the product, and anti-doping measures are to make the product cleaner. The Olympic Congress of Paris 1994 decided that coaches, doctors, and biochemists should step back to leave the spotlight to athletes alone. The athlete who is not just a dumb clown, but can speak up for him- or herself, can gain the best sponsors, since in these postmodern days it is individuality that is required, the athlete who in all areas of life is sufficiently spontaneous to 'just do it'.

References

Alkemeyer, T. (1996) *Körper, Kult und Politik. Von der 'Muskelreligion' Pierre de Coubertins zur Inszenierung von Macht in den Olympischen Spielen von 1936*, Frankfurt: Campus.

Boix, J. and Espada, A. (1991) *El deporte del poder. Vida y milagro de Juan Antonio Samaranch*. Madrid: Ediciones temas de hoy.

Boulogne, Y.-P. (1975) *La vie et l'œuvre pédagogique de Pierre de Coubertin* Ottawa: Leméac.

——(1994) The Presidencies of Demetrius Vikelas and Pierre de Coubertin, in *The International Olympic Committee – One Hundred Years*, vol. 1, Lausanne: IOC, 13–207.

Coubertin, P. de (1935) *Les assises philosophiques de l'olympisme moderne. International Radio Message on year before the Olympic Games*, Lausanne: IOC.

——(1936) 'La symphonie inachevée', in Boulogne, Y.-P. (1975) *La vie et l'œuvre pédagogique de Pierre de Coubertin*, Ottawa: Leméac, 462–4.

Edwards, H. (1969) *The Revolt of the Black Athlete*. New York: Free Press.

Espy, R. (1981) *The Politics of the Olympic Games*. Berkeley, CA: University of California Press.

Goksoyr, M. (1991) 'An image of the Third World in the white man's arena. The anthropological days in St. Louis 1904, and their aftermath', in *The Olympic Games through the Ages: Greek Antiquity and its Impact on Modern Sport* (eds R. Renson *et al.*), Athens: Hellenic Sports Research Institute, 229–40.

Guttmann, A. (1984) *The Games must go on. Avery Brundage and the Olympic Movement*, New York: Colombia University Press.

Guttmann, A. (1992) *The Olympics. A History of the Modern Games*, Champaign, IL: University of Illinois Press.

Hulme, D. L. Jr. (1990) *The Political Olympics. Moscow, Afghanistan and the U.S. Boycott*. New York: Praeger.

Kamper, E. (1972) *Encyclopedia of the Olympic Games*, Dortmund: Harenberg Verlag.

Kanin, D.B. (1981) *A Political History of the Olympic Games*. Boulder, CO: Westview Press.

Krüger, A. (1975a) *Dr. Theodor Lewald. Sportführer ins Dritte Reich*, Berlin: Bartels & Wernitz.

——(1975b) *Sport und Politik. Vom Turnvater Jahn zum Staatsamateur*. Hannover: Fackelträger Verlag.

——(1979) 'Mens fervida in corpore lacertoso oder Coubertins Ablehung der schwedischen Gymnastik', in *HISPA 8th Int. Congress. Proceedings*, Uppsala: University Press, 145–53.

——(1980) 'Neo-Olympismus zwischen Nationalismus und Internationalismus', in *Geschichte der Leibesübungen*, vol. 3/2, (ed. H. Ueberhorst), Berlin: Bartels & Wernitz, 522–68.

——(1982) 'Deutschland und die olympische Bewegung (1918–1945)', in *Geschichte der Leibesübungen*, vol. 3/2, (ed. H. Ueberhorst), Berlin: Bartels & Wernitz, 1026–47.

——(1986) 'War John Astley Cooper der Erfinder der modernen Olympischen Spiele?', in *Sport und Kultur*, vol. 6, (eds L. Burgener *et al.*), Bern: Lang Verlag, 72–81.

——(1994a) '"The Olympic spirit of the modern world has given us a symbol of world war". Sport and national representation at the eve of World War I', in P. Arnaud and A. Wahl (eds) *Sport et rélations internationales*. (Centre de Recherche Histoire et Civilisation de l'Université de Metz, vol. 19), Metz, 47–64.

——(1994b) '"Dann veranstalten wir eben rein deutsche Olympische Spiele." Die Olympischen Spiele 1936 als deutsches Nationalfest', in Breuer, H. and Naul, R. (eds) *Schwimmsport und Sportgeschichte. Zwischen Politik und Wissenschaft. Festschrift für Hans-Georg John zum 65. Geburtstag*, St. Augustin: Academia, 127–49.

——(1995) '"Buying victories is positively degrading." The European origins of Government Pursuit of National Prestige through Sports'. *International Journal of the History of Sport* 12(2), 201–18.

——(1996a) 'Sport, Kommerzialisierung und Postmoderne am Beispiel der IOC, Inc.', in H. Sarkowicz (ed.) *Schneller, höher, weiter. Eine Geschichte des Sports*, Frankfurt: Insel Verlag, 79–92.

——(1996b) 'The History of the Olympic Winter Games. The invention of a tradition', in M. Goksøyr, G. v.d. Lippe, K. Mo (eds) *Winter Games. Warm Traditions*, Oslo: Norsk Idrettshistorisk Forening, 101–22.

——(1996c) 'Mit Coca-Cola zum Gold. Olympia und Kommerz', in *Schulfernsehen Südwest* 5(3) 59–65.

Krüger, A. and Ramba, D. (1991) 'Sparta or Athens? The Reception of Greek Antiquity in Nazi Germany', in *The Olympic Games Through the Ages: Greek Antiquity and its Impact on Modern Sport* (eds R. Renson *et al.*), Athens: Hellenic Sports Research Institute, 345–56.

Krüger, A. and Riordan, J. (eds) (1996) *The Story of Worker Sport*, Champaign, IL: Human Kinetics.

Lennartz, K. (1994) 'The presidency of Henri de Baillet-Latour', in *The International Olympic Committee – One Hundred Years*, vol. 1, Lausanne: IOC, 209–93.

Lennartz, K. (1995) 'The presidency of Sigfried Edström (1942–1952)', in *The International Olympic Committee – One Hundred Years*, vol. 2, Lausanne: IOC, 13–76.

Lennartz, K. (ed.) (1974) *Kenntnisse und Vorstellungen von Olympia und den Olympischen Spielen in der Zeit von 393 – 1896*, Schorndorf: Hofmann Verlag.

Lucas, J. A. (1982/3) 'Theodore Roosevelt and Baron Pierre de Coubertin: entangling Olympic games involvement', *Stadion* 8/9 (1982/3), 137–50.

Lindroth, J. (1974) *Idrottens väg till folkrörelse*, Uppsala: Universitet.

Mayer, O. (1960) *A travers les anneaux olympiques*. Geneva: Cailler.

Miller, D. (1992) *Olympic Revolution. The Olympic Biography of Juan Antonio Samaranch*. London: Pavilion Books.

Moore, K. (1991) 'A neglected Imperialist: The Promotion of the British Empire in the Writings of John Astley Cooper', *International Journal of the History of Sport* 8(2), 256–69.

Pound, R. W. (1994) *Five Rings over Korea*, Boston: Little, Brown.

Quanz, D. (1993) 'Civic Pacifism and Sports-based Internationalism: Framework for the Founding of the International Olympic Committee', *Olympika* 2, 1–24.

Quercetani, R. L. (1990) *Athletics. A History of Modern Track and Field. 1860–1990. Men and Women*, Milan: Vallardi.

Reich, K. (1986) *Making It Happen. Peter Ueberroth and the 1984 Olympics*. Santa Barbara, CA: Capra Press.

Rühl, J. K. (1975) *Die 'Olympischen' Spiele Robert Dovers*, Heidelberg: Carl Winter Universitätsverlag.

——(1991) 'L'idéal de l'amateurisme et l'influence de la Grèce sur les "jeux olympiques" à Much Wenlock', in *The Olympic Games through the Ages: Greek Antiquity and its Impact on Modern Sport* (eds R. Renson *et al.*), Athens: Hellenic Sports Research Institute, 129–42.

Rürup, R. (1996) *1936. The Olympic Games and National Socialism*. Berlin: Argon Verlag.

Schantz, O. (1995) 'The Presidency of Avery Brundage (1952–1972)', in *The International Olympic Committee – One Hundreds Years,* vol. 2, Lausanne: IOC, 77–200.

Scherer, K. A. (1996) *100 Jahre Olympische Spiele. Idee, Analyse und Bilanz*. Dortmund: Harenberg Verlag.

Teichler, H. J. (1991) *Internationale Sportpolitik im Dritten Reich*. Schorndorf: Hofmann Verlag.

Varela, A. M. (1992) *Pierre de Coubertin*. Barcelona: Edicions 62.

Young, A. (1987) 'The origins of the modern Olympics: a new version', *International Journal of the History of Sport* 4(3), 271–300.

2 FIFA

Bill Murray

Introduction

FIFA, the controlling body for football throughout the globe, has an influence in the sports world that can be matched only by the International Olympic Committee (IOC). When it was founded in Paris in 1904, it had seven members; today that number is close to 200, more than the member nations of the United Nations. The IOC presides over what once was amateur sport, and its Olympic Games acts every four years in tandem with FIFA's showpiece, the World Cup. Much of the IOC's time is spent gearing up for its quadrennial feast of sport, and it is only in the bidding for the host city for the games, and the four weeks or so of the actual games, that it occupies centre stage. FIFA, on the other hand, presiding over the world's most popular game, has no off-season: the World Cup may be the climax, but hardly has it been played than other competitions in each of the six confederations under its control take over; throughout the world at any one time a league or a cup championship is being played with all the fury and devotion that see Association Football dominating the sporting pages and television screens of the media throughout the world. Countries within each of the confederations controlling specific areas of the globe have their own autonomy in certain matters, as have the confederations within FIFA, but it is FIFA that is the ultimate arbiter in all matters concerning the world game.

Origins

The Football Association that gave the rules to what became known as Association Football was founded in London in October 1863; it was followed by a Scottish Football Association in 1873, a Welsh Football Association three years later and an Irish Football Association in 1880. Two years later the International Board was established to standardize the rules of the game among the four 'nations' of the United Kingdom and to set up the Home International Tournament to be played on an annual basis – the games between Scotland and England, begun in 1872, would last until 1988. At the turn of the century, football in Great Britain, particularly in England and Scotland, was so far ahead of the rest of the world that the authorities in these countries did not take seriously the growth of the game elsewhere. This supremacy was recognized everywhere the game was played at the turn of the century, and through until today the (British) International Board has had a disproportionate influence within FIFA, while the division of the single political entity of Great Britain into four 'home' nations is still recognized, albeit as a subject of recurrent debate both within Britain and abroad.

It was perfectly natural, then, that when some ambitious individuals on the Continent had the idea of setting up a body to oversee the progress of the game on the international stage, they should look to the homeland of the game for advice. This attention was not welcomed and the advice was not forthcoming, but the enthusiasts from the other side of the Channel went ahead with their plans anyway. The idea of a body to control international football was first voiced by the Belgians in the late 1890s, and the Dutch banker, C. A. W. Hirschman, raised the matter again in 1902. The main force behind what was to become the controlling body of world football, however, was the French engineer and newspaper man, Robert Guérin. Guérin was a member of one of the major French sporting societies, the USFSA (Union of French Sports and Athletics Societies) and they hosted the inaugural meeting of what became the Fédération Internationale de Football Association (FIFA), in Paris on 21 May 1904.

The inaugural meeting of FIFA was chaired by M. Fringnet, vice-president of USFSA, and seven nations were represented in person or by proxy: M. Hirschman (Netherlands Football Union, Holland); V. Schneider (Swiss Football Association); M. Sylow (Danish Football Union); R. Guérin and A. Espir (USFSA); P. Muhlinghaus and M. Kahn (Union of Belgian Athletics Societies). M. Fringnet welcomed the foreign delegates and read letters from Dr Karting, announcing the replacement of M. Manning by M. Henschen, to represent the German Football Association (DFB), and from the FA in London, offering its apologies and announcing the calling of a congress in London for 1905. There was also a letter of apology from the Madrid FC, unable to send a delegate, but offering its support. Spain not having a national association at this time, M. Espir was allowed to represent that country. The secretary of the Swedish FA, M. Kornerupt, was also unable to be present, but he too expressed his support and agreed that his country be represented by M. Sylow from Denmark.

The aim of this grandiloquently titled body, free from any 'European' qualifier – Argentina and Uruguay were arguably more advanced in football than any other country outside the United Kingdom at this time, but were not consulted about its formation – was to resolve disputes within nations concerning the authority of the national federation or association, and to organize regular international competitions. The seven founding nations at Paris in 1904 had grown to 24 in 1914, by which time Argentina, Chile, the United States and South Africa had joined, giving the new body a world dimension. The British associations also joined: England in 1905 to keep some sort of control over its wayward progeny, while Scotland and Wales joined in 1910, Ireland a year later. The support of the British associations was at best lukewarm, and their insular arrogance would be a source of continuing conflict until the pupils turned the table on the masters in the 1950s. Despite this, the soccer disciples went to exceptional lengths to welcome the British: Daniel Burley Woolfall, an Englishman, replaced the first president of FIFA, Robert Guérin, in 1906; the (British) International Board remained the controller of the laws of the game, with only two members from FIFA added to it, in 1912; the percentage of receipts that other countries paid to FIFA from all international matches did not apply to the Home Internationals; and throughout the life of FIFA, most of which has been with few English speaking countries as members, although French was the first official language, English has been the language to decide in cases of linguistic dispute. Attempts to rally anti-English feeling, as the French tried to do in 1908, and the German delegates in 1913, were unsuccessful.

Britain vs. France

FIFA, despite the obvious problems of such international bodies, soon set down firm roots and thereafter went from strength to strength. From its earliest days, international competition was a major concern, and from the first the idea of a 'world cup' was raised. One of the main problems facing FIFA over the next half century, however, was the unwillingness of the British FAs to give it due recognition. The world body was also beset by the personal jealousies and national sensitivities inevitable in such institutions, and within the first few years of its founding, France was expelled from its own creation. This resulted from the spill-over of French domestic problems, where the two major bodies controlling sport in France were fiercely divided: the one dominated by the Church (FSGSP), the other virulently anti-clerical (USFSA). It was representatives from the secular USFSA who represented France on FIFA, but it was they who suffered when they allowed their domestic antagonisms to show up in the world body. As fanatical in their attitude to amateurism as they were in regard to anti-clericalism, the French representatives urged support for the English amateur FA when that body broke from the London FA over its recognition of professionalism, and supported its admission to FIFA, despite the FA already being a member. At the 1908 Congress in Vienna they played on anti-British prejudice, pointing to that country's dictatorial attitude and linguistic imperialism, but when they tried to form a rival body they were unable to persuade the Swiss, Italians and Hungarians to follow them. FIFA could not tolerate this and the

French delegates had to resign. This left the way for the rival FSGSP, which had amalgamated with several regional and other bodies into a French Interfederal Committee (CFI) in 1907, to apply for membership. In 1910 they were accepted into FIFA.

FIFA had survived its first major power struggle; the teams of USFSA suffered from not being allowed to play teams not associated with FIFA and were told that the only way to overcome this was by joining its detested rival. A similar fate would await other bodies that challenged the authority of the world body: Colombia in the 1950s and Australia a decade later were forced to make their peace with FIFA after leaving it, and the frequent threats of the Latin American countries to break away, usually over what they saw as the Eurocentricism of the world body, were never carried out.

The individual who benefited most from the French dispute within FIFA was Jules Rimet, at that time president of Red Star and leading light within the Catholic FSGSP. He would later preside over the French Football Federation and the French National Council for Sport, but it is as president of FIFA from 1921 until 1954 that he is best known. He is also recognized as the founder of the World Cup, the first world-wide international sporting competition open to amateur and professional alike, first played in 1930, and from 1950 called after Rimet.

The major splits ahead for FIFA would be in regard to the British associations, but from 1904 its story is one of continuous growth. By 1914 it had 24 members, four of whom came from outside Europe: South Africa (1909–10), Argentina (1912), Chile (1912) and the USA (1913). On the eve of the Second World War there were 51 members, and between 1950 and 1984 membership more than doubled, from 73 to 150. The draw for the 1994 World Cup included 143 of FIFA's 168 member nations and by the time the competition had ended there were 191. This rapid increase came mainly from the break-up of the former communist empires and regimes, and as this process continues the number of members continues to grow. Today there is barely a flag in the world that does not fly around the FIFA offices in Zurich. FIFA has not been exempt from the problems of international bodies committed to high ideals, but it has a power that none could resist: the French delegates were the first to discover this, later there would be others. When the British associations left FIFA in the 1920s (twice) it was the British rather than FIFA who suffered most.

The British associations left FIFA shortly after the end of the First World War, rejoined it again in 1924, but left again in 1928, not to rejoin until after the Second World War. Politics and amateurism were two of the main stumbling blocks, but underscoring this was a fundamental difference in the approach to the game among most of the countries comprising FIFA and those of the home associations. Traffic in footballing ideas was all one way before the Second World War, and the few voices suggesting that the Europeans had something to teach the masters were lost in the wilderness of British apathy and indifference.

A major criticism by the British of the Europeans was in regard to political intrusions in the continental game. And yet it was the British FA's wish to inject a specifically political note that led to their first split with FIFA. This was on 29 December 1919 when it was proposed by the UK associations, supported by France, Belgium and Luxembourg, that they would have no contacts with the defeated belligerents in the recent war. They wanted to leave FIFA to form their own Federation of National Football Associations and pressured even neutrals not to play against the defeated central powers of Germany, Austria and Hungary. Switzerland was the first nation to play against Germany, as it would be after the Second World War, mainly because the much larger German-speaking part of the Federal Republic carried the day over the smaller francophone region. Other neutral nations, encouraged by Hugo Meisl, the driving force of football on the continent, were unwilling to cut off their sporting contacts with nations which had not been their enemies. Italy, which had joined the Allies later in the war, expressed its opposition to the boycott. And so it was that the champions of sport for sport's sake left FIFA on 23 April 1920 and expelled FIFA's two members from the International Board. For two years they refused to allow their members to compete with FIFA teams. When the British associations rejoined FIFA on 14 June 1924, it was again for political reasons, this time closer to home: Ireland.

In the tensions and civil war that led to the creation of a divided Ireland in 1927, with a basically Protestant north and the essentially Catholic Irish Free State (Eire) in the south, teams from the southern states seceded from the IFA, run from Belfast, to create their own Football Association of Ireland (FAI) in June 1921, followed by the creation of their own League two months later. There followed disputes over the right to use the title 'Ireland', with Eire objecting to 'Northern Ireland' calling itself 'Ireland' when it controlled only six counties; moreover, some teams in Ulster, of Catholic inspiration, wanted to play in the FAI. The IFA, for its part, insisted that the Dublin-based Association call itself the Football Association of the Irish Free State. The problem, to become familiar enough after 1945 when other nations claimed sole right to a national title, was brought to FIFA when the FA of Eire asked for affiliation with the world body and representation on the International Board. Recognition one way or the other was loaded with political implications. In this case the FAI was accepted into FIFA in August 1923, and this was recognized by the International Board, but not its place with the Board. Teams in Ulster, and this with the powerful Belfast Celtic particularly in mind, were forbidden from playing in the Eire League. Moves to have an international team picked by a joint IFA/FAI committee were rejected by Belfast.

Amateurism

The main issue bedevilling relations between the UK and FIFA on its return in 1924 was that of amateurism, particularly payment for broken time, but it was also, as the official history of the FA admits, 'partly because of the suspicion that [FIFA] was aiming to become the final authority of the game'. The FA was peeved that in the organization of soccer for the Olympic Games, FIFA had made the 'inflammatory' statement that it was 'the final authority on the game'. However, it was the issue of amateurism that provoked the split.

On this issue the British, still controlled by those who had accepted professionalism more or less as a necessary evil, wanted a definition of amateurism that restricted payments to necessary travel and hotel expenses. Players could pay a coach or trainer, but all other training expenses had to be paid for by themselves. They were forbidden to play for any football prize 'in a football context', nor were they allowed to be paid or compensated for time lost at work. This effectively restricted teams playing soccer in the Olympic Games to the rich, and it was obvious that the brilliant young Uruguayans who had won gold in the 1924 and 1928 Olympic Games were not in that category. Apart from the time taken to sail from their homeland to Europe, it was well known that they had been practising together for months. For the British associations, niggardly in the expenses granted to their own professionals, and who looked on serious training as some form of blasphemy, this was too much, and they left FIFA on 17 February 1928. This time the break was not so complete, and sporting contacts continued at club and even international level. There was no suggestion, however, that they take part in the first World Cup to be played in Montevideo, the capital of Uruguay, in 1930. This was the first international sporting competition open to professional and amateur alike, and despite the problems of that first competition, played in a country remote from the main centres of football in Europe, this quadrennial competition continued to progress over subsequent years, interrupted only by the European war of 1939 that became a world war two years later. Its success, overlooked by the British press and public before 1950, was assured long before Britain sent any teams to take part in it.

The World Cup

In this time football advanced despite the obvious problems of bringing together on the sporting arena all the tensions and frustrations of the world. Soccer has become synonymous in some non-soccer countries with riots and spectator violence, yet only soccer, of all the football codes, has produced not only a genuine global competition, but one which has continued to flourish since its modest début in far from modest surroundings in 1930. Jules Rimet is the man most associated with the

World Cup, but his compatriot Henri Delaunay was an enthusiastic supporter. Known as 'Sir Henry' for his British airs, his pipe and his cocker spaniel, as well as his predilection for British names over the 'Racing', 'Olympique', 'Stade' and 'Union Sportive' favoured by the French. Delaunay stood out in contrast to Rimet, who spoke only one language and who, despite his achievements, was a man of remarkably narrow vision.

Rimet and Delaunay began their campaign for a world competition at the Paris Olympics in 1924 and finally won acceptance for their idea at Amsterdam four years later. Uruguay was the obvious choice to host the first competition, to be held in 1930, not just because of its stunning success in the Paris and Amsterdam Olympics, but because it was prepared to pick up the bill for travel and accommodation for all competing countries. Uruguay was particularly anxious to host the event as part of the celebrations for the centenary of its constitution, and promised to build a special stadium for the event, the Estadio Centenario.

The competition was held just as the effects of the Depression were being felt in the western economies, but the major problem was that of convincing Europeans to send their teams on the long sea journey and staying in the southern continent for the two weeks of actual competition – a minimum of six weeks. The best European nations, Austria, Czechoslovakia and Hungary, were now professional, and although Uruguay had generously agreed to pay for all expenses while in that country, they were still faced by a heavy wages bill. The outcome was that only Belgium, Yugoslavia and France, all still nominally amateur, made the journey from Europe, to join the United States of America and the Latin American teams which comprised the thirteen entrants who finally lined up for the first World Cup.

Despite the novelty of the occasion, the competition was successfully completed, helped by a final which saw the old rivals, Argentina and Uruguay pitted against each other. The host nation won, sparking off unprecedented scenes of joy and despair on the opposite banks of the Rio Plata. Prior to this there had been the usual problems on the field, much national posturing and political side-effects, but the Uruguayans could well reflect proudly on their accomplishments. It is doubtful if this could be said of the next World Cup, held in Italy in 1934 and overhung from the start by the politics of Mussolini's fascism.

FIFA tried hard to ignore the external politics crowding in on the game throughout the 1930s, particularly as it had problems enough of its own at this time. Many of the South American nations were in an upheaval over the issue of amateurism and professionalism, with the splits and secessions that usually accompany such disputes. Some were unhappy about the control of the game from Europe. Uruguay refused to send a team to the 1934 World Cup because of what it believed was the insult of the Europeans in sending only three teams in 1930, while Argentina sent a weakened team, in protest at the way its best players had been plundered by Italy since the late 1920s. Brazil, also split by the amateur/professional issue, was as yet only on the threshold of its spectacular entry on to the world stage. Like Argentina it was eliminated in the first round.

The political problems of 1934 expanded to form a darkening cloud that hung over the 1938 World Cup held in France. Spain was racked by civil war, Austria had been annexed by Germany, and Czechoslovakia was about to be sold out to the Nazis. FIFA tried hard to imagine that none of this was happening and valiantly tried to keep together what it was already calling its 'family'. In the early 1930s FIFA's publications had come out with some vapid statements about soccer having nothing to do with politics, and even when the European civil war had begun it still tried to convince itself of this.

South America

Much of the coming conflict could be seen in the Civil War in Spain, which began in 1936 and continued on its bloody way until 1939. FIFA banned all international matches there, but when Franco started to gain the ascendancy it changed its mind and supported him. Franco then demanded that no games be permitted against a Basque team that had gone on a world tour, in part to avoid the conflict, in part to raise funds for its compatriots. FIFA agreed to Franco's demands, but the issue raised a storm in South America where the Basques were due to play and where there was already a strong body of opinion against the European-based football body. Several countries threatened to ignore the ban, above all Chile supported by Bolivia, Paraguay, Peru and Uruguay. A debate raged in the Argentine press, but eventually they sided with FIFA. Argentina had been irritated that their (late) application to host the 1938 World Cup had been unsuccessful (when they withdrew from the competition their offices were attacked by infuriated fans). The power of FIFA was to prevail against the Basques, however. When they arrived to play their games they had to make do with a civil presentation to the crowd, and none of the five games scheduled was played. Uruguay and Chile did not carry out their threat to secede.

In February 1939, Rimet, the president of FIFA, made a special visit to South America to help solve the problems, and allay the suspicion noted in FIFA's official publication, *Football World/Football Mondial/Fussball Welt* (April 1939), regarding the 'reproach sometimes made by South America, of [FIFA] being too European' – in fact there was only one South American on the FIFA executive, but that was said to be because of the problem of communication. It was too late for Rimet to get Argentina to enter the 1938 World Cup, but he did smooth a few ruffled feathers and in the end kept the malcontents within 'the great football family'. He was given a particularly warm welcome by the Argentina FA, itself in dispute with Uruguay, which had first issued the invitation to him. Argentina's hurt at losing the 1938 finals to France was obviously forgotten, as it pledged its presence at the 1942 games, which FIFA suggested it should host if Germany pulled out. Rimet also raised the possibility of a game between Europe and South America, but more realistically it was decided by FIFA that a game between the best clubs of Europe and South America would be a better idea. Brazil was the only South American (CONMEBOL) country to go to the World Cup in France, and was quick to pledge its loyalty to FIFA – which did not prevent it threatening to leave the 'football family' when it was eliminated from the competition on a disputed penalty.

The South Americans were left to their own devices in the early 1940s as Europe tore itself apart, but no sooner had the guns fallen silent in Europe than arrangements were being made for football matches to resume. Shortly after the victories in Europe and Asia, the British FAs made their peace with FIFA, returning to the fold in 1946. One of their first acts was to arrange a Great Britain vs. Rest of Europe spectacular which was played at Hampden Park, Glasgow before 134,000 spectators in May 1947. This match netted the depleted FIFA coffers £30,000, and football in Europe prepared to enter another boom period. When the question of the next World Cup was raised, however, South America was the only choice, and that fell to Brazil. With the successful completion of this tournament the future of the World Cup, now called the Jules Rimet World Cup, was assured. Thereafter its main problems would come with its very success.

The rise of Africa and Asia

International football entered a new phase in the 1950s as improvements in land and air travel brought the nations of the word closer together. Floodlit matches, common in South America in the 1930s, became the norm in Europe during this time, allowing mid-week competitions, and while it would not be until the 1960s that television crossed the oceans, from the early 1950s it was able to link up whole continents. The new competitions encouraged by the technological changes gave an added impulse to continental competitions, but this in no way diminished the power of FIFA. FIFA, however, faced new problems as it absorbed the nations of Asia and Africa, freed from colonialism or European control and which sought through football to proclaim their national identity. Europe and South America, however, continued to dominate a world game that had become truly global.

In the mid-1950s FIFA had eighty affiliated members, only eighteen of whom were from Asia and five from Africa; two decades later membership had almost doubled, to 141, but the Afro-Asian members had risen to thirty-nine countries from Africa (including suspended members South Africa and Rhodesia) and thirty-three from Asia; by 1990 there were 166 member nations, forty-eight from Africa and thirty-six from Asia. By then soccer was represented in every part of the globe, with FIFA presiding over six regional confederations. The first of these had been formed in South America in 1916 (CONMEBOL), the others came much later, Europe not forming its UEFA until 1954. In that same year the Asian Football Confederation (AFC) was formed, and two years later the Confédération Africaine de Football (CAF). The North and Central American powers finally came together to form CONCACAF in 1961, and four years later the last outposts of the football world were brought under the international umbrella when the islands of Oceania agreed to federate in 1965/6.

The strength of the African, Asian and Middle-Eastern nations on the football field was not very impressive in the 1950s, and it was not until the 1970s that their voting power off it would have spectacular results. They brought to FIFA impressive statistics in the number of people playing football, but before they began to show their talents on the field, above all with the impact of the Middle-Eastern nations boosted by the windfall profits of their oil reserves after 1973, and the sheer natural talents of the Africans from the early 1980s, they brought a host of political problems.

The first of these came with the creation of the state of Israel in 1948 and the subsequent Arab-Israeli conflict; the second with the triumph of the Communist Revolution in China in 1949. The communist takeovers in Eastern Europe did not cause the same problems as they did in Asia, where North and South Korea and China continued to claim total rights to their divided countries. In South Africa problems of a more strictly sporting nature were emerging as the white regime insisted on treating its non-white inhabitants as lesser beings, in sport as much as in the political system that became official policy under the name of apartheid after 1948. On all of these issues the African and Asian nations would form a block of opinion that the Europeans, above all the Anglos, saw as bad form, bringing as it did a brand of politics into sport that they did not like.

After the revolution of 1949 that brought Mao and the Communists to power in China, many of the middle-class players and millionaire supporters of the game left the mainland. Many settled in Hong Kong and they were prominent in the foundation and early days of the Asian Football Confederation. On the mainland the new governing body for sport, the All-China Athletic Federation, controlled soccer, and it was recognized as a member of FIFA from its inception, since the geographical area it controlled was that of the pre-existing China. On the island of Taiwan (Formosa), where Chiang Kai Shek tried to set up a new China with the help of the US, soccer played second fiddle to baseball and basketball, but it served to cause confusion when Taiwan, calling itself China, was admitted to FIFA in 1954. Four years later the People's Republic resigned in protest. The communist regime was not to allow its sporting flowers to bloom in the free market, and its footballers had to be content at first with games against communist neighbours North Korea and the USSR.

China's sporting contacts opened out to games against countries like Tanzania and other African countries where China was trying to exert influence, but disappeared when the ideological fanatics of the Cultural Revolution took over from 1966 to 1970. Then came that early form of glasnost, the 'ping-pong diplomacy' of the early 1970s, which saw China anxious to re-enter the world body of football. This posed a problem for FIFA since Taiwan was an affiliated member. However, new president Joao Havelange made it clear when he took over in 1974 that he wanted Communist China brought into the FIFA family, an ambition shared by the Hong Kong millionaire businessman, Henry Fok, who won the support of the Middle Eastern countries by pledging his opposition to Israel. In 1974 the AFC expelled Taiwan to allow China to enter its confederation, and this faced FIFA with the even greater problem of having to expel the AFC, its biggest confederation. Nelsonian diplomacy continued to prevail, as FIFA bartered the fate of Israel, also expelled, by moving it to Oceania if Taiwan could be restored.

None of this prevented teams from England, Portugal and Italy visiting the People's Republic in the late 1970s, while teams from China were invited to play games in Europe in return. This was in breach of FIFA's rules about playing with non-members, but was overlooked. China was even allowed to enter the draw for the 1982 World Cup before it became a member of FIFA, which it did in 1979. Other, much smaller, nations, had been expelled for not paying their dues. Havelange's support for China came in large measure because of the step it would represent in making the game truly global. Through to the 1960s India promised to be the giant of Asian soccer; in the late 1970s that mantle fell on the People's Republic of China, but whatever the world body gained in statistics there was little reward in quality. For while more than 20 million were added to the list of FIFA's registered players in the 1980s, China's performance in Asian and World competition has been mediocre.

Middle-Eastern politics made their first serious entry into the World Cup in 1958 when Indonesia, Egypt and Sudan refused to play against Israel in the preliminary rounds. Israel then looked like qualifying without playing a game, but FIFA decided that they would have to play one of the teams who had lost, and so Wales qualified. Israel as a nation and its club teams were shunted from confederation to confederation to avoid the hatred of the Arabs and their Asian and African supporters who would refuse to play them. It was not until they were accepted into the Union of European Football Associations (UEFA) in 1991 that Israel found a confederation it could call its own.

The African nations had many regional, linguistic and other divisions to overcome since the foundation of the Confederation of African Football in 1957, but on two issues they were in complete union of views: the evils of colonialism and the existence of apartheid in South Africa. Under Sir Stanley Rous, president of FIFA from 1962 to 1974, FIFA tried not to see this as a serious problem, but its fundamental contradiction with the ideals of fair play meant that even administrators who had still to come to terms with the end of colonialism had to do something about it. In their anxiety to stay within FIFA the Football Association of South Africa offered to send a black team to the World Cup in 1966 and a white team in 1970. The non-white-controlled South African Soccer Federation refused to agree with this and in 1962 FIFA suspended South Africa: expulsion came in 1976 after Rous had been replaced by Havelange.

Throughout the 1960s the political power of the Afro-Asian nations made little impact on FIFA, and when most of them boycotted the 1966 World Cup in England over the allocation of only one place between them (and Oceania), their absence was barely noticed – especially since the highlight of the World Cup was the performance of the Asian nation that ignored the boycott: North Korea.

Across the Atlantic another major row was brewing which FIFA could not ignore, when rival groups impressed by the commercial possibilities of the game that had drawn so much enthusiasm in the 1966 World Cup sought to create a similar market potential in the United States. Three groups set up leagues of their own and then applied to join FIFA. Only one could be affiliated with the world body, and so the United States Soccer Football Association (along with the Canadian FA) found itself arbiter in the bestowal of the franchises that would gain the approval of FIFA. The two losing groups merged to found a pirate league, called the National Professional Soccer League (NPSL). Operating outside FIFA, and so deprived of international competition, the outlaw NPSL comforted themselves with a CBS contract to televise one game per week. The two warring bodies soon cut their losses and came together to form the North American Soccer League, and, after a sticky start, attracted massive crowds to soccer in the 1970s, thanks mainly to importing stars from Europe and South America, above all Pelé. The heady days of the late 1970s proved to be a false dawn and the dreams of the romantics and profit-seekers ended in a crash in 1984. FIFA, however, never lost sight of a land that represented a mission area to be converted and a gold-mine to be tapped.

Joao Havelange

In the 1970s FIFA moved into new and more luxurious offices in Zurich and the world body entered into a new era of expansion throughout the world, as the Asian and African nations that had been a problem in Rous's time became a solution to the ambitions of the new president, Joao

Havelange. On the eve of the World Cup final of 1974 in West Germany the nations of the Third World exercised their democratic rights to elect a president who was committed to promoting the game in their countries. Ironically the transfer of power away from its European, and particularly British, influence, came at a time when Europe itself was about to take an unhealthy grip on the field of play, attracting to its domestic leagues, particularly in Italy and Spain, the cream of world soccer talent.

Jean Marie Faustin Godefroid Havelange, better known as Joao Havelange, Olympic representative for Brazil in swimming in 1936 and water polo in 1952, president of the Brazilian FA, recipient of a multitude of titles, and multi-millionaire businessman, stood in stark contrast to the man whom he replaced: Stanley Rous, one time schoolteacher, esteemed referee and long-time secretary of the FA. To win the votes of the Third World countries Havelange had used all the power and influence at his disposal, and yet his victory was a narrow one. This was due to the man who worked behind the scenes for Rous, Horst Dassler, owner of the Adidas sporting goods empire that was then making massive inroads into the Olympic market and intended to do the same in soccer. Shrewdly, the new president brought Dassler into his own camp, and the dynamic entrepreneur then showed Havelange how to finance the promises he had made to the Third World countries as part of his election platform, from coaching assistance and other financial help to wider participation in world competitions. The essential part of Dassler's plan was to win over Coca-Cola to a massive sponsorship deal that financed the new world youth tournaments introduced by FIFA to help the underdeveloped football countries.

Many European commentators resented the power of the Afro-Asian nations, and when Asia and Africa were each granted an extra place for the 1982 World Cup FIFA was accused of giving in to clamorous voices out of tune with their footballing ability. After their boycott over representation in 1966, Asia and Africa were granted a place each in the 1970 World Cup. Havelange now promised to double this, and did so by having the finals of the World Cup enlarged from a comfortable sixteen teams easily divided by four, into a cumbersome twenty-four that resulted in many crowded fixtures. Havelange was also said to have called in a political favour from Samaranch, whom he is said to have helped, through his power with Third World countries, to get elected president of the International Olympic Committee in 1980: Samaranch was said to have encouraged the Spanish organizers of the 1982 World Cup to increase the number of participants.

By then Havelange had gone a long way towards fulfilling other promises to promote the game in underdeveloped countries. However dubious the role of Dassler in this, and whatever the fears about commercial intrusion, the partnership of Coca-Cola and FIFA in the expansion of various world competitions outside the World Cup and the Olympic Games has been a spectacular success. There had been many regional competitions under the control of their particular confederation long before Havelange, of course, but the age of jet travel and instant communication by phone, fax and satellite meant that these could be expanded on a world-wide basis.

The first World Youth Cup, for players under 20 years old, was held in Tunisia in 1977, and thereafter has been played in many parts of the world with particular benefit to the underdeveloped football countries, as the Europeans and South Americans at first tended to ignore them. When Portugal as home nation in 1991 survived a brilliant Brazilian onslaught to retain the trophy on penalties, they did so before 127,000 adoring fans, the biggest crowd at a FIFA competition since Brazil in 1950.

The under-17 world championship began as a schoolboy competition, with equal representation, three places each, to the five biggest confederations, regardless of their standing in the football world. (To make up the sixteen, the last place is given to Oceania.) As in the other under-age tournaments, Europe and South America did not take this competition seriously to begin with, but as the search for talent to tempt the insatiable greed of the Europeans continues unabated, no final is now complete without the agents from Europe with their open cheque books.

It was also by making the Olympics an under-age competition that FIFA finally came to terms with the constant problems with the one-time amateur body. Soccer at the Olympic Games, besmirched by professionalism, but too popular and too much of a money-spinner to be left out, has always posed a problem. From 1930 the major soccer nations lost interest in the games, but from 1952 the state amateurs of the Communist nations took them seriously as a means of proving the superiority of their political systems. In 1978 FIFA tried to get rid of some of the anomalies of star professionals appearing in the Olympics at the same time as it sought to win the favour of the Afro-Asian countries, by decreeing that any European or South American who had represented his country would be banned from the Olympics. This, however, did not apply to the other confederations. The countries of the state amateurs, whose players floated freely between Olympic and World Cup selection, were the most affected, and the most indignant, but the Afro-Asian countries still placed more credit on the World Cup. The issue was finally resolved by decreeing that from 1992 soccer at the Olympic Games would be restricted to players under 23 years, a sensible solution that has offended the inglorious ambition of the Olympics custodians to see every sport represented in the Olympic Games at the highest level, regardless of whether they already have their own world competition.

The problem of over-age players in such competitions is obvious, and FIFA have come down hard on known abuses, issuing bans and long suspensions on nations found guilty.

FIFA introduced an international five-a-side competition in 1989, but this is unlikely to interest anyone other than those directly involved. On the other hand, the FIFA Women's World Cup promises to win as much interest as the youth competitions. First held in China in November 1991, it was played· before capacity crowds of over 60,000 and millions more who watched on television. China were beaten by Norway, who reached the final only to lose to the USA, that most underdeveloped of soccer nations, who were run-away winners in all their games. In Sweden four years later Norway had their revenge with a victory over Germany in the final; a rather embittered US team had to be content with third place with a 2–0 victory over China. One of the more welcome additions to the Atlanta Olympic Games in 1996 was women's football, and to the delight of the home crowd the US stormed their way to gold, beating China 2–1 with a 'golden goal' in extra time before 76,481 ecstatic fans in Athens, Georgia, said to be the highest number ever to watch a women-only sports event.

Changes and problems: 1970s–1990s

Football and the Olympic Games provide the world's two most popular international sporting entertainments, and share the problems that such events attract. However, while the Olympic Games have constantly been threatened with and seriously weakened by boycotts, the boycotts in soccer have usually been by particular nations over particular grievances, above all concerning Israel and Taiwan, but also about the claims of the Afro-Asian nations for more representation. This barely affected the major tournaments. The only time the World Cup had to face a potential boycott was in Argentina in 1978, in protest at the brutality of the Videla regime that came to power in 1976 and embarked on a relentless regime of terror epitomized in the 'disappeared', the young men picked up by the secret police and who never saw their families again. This was also the first World Cup since Italy in 1934 to be played with blatantly political involvement. The Videla regime had inherited the 1978 Mundial from its predecessor, but lost no time in trying to show how they could organize a world-class event. They spent vast sums of money to impress visitors, but whatever success they had in convincing visitors that Argentina was a modern nation, their success in raising the moral approval of the regime was slight. And despite the protests by leftists throughout the world, in Argentina itself guerrilla groups said they would not upset the Mundial because it was a 'feast of the people'. Cesar Menotti, the manager of the team, was no lover of the generals, and such was his power as the man who had guided Argentina to World Cup victory, that he was able to criticise them with impunity for trying to usurp the glory. The Dutch runners-up too, refused to shake hands with the Argentine dictator. There had never been any question of FIFA transferring the games from Argentina: it ignored the protests of the Soviet Union at having to play in Chile in stadiums that had been used as prison camps and places of torture when the Pinochet regime ousted Allende in 1973, and it was no more put out by the atrocities committed in Argentina in the years to come.

To the taint of politics in Mundial 1978 was added that of corruption, when Argentina secured their place in the final against a somewhat supine Peru team who were already out of the competition. Four years later, in Spain, grave doubts hung over the result of the Austria–Germany game that assured the qualification from the preliminary group of the two European neighbours ahead of a justifiably enraged Algeria. Algeria's complaints about European complicity were overlooked by FIFA. In that same competition Germany was involved in another controversy when goalkeeper Harald Schumacher violently charged France's Patrick Battiston, causing him serious injury, without as much as the referee issuing a caution. This happened in full view of a world-wide television audience, but the suggestion that FIFA should use this evidence against Schumacher was not even contemplated: this would change by USA 1994.

In the meantime the normal problems of international competition continued to create irritations and occasional outrage, from suspicions about the commercial and other motives that gave the 1986 World Cup to Mexico and its unpopular media barons when Colombia pulled out, to dealing with nations whose pride or pocket was hurt in failure to win games or the right to host particular tournaments. All of this would be overshadowed by the decision to award the 1994 World Cup to the United States.

There was little FIFA could do about the dismal play in most of the games at Italia 1990, but its motives in giving the honour of the next World Cup to a nation notoriously ignorant of the spirit and rules of the world game raised fears among the soccer faithful wherever the game was played. Such fears turned out to be misplaced, and while commerce undoubtedly played a major role in FIFA's decision, the world body was also motivated by a sense of mission in taking the game's show-piece to the darkest corner of the soccer world.

USA 1994 was one of the most successful World Cups, and while it was the players who provided the actual spectacle, the much maligned FIFA has to be given praise for making it possible. After flying a few kites about changes in the game to make it more palatable for what it saw as American tastes, FIFA's final changes and instructions to referees were all positive.

Awarding three points for a win instead of two discouraged playing for a draw, and the ban on the goalkeeper handling a back-pass, introduced two years earlier, eliminated the most frustrating of the several ways of wasting time. That other bane of the soccer spectator's life, watching players roll around in histrionic agony at the slightest touch from an opposing player, was virtually eliminated by the arrival of stretchers to take them from the field to perform in private. Linesmen were told to ignore 'passive' offside and favour the attacking player, which could not solve the eternal problem of the offside rule, but at least made mistakes more likely to favour attack. Stoppage time was meticulously recorded, so that most games went a few minutes beyond the ninety. Unfortunately, FIFA did not proceed with the decision to introduce sudden-death in extra-time to help avoid that most exciting but farcical way of deciding a game, the penalty shoot-out. As it turned out, the most disappointing game to go into extra-time, the final between Italy and Brazil, was unable to produce a goal in any case.

FIFA's instructions to referees to protect the ball players had the most exhilarating consequences, as referees came down on foul play with a severity never before seen. The result was that key players like Romario of Brazil and Baggio of Italy did not have to suffer the outrages committed against the great players of previous tournaments – such as Pelé in 1966, or Maradona, a kicking-bag for cynical defenders throughout his career. Nor were there any of the on-field 'battles' that had scarred the 1938 and 1954 competitions, or the gross indiscipline that went beyond the control of referees in 1962 and 1970. Some referees were woefully incompetent, and paid the price for it in being sent home early, but on the whole, and despite a questionable flourishing of red and yellow cards on occasion, they performed admirably.

More controversial was the use of the TV camera to dispense justice for offences that the referee missed. Television replays mostly showed the referee to be correct, but when referee Sandor Puhl at the Italy/Spain game failed to see the elbow from an Italian defender that broke the nose of Spain's Luis Enrique in the penalty area, FIFA, acting on the video evidence, severely punished the offender. What they did not do, and which has been used controversially twice in Bundesliga games in Germany, was to have the game replayed, on the grounds that Spain should have been given a penalty that would almost certainly have won them the game. That would be to open up a veritable Pandora's Box, and even in the Bundesliga it has been used only in cases where a goal was or was not clearly scored. No sports lover can have sympathy for the player who attacks an opponent behind the referee's back, but cases where a goal is clearly scored but not given are worth consideration. The issue of video evidence was brought to light in England during Euro-96, when a clear goal by Romania against Croatia was missed by the referee and his linesmen, but not by the television camera. Romania protested, and had the sympathies of all who watched the incident on TV replays, but FIFA rightly dismissed their complaints: if video evidence is ever used it will have to be at the time of the incident, and on the rarest of occasions.

'Gigantism'

Football and the Olympic Games have grown to immense proportions in recent years, encouraged by television and the seemingly endless floods of money that it allows to pour into the sport, at least in its upper reaches. Accusations of money spoiling sport, and football in particular, have been with the game since its earliest days, but in recent years commerce seems to be in danger of taking over the game itself. FIFA has made noises about preserving the game, or some of its major competitions, for the ordinary spectator, but more and more the top games look like being reserved for the wealthy, with even television signing up the top games for subscription viewing. Along with this is the gigantism in individual competitions, especially the World Cup, and the proliferation of increasingly meaningless competitions that overload the playing season of players who are generally well paid for their efforts.

FIFA's move towards gigantism has been pushed by the pressure of the developing soccer nations demanding a place in the final, but FIFA under Havelange has willingly gone along with this. In France in 1998 there were thirty-two teams in the final, twice as many as in 1978. Four weeks of intense competition in the middle of the day in stadiums that were like ovens to the players made the outcome of USA 1994 in part a test of endurance. Summer games in the northern hemisphere are to suit the European off-season, and playing at the hottest time of the day was to suit European television audiences; these are realities FIFA has to come to terms with, but changes have to be made.

The problem of a final pool of twenty-four, and now thirty-two, is a more general problem, arising wherever the finals are played. While the increased numbers might please the smaller nations, and the players are always happy to take the increased money from television, there is too much pressure on the players, most of whom have just completed a strenuous league programme. Somehow the finals have to be brought back to sixteen, perhaps by playing two semi-final qualifying groups of sixteen in two different countries, in the year before the final. This would have the added advantage of allowing two other countries to take part in hosting the world competition. Japan and South Korea have been jointly appointed to host the World Cup in 2002, but the details of how this is to be carried out have yet to be decided. FIFA has to be credited for the idea of sharing the competition, but it remains to be seen if the wounds left by Japanese atrocities in Korea before 1945 will be opened up again or helped to heal over.

Much of the elephantine growth of the game has been linked ineluctably to the development of technology, but FIFA seems to have done little to resist it. Again, in a world where greed is the ruling religion, at least among the rich and the powerful, FIFA can be seen as doing little more than following the fashionable trend. For an organization whose principle of fair play is constantly touted, however, one might expect higher standards of morality.

Much of the blame for the gigantism and commercialization of the world game has been laid at the feet of FIFA's president since 1974, Joao

Havelange. In 1996 he turned eighty, and many in the football world hoped that he would retire, but such was not to be the case. His authoritarian rule, wielded with all the power of a man who made millions amidst the poverty of his home nation, and whose treatment of even the greatest players the game has seen smacks of Third World dictatorship, has made him unpopular in many circles, none more so than in Brian Glanville's column in *World Soccer*, where this most notable of international football writers has waged a relentless campaign against him. All of this Havelange has shrugged off, helped in part by the absence of a likely replacement, and the realization that the western world is turning away from concerns of social justice towards a more Brazilian organization of economics and society. Africa's Issi Hayatou had pretensions to the top post, and more recently it seemed as though Lennart Johannsen, UEFA's president, would mount a successful challenge, but the best he could do was thwart FIFA's wish to have the 2002 World Cup held in Japan. The job went instead to Sepp Blatter of Switzerland.

Post-Havelange?

Havelange cannot go on for ever, but there is little to suggest that FIFA will not. The world body is stronger today than it ever was, the game more popular than it ever was. Whether or not it is healthier is perhaps another matter. Traditionally the soccer countries that have paid the highest salaries to star players have been those with little concern for poverty in society at large, with the more equitably organized societies, as in the Scandinavian countries, Germany or even Britain, paying a pittance in comparison. It is a sign of the times and perhaps of the future that football teams in England and Scotland are paying the world's highest transfer fees for players at a time when poverty and social unease have hardly been worse in these countries.

A historian seeking comfort in the past for the trend that football seems to be taking could look to how the FA and other amateurs tried to hold the moral high ground against claims by the players for fair wages at the turn of the century, and how the League and the FA tried to maintain players in servitude thereafter. It is cold comfort however; it seems more likely that football has finally fallen into the hands of the profit-seekers, the rich getting greedier the richer they become, and the poor being left with the crumbs. The FA, the one-time guardian of fair play, and FIFA that once tried to follow its example, have joined wholeheartedly in the Gadarene rush that threatens to see the people's game transformed into a pastime for business and leisured-class élites.

References

Much of the above is based on material that has appeared in my two books on the history and the growth of association football throughout the world:

Murray, B. (1994) *Football. A History of the World Game*, Aldershot: Scholar Press.
——(1996) *The World's Game. A History of Soccer*, Urbana and Chicago: The University of Illinois Press.

Despite the similarity of title and subject matter, these are two quite different books. The Bibliographies of these books should be consulted for a full coverage of the sources on which this work is based. See in particular, however:

FIFA (1984) *FIFA: 1904–1984*, Zurich: FIFA. (An official history.)

3   The impact of communism on sport

James Riordan

Introduction

Communist sports policy in Europe is dead. It lives on in China, Cuba and North Korea. It was not everywhere identical; nor did it feature highly in terms of national priorities in the less economically advanced communist nations, such as Albania, Vietnam and Cambodia. Nevertheless, it did contain certain discernible similarities that marked it off from sports policies elsewhere in both the developed and the less developed world. This chapter examines these similarities, as well as the implications of the rapid volte face in sport in virtually all the erstwhile communist states following the revolutions in 1989 throughout eastern Europe.

The rapid collapse of Soviet-style communism in eastern Europe and of the nine nations there that subscribed to it (with variations in Albania and Yugoslavia on the totalitarian or 'state socialism' model) provides an opportunity to examine the 'communist sports policies' and the impact they had on sport and popular perceptions.

One reason for virtual universal interest in communist sport was that its success, particularly in the Olympic Games, drew considerable attention and admiration. The Soviet Union and the German Democratic Republic (East Germany) provided exciting competition with the USA and West Germany, as did other East versus West, communist versus capitalist sports confrontations.

A less remarkable, though perhaps more far-reaching, aspect of communist sport, however, was the evolution of a model of sport or 'physical culture' for a modernizing community, employing sport for utilitarian purposes to promote health and hygiene, defence, labour productivity, integration of a multi-ethnic population into a unified state, international recognition and prestige; what we might call 'nation-building'. After all, with the exception of East Germany and, partly, Czechoslovakia, communist development was initially based on a mass illiterate, rural population. It was this model that had some attraction for nations in Africa, Asia and Latin America.

In most communist states, therefore, sport had the quite revolutionary role of being an agent of social change, with the state as pilot. In any case, after revolution or liberation there was rarely a leisure class around to promote sport for its own disport, as there was, say, in Victorian England.

Furthermore, partly under the influence of Marxist philosophy stressing the interdependence of the mental and physical states of human beings, many communist states emphasized the notion that physical culture is as vital as mental culture in human development, and that it should be treated as such both for the all-round development of the individual and, ulti- mately, for the health of society. In the classic treatment of this issue back in 1917, the year of the Russian Revolution, Mao Zedong actually placed physical culture before mental culture:

> Physical culture is the complement of virtue and wisdom. In terms of priorities, it is the body that contains knowledge, and knowledge is the seat of virtue. So it follows that attention should first be given to a child's physical needs; there is time later to cultivate morality and wisdom.

Sport, or rather physical culture, then evidently had particular social and political significance in the development of communist societies. This is all the more so because the place of sport has been more central in their social systems and has been controlled and directed by the state. The following would seem to be the main state priorities assigned to sport in communist development.

Major priorities in sports policies

Nation-building

All communist states faced problems of political stabilization and of economic and social development; some were confronted with the serious problem of national integration of ethnically diverse populations into a new unified state. A key issue here is that of nation-building: the incul- cation of political loyalties to the nation as a whole, transcending the bounds of kinship, race, language, religion and geographical location. Not only was this a key problem facing post-revolutionary Russia, China and Cuba, it has been equally relevant to post-liberation modernizing societies in Africa and Asia.

What better than sport to help the regimes in such societies promote the building of strong nation-states? After all, sport, with its broad relevance to education, health, culture and politics, and its capacity to mobilize peo- ple (predispose them towards change), may uniquely serve the purpose of nation-building and help foster national integration. It extends to and unites wider sections of the population than probably any other social activity. It is easily understood and enjoyed, cutting across social, economic, educational, ethnic, religious and language barriers. It permits some emotional release (reasonably) safely, it can be relatively cheap and it is easily adapted to support educational, health and social-welfare objectives.

And it is here that the sports introduced by Westerners at the turn of the century in China, Russia, Cuba and other developing states have some advantages over indigenous folk-games in that the latter are often linked to festivals which mainly take place annually in the various communities. Indigenous sports have therefore served only as a means of expressing tribal or ethnic identity. Modern sports have served as a means of expressing national identity. It has therefore been the modern sports that the communist nations have taken up and promoted.

Integration

Bound up with nation-building has been the state-desired aim of integrating a multinational population, often in transition from a rural to an urban way of life, into the new nation-state. Many communist societies were loose confederations of diverse ethnic groups: different colours, languages, traditions, religions, stages of economic growth, prejudices. Let us take the world's two largest communist countries.

The billion people of China consist of at least a dozen distinctly different ethnic groups; the country is divided into twenty-one provinces and five ethnic autonomous regions. The minorities constitute aborigines (Chuan, Yi, Maio, Manchu, Puyi) and Koreans in the east; Mongols, Turks (Uighurs) and Tibetans in the west.

The USSR was a multinational federation of over 290 million people containing 100 or more nationalities. The country was divided into 15 Union Republics, each based on a separate ethnic group, and many other administrative divisions (autonomous republics, autonomous regions, territories and national areas). Every weekday children studied in as many as 87 different languages and daily newspapers came out in 64 languages.

The governments of both these great nations quite deliberately took western sports from town to country and, in the case of the USSR, from the European metropolis to the Asiatic interior, and used them to help integrate the diverse peoples into the new nation and to promote a patriotism that transcended mere nations and ethnic affiliations.

In Soviet history, for example, even before the Civil War (1917–21) was over, the new Soviet regime organized the First Central Asian Games in the ancient Islamic centre of Tashkent in October 1920. This was actually the first time in history that Uzbeks, Kazakhs, Turkmenians, Tadzhiks, Kirgiz and other Muslim peoples, as well as Russians, Ukrainians and other Europeans, had competed in any sporting event together. As Rodionov (1975) made clear later, 'The integrative functions of sport are immense. This has great importance for our multinational state. Sports contests, festivals, spartakiads and other forms of sports competition have played a key role in cementing the friendship of Soviet peoples.'

In China, similarly, the ethnic games festival held in Beijing in September-October 1985 was, in the view of Chris Hann (1987),

> designed to help integrate the diverse peoples of the state: in this case a rather subtle kind of integration, for it appeared to be predicated on assertions of ethnic difference, but conducive nonetheless to integration in the framework of the socialist state and legitimation of nationalist policies.

As we shall see below, the integrating functions of sport are just as clearly evident when the competitive elements are added: in the case of the USSR these became important from the end of the 1920s, in China only from the late 1970s. Both internally and externally sport was used to mobilize people in ways which actively contributed to the raising of group consciousness and solidarity, goals explicitly favoured by the leadership.

Defence

Since many communist states were born in war and lived under the constant threat of war, terrorism and subversion (for example the Soviet Union, China, Cuba), it is hardly surprising that defence has been a prime consideration. Sport, therefore, was often subordinated to the role of military training. In some countries the system was best described as the 'militarisation of sport'. The role of the military in sport was further heightened by centralized control of sports development. Even before their revolutions, however, China and Russia had military personnel playing a prominent part in sports administration largely because of their countries' geopolitical situation and history of foreign invasion. It has to be remembered that both countries have had extensive borders with foreign states – fourteen in the case of China and twelve in that of the Soviet Union. Further, even in relatively recent times both countries lost immense numbers of people in wars. For example, China lost 13 million and the USSR some 27 million in World War II, far and away the greatest human war losses in history.

In both nations, as well as certain other communist states (for example North Korea and Cuba), the sports movement was initially the responsibility of the armed forces and even recently was dominated by instrumental defence needs and military or paramilitary organizations. All the communist nations had a nationwide fitness programme with a bias towards military training, modelled on the Soviet 'Prepared for Work and Defence' (*GTO*) system (originally taken from the standards set by Baden-Powell for the Boy Scout 'marksman' and 'athlete' badges, and significantly called 'Be Prepared for Work and Defence'). Thus, in China, as Glassford and Clumpner (1973) attest, 'A major component of physical culture in Chinese schools is the military preparation program based on the Soviet *GTO* system. Route marches of 10 to 20 kilometres, grenade throwing, dashes, mock and real rifle training form the core of this program.'

Even in a relatively industrially advanced country like East Germany, albeit a 'front-line state', it was the Soviet military-oriented fitness system that was employed, particularly for young people: Childs (1978) writes,

> The performance objectives of the sport and physical educational programmes are based on the requirements of a graded sports badge, the pattern of which was adopted from the Soviet Union . . . . Initially this badge carried the imposing title of 'Ready to Work and Defend Peace' and was heavy with militaristic and ideological requirements . . . [it has since become] 'Ready to Work and Defend the Homeland'.

All communist and some non-aligned states have had a strong military presence in the sports movement through armed and security forces' clubs (see below), have provided military sinecures for more-or-less full-time athletes and, at times, have established direct military supervision over sport and physical education, such as in the USSR in the periods 1918–22 and 1940–46. They were also linked through the Sports Committee of Friendly Armies, set up in Moscow in 1958.

In many communist states, therefore, the armed and security forces have provided many of the funds and facilities that enabled people to take up and pursue a sport, especially full-time and in sports involving expensive equipment (ice hockey, soccer, gymnastics, weightlifting, equestrianism). They thereby helped to ensure that as many people as possible were physically fit, mentally alert and possessed the qualities (patriotism, will-power, stamina, ingenuity) regarded as being of particular value for military preparedness (and for internal policing against dissidents and deviants). Furthermore, military organization of sport appeared to be an efficient way of deploying scarce resources in the most economical fashion and using methods of direction that were more effective coming from paramilitary than from civilian organizations.

Health and hygiene

Of all the functions of state-run sport in communist societies, that to promote and maintain health always took priority. In many communist states sport came under the aegis of the health ministry. In so far as sports development was based for much of Soviet development on a population at a comparatively low health level, and as it has served as a model for

most other communist societies, it will be instructive to examine briefly
that experience.

When the Russian Communists (Bolsheviks) took power in October
1917, they inherited a semi-feudal, 80 per cent peasant and illiterate empire
of over 100 different ethnic groups. The country was in a state of war-
ruin and chaos, it was a land with an overwhelmingly inclement climate,
where disease, epidemics and starvation were common, and where most
people had only a rudimentary knowledge of hygiene. The new rulers well
knew it would take a radical economic and social transformation to alter
the situation significantly. But time was short, and able-bodied and
disciplined men and women (children too) were needed urgently, first for
the country's survival, then for its recovery from the ravages of war and
revolution, its industrial and cultural development, and its defence against
further expected attacks.

Regular participation in physical exercise, therefore, was to be one
means – relatively inexpensive and effective – of improving health standards rapidly and a channel by which to educate people in hygiene,
nutrition and exercise. For this purpose a new approach to health and
recreation was sought. The name given to the new system was *physical
culture.*

The pre-revolutionary and Western conception of sport and physical
education was thought to be too narrow to express the far-reaching aims
of the cultural (mental and physical) revolution under way. Physical culture
was to embrace health, physical education, competitive sport, and even
civil defence and artistic expression. The acquisition of that culture was
said to be an integral process that accompanied a person throughout life.

As Nikolai Semashko, himself a doctor and the first Health Minister
(also concurrently Chairman of the Supreme Council of Physical Culture),
made plain in 1928,

> Physical culture in the Soviet understanding of the term is concerned
> not with record breaking, but with people's physical health. It is an
> integral part of the cultural revolution and therefore has personal and
> social hygiene as its major objective, teaching people to use the natural
> forces of nature – the sun, air and water – the best proletarian doctors.

In other words, physical culture was to be a plank in the health campaign, encouraging people to wash, to clean their teeth, to eat and drink
sensibly, to employ a rational daily regime of work, rest and sleep (hence
Semashko's 1926 slogan of 'Physical Culture 24 Hours a Day' – eight
hours' work, eight hours' sleep and eight hours' recreation). Even
more than that: the country was in the grip of a typhoid epidemic, had
long suffered from such near-epidemic diseases as cholera, leprosy,
tuberculosis and venereal disease; it suffered, according to Semashko
(1928), from 'dreadfully backward sanitary conditions, the ignorance and

non-observance of rules for personal and public hygiene, leading to mass epidemics of social diseases such as syphilis, trachoma, scabies and other skin infections'.

Physical culture, therefore, was to help combat serious disease and epidemics. The therapeutic value of regular exercise, for example, was widely advertised in the intermittent anti-TB campaigns of the late 1920s. But physical culture was not confined to improving only physical health; it was regarded as important in combating what the leaders defined as antisocial behaviour in town and country. If young people could be persuaded to take up sport and engage in regular exercise, they might develop healthy bodies *and* minds. Thus, the Ukrainian Communist Party issued a resolution in 1926, expressing the hope that 'physical culture would become the vehicle of the new life . . . a means of isolating young people from the baneful influence of the street, home-made alcohol and prostitution'. The role assigned physical culture in the countryside was even more ambitious; it was

> to play a big part in the campaign against drunkenness and uncouth behaviour by attracting village youth to more rational and cultural activities. . . . In the fight to transform the village, physical culture is to be a vehicle of the new way of life in all measures undertaken by the authorities – in the campaign against religion and natural calamities.
>
> (Landar 1972: 11)

Even in the 1980s, the name of sport was still being invoked to combat alcoholism and religion (Nekrasov 1985).

Physical culture, then, stood for 'clean living', progress, good health and rationality, and was regarded by the authorities as one of the most suitable and effective instruments for implementing their social policies, as well as for the social control implicit in the programme.

As industrialization got under way at the end of the 1920s, physical exercise also became an adjunct, like everything else, of the Five-Year Plan. At all work-places throughout the country a regime of therapeutic gymnastics was introduced with the intention of boosting productivity, cutting down absenteeism through sickness and injury, reducing fatigue and spreading hygienic habits among the millions of new workers who had only recently inhabited bug-infested wooden huts in the villages.

This Soviet-pioneered health-oriented system of sport was either imposed upon or adopted by every other state that took the road to communism.

Social policies

There are many facets of social policy relevant to sport that concern communist states. Some have been referred to above: combating crime, particularly juvenile delinquency; fighting alcoholism and prostitution; and attracting young people away from religion, especially from all-embracing faiths like Islam that impinge upon large segments of social life. One aspect of the use of sport for social policies is the concern that it can make some contribution to the social emancipation of women.

A strong motivation here can be the desire by the leaders for national recognition through international sports success. The attention paid by some eastern European nations to women's sport sometimes contrasted with the relative neglect in both the more 'enlightened' nations of the West and in developing states. As an East German sports official, Otto Schmidt (1975), noted, 'While other nations can produce men's teams as good as, if not better than, ours, we beat them overall because they are not tapping the full potential of their women.'

The impact of women's sport is even greater – though emancipation is far more protracted and painful – in communities in which women have, by law or convention, been excluded from public life and discouraged from baring face, arms and legs in public. Some multi-ethnic communist countries quite deliberately used sport to break down prejudice and gain a measure of emancipation for women. This was a conscious policy in communist states with a sizeable Muslim population, like Albania, the USSR and Afghanistan. In reference to women of Soviet Central Asia (bordering on Iran, Turkey and Afghanistan), a Soviet sports official Davletshina (1976) asserted that 'sport has become an effective and visible means of combating religious prejudice and reactionary tradition; it has helped to destroy the spiritual oppression of women and to establish a new way of life'. It is a sobering thought that had the grandmothers of such Soviet Uzbek gymnasts as Nelli Kim or Elvira Saadi appeared in public clad only in a leotard, they would almost certainly have been stoned to death.

It was mounting western official (as well as western women's) awareness of losing out to communist nations that evidently contributed to the encouragement, *inter alia*, of heightened interest in women's sport and employment of training methods for women employed in eastern Europe. But the influence has sometimes been the other way. For example, it was the US women's example that encouraged Chinese women to take up weightlifting and bodybuilding (even boxing) in the early 1980s. Similarly, it was Western women's example that overcame the prejudices of some (male) communist leaders against such sports as women's soccer and long-distance running.

International recognition and prestige

For all young countries trying to establish themselves in the world as nations to be respected, even recognized, sport may uniquely offer them an opportunity to take the limelight in the full glare of world publicity. This is particularly important for those nations confronted by bullying, boycott and subversion from big powers in economic, military and other areas. This has applied as much to the Baltic states in regard to Soviet Russia as it has to Cuba and Nicaragua in regard to the United States. As Fidel Castro (1974: 290) has said of imperialist states in regard to Latin America, 'Imperialism has tried to humiliate Latin American countries, has tried to instil an inferiority complex in them; that is part of the imperialists' ideology to present themselves as superior. And they have used sport for that purpose.'

This has put particular responsibility on athletes from communist nations in that they have been seen by political leaders as encouraging a sense of pride in their team, nationality, country and even political system. Not all communist athletes accepted that role, as witnessed by the post-communist outbursts in post-1989 eastern Europe.

The role that sport has played in communist foreign policy is dealt with in more detail below.

Sport and foreign policy

Ever since the first communist state came into existence in 1917, communist leaders made explicit the dependence of external sports relations on foreign policy. It could hardly be otherwise in countries where sport was centrally directed and employed in the pursuit of specific socio-political objectives, including those of foreign policy. We have already seen that sport was a political institution run by the state, and that overall sports policy was laid down by the communist government. Decisions of national import concerning foreign sports policy – such as participation in the Olympic Games or in particular states disliked by the ruling Communist Party – were therefore made by the Party and government. On occasion it was a supranational body, like the Warsaw Pact, rather than a national government, that decided policy, as in the case of the Soviet-led boycott of the Los Angeles Olympics in 1984. For those communist states in eastern Europe that had been closely tied to the USSR, it was often the Soviet Politburo that imposed a 'fraternal' sports policy upon them.

That is not to say that all communist leaderships acted in accord or collusion. China, Yugoslavia and Romania took part in the Los Angeles Olympics in the face of Soviet opposition. Cuba and Marxist-governed Ethiopia acted in solidarity with North Korea in boycotting the Seoul 1988 Summer Olympics, while all other communist states (save Albania which boycotted all Olympic Games up to Barcelona in 1992) competed.

The role of sport in communist foreign policy varied in importance over the years, reflecting both shifts in domestic and foreign policies and the rapidly changing world situation. In the years from 1917 to 1948–9, when the Soviet Union either constituted the sole communist state in the world or held undivided sway over the communist movement, it was Soviet policy that dictated communist involvement in world sport. But following the Soviet break with Yugoslavia in 1948 and the communist revolution in China in 1949, the Soviet monopoly was broken.

Since the end of World War II, a major aim of several communist states was to attain sports supremacy over capitalist nations, particularly through the Olympic Games.

Where other channels have been closed, success in sport would seem to have helped such countries as the USSR, China, Cuba and East Germany as well as many other states in the developing world to attain a measure of recognition and prestige internationally, both at home and abroad. Sport here is unique in that for all communist societies, including the USSR and China, it is the only medium in which they have been able to compete with and beat the economically advanced nations. This took on added importance in view of what their leaders traditionally saw as the battle of the two ideologies for influence in the world. An official Soviet government resolution published in the monthly *Kultura i zhizn* in 1949 claimed that 'The increasing number of successes achieved by Soviet athletes . . . is a victory for the Soviet form of society and the socialist sports system; it provides irrefutable proof of the superiority of socialist culture over the moribund culture of capitalist states.'

Cuba's leader, Fidel Castro (1974: 91), looks forward to the day when Cuba can prove the superiority of its national sport, baseball, over that of US baseball: 'One day, when the Yankees accept peaceful coexistence with our country, we shall beat them at baseball too and then the advantages of revolutionary over capitalist sport will be clear to all.'

Despite some setbacks, there is ample evidence to show that the economically advanced socialist states went a long way to achieving their aim of world sporting supremacy, especially in the Olympic Games, as Table 3.1 testifies. They provided two of the top three nations in the summer Olympics since 1968 (except 1984, when they provided two of the top four despite the overwhelming communist boycott of the Los Angeles Olympics) and in the winter Olympics since 1972. Even in the Barcelona summer Olympics of 1992, when the USSR had already broken up (it performed as the 'Unified Team', which excluded athletes from the three Baltic states of Latvia, Lithuania and Estonia) and other eastern European countries were in disarray, the Unified Team beat its nearest challenger, the USA, and the two communist nations, China and Cuba, came fourth and fifth respectively.

The Soviet Union dominated the Olympic Games, summer and winter, ever since it made its debut in the summer of 1952 and the winter of

Table 3.1 Medals won by the top six Olympic teams, 1952–92

Year and venues of Olympic Games	Summer Olympics				Winter Olympics			
	National Olympic teams	Medals			National Olympic teams	Medals		
		Gold	Silver	Bronze		Gold	Silver	Bronze
1	2	3	4	5	6	7	8	9
1952	USSR	22	30	19	Norway	7	3	6
	USA	40	19	17	USA	4	6	1
Helsinki	Hungary	16	10	16	Finland	3	4	2
	Sweden	12	13	10	Austria	2	4	2
Oslo	West Germany	0	7	17	West Germany	3	2	2
	Finland	6	3	13	Sweden	0	0	4
1956	USSR	37	29	32	USSR	7	3	6
	USA	37	25	17	Austria	4	3	4
Melbourne	Austria	13	8	14	Finland	3	3	1
	Germany	6	13	7	Sweden	2	4	4
Cortina	Hungary	9	10	7	USA	2	3	2
d'Ampezzo	Great Britain	6	7	11	Switzerland	3	2	1
1960	USSR	43	29	31	USSR	7	5	9
	USA	34	21	16	USA	3	4	3
Rome	Germany	12	19	11	Sweden	3	2	2
	Italy	13	10	13	Germany	4	3	1
Squaw	Hungary	6	8	7	Finland	2	3	3
Valley	Poland	4	6	11	Norway	3	3	0
1964	USSR	30	31	35	USSR	11	8	6
	USA	36	26	28	Norway	3	6	6
Tokyo	Germany	10	22	18	Austria	4	5	3
	Japan	16	5	8	Germany	3	2	3
Innsbruck	Italy	10	10	7	Finland	3	4	3
	Hungary	10	7	5	Sweden	3	3	1
1968	USA	45	28	34	Norway	6	6	2
	USSR	29	32	30	USSR	5	5	3
Mexico City	GDR	9	9	7	Austria	3	4	4
	Hungary	10	10	12	Sweden	3	2	3
Grenoble	Japan	11	7	7	France	4	3	2
	West Germany	5	10	10	Holland	3	3	3
1972	USSR	50	27	22	USSR	8	5	3
	USA	33	31	30	GDR	4	3	7
Munich	GDR	20	23	23	Norway	2	5	5
	West Germany	13	11	16	Holland	4	3	2
Sapporo	Hungary	6	13	16	Switzerland	4	3	3
	Japan	13	8	8	West Germany	3	1	1
1976	USSR	49	41	35	USSR	13	6	8
	GDR	40	25	25	GDR	7	5	7
Montreal	USA	34	35	25	USA	3	3	4
	West Germany	10	12	17	West Germany	2	5	3
Innsbruck	Poland	7	6	13	Austria	2	2	2
	Romania	4	9	14	Finland	2	4	1

Table 3.1 Contd.

Year and venues of Olympic Games	National Olympic teams	Medals			National Olympic teams	Medals		
		Gold	Silver	Bronze		Gold	Silver	Bronze
				Summer Olympics				Winter Olympics
1	2	3	4	5	6	7	8	9
1980	USSR	80	69	46	GDR	9	7	7
	GDR	47	37	42	USSR	10	6	6
Moscow	Bulgaria	8	16	17	USA	6	4	2
	Poland	3	14	15	Norway	1	3	6
Lake	Hungary	7	10	15	Austria	3	3	2
Placid	Romania	6	6	13	Finland	1	5	3
1984	USA	83	61	31	GDR	9	9	6
Los Angeles	Romania	20	16	17	USSR	6	10	9
	West Germany	17	19	23	USA	4	4	0
	China	15	8	9	Finland	4	3	6
Sarajevo	Italy	14	6	12	Sweden	4	2	2
	Canada	10	18	16	Norway	3	2	4
1988	USSR	55	31	46	USSR	11	9	9
Seoul	GDR	37	35	30	GDR	9	10	6
	USA	36	31	27	Switzerland	5	5	5
	South Korea	12	10	11	Finland	4	1	2
Calgary	West Germany	11	14	15	Sweden	4	0	2
	Hungary	11	6	6	Austria	3	5	2
1992	Unified Team	45	38	29				
Barcelona	USA	37	34	37				
	Germany	33	21	28				
	China	16	22	16				
	Cuba	14	6	11				
	Spain	13	7	2				

1956, challenged only by the German Democratic Republic which gained more medals than the USA in the 1976 and 1988 summer Olympics, and more medals than the USSR in the 1980 and 1984 winter Olympics. The only interruption to communist victory was in 1968, when the USSR took second place to Norway in winter and to the USA in summer, and in the summer of 1984 when the major communist sporting nations did not compete.

China placed fourth in the 1984 summer Olympics and again in 1992; Cuba has moved steadily up to fifth position in the summer Olympics and consistently won more medals than all the countries of South America put together.

The example of East Germany, with a population of under 17 million, is particularly instructive. An overriding problem facing East Germany after the war was that of gaining international acceptance as an independent state. Its leaders further had to contend with attempts to impose

Soviet institutions and values upon the country, on the one hand, and western hostility, subversion and boycott, on the other. The rivalry with West Germany was evidently to become a testing ground for proving the viability of either capitalism or socialism in all spheres, including sport.

Success in sport was seen in East Germany as one means, perhaps the most accessible and 'popular', of gaining acceptance of the regime and enhancing its image at home and abroad while other channels were closed. It was not easy. In the winter Olympics of 1960, for example, the USA refused visas to East German athletes to travel to Squaw Valley where the games were being held. Such denial of visas was made thirty-five times by the USA and its NATO allies between 1957 and 1967. In other instances, when East German athletes won competitions, the awards ceremony was cancelled; and often western officials refused permission for the GDR to display its flag and emblem.

But its leadership persisted and quite demonstrably poured funds into sport to try to establish the nation as a world power to be recognized and reckoned with. As Party Chairman Erich Honecker (1976: 133) made clear,

> Our state is respected in the world because of the excellent performance of our top athletes, but also because we devote enormous attention to sport in an endeavour to make it part of the everyday lives of each and every citizen.

It is impossible to make any study of East German sport without seeing it in the wider context of, first, the striving to establish the nation as the equal of its fellow German state, the Federal Republic of Germany and, second, trying to achieve both political and sporting status in the world, above all within the Olympic movement and the United Nations. It is a measure of the success of those objectives that final acceptance by the IOC came in 1972, for the Olympic Games held in West Germany (Munich), to be followed the year after by membership of the United Nations. Both were the result of twenty-five years of intensive diplomatic activity, sporting and political.

Although the IOC had recognized the East German National Olympic Committee in October 1965 and granted it the right to enter a team separately from West Germany in the Mexico Olympics of 1968, it was only in Munich in 1972 that East Germany for the first time possessed its own national team, flag and anthem. This sporting autonomy and success led to mounting diplomatic recognition of the country throughout the world. Table 3.2 shows the steady change-round in Olympic success between the two German states. While West Germany was overwhelmingly successful in the 1950s, the gap closed in the 1960s, then East Germany forged well ahead in the 1970s and 1980s. It is worth mentioning in passing that the united team of Germany came third in the 1992 summer Olympics, though

Table 3.2 Olympic results, GDR and FRG, 1952–88

Games	GDR				FRG			
	Gold	Silver	Bronze	Total	Gold	Silver	Bronze	Total
1952 Summer	–	–	–	–	0	7	17	24
Winter	–	–	–	–	3	2	2	7
1956 Summer	1	4	2	7	5	9	6	20
Winter	0	0	1	1	1	0	0	1
1960 Summer	3	9	7	19	10	10	6	26
Winter	2	1	0	3	2	2	1	5
1964 Summer	3	7	6	16	7	15	12	34
Winter	2	2	0	4	1	0	3	4
1968 Summer	9	9	7	25	5	10	10	25
Winter	1	2	2	5	2	2	3	7
1972 Summer	20	23	23	66	13	11	16	40
Winter	4	3	7	14	3	1	1	5
1976 Summer	40	25	25	90	10	12	17	39
Winter	7	5	7	19	2	5	3	10
1980 Summer	47	37	42	126	–	–	–	–
Winter	9	7	7	23	0	2	3	5
1984 Summer	–	–	–	–	17	19	23	59
Winter	9	9	6	24	2	1	1	4
1988 Summer	37	35	30	103	11	14	15	40
Winter	9	10	6	25	2	4	2	8

with twenty medals fewer than East Germany had won at the Seoul Olympic Games in 1988.

The success of East Germany in cultivating élite athletes is apparent in the fact that during the 1980s, in Olympic and world championship terms, calculated in per capita medals, the country won one gold medal for every 425,000 citizens, by contrast with approximately one gold per 6.5 million citizens in both the USSR and the USA. In short, that means that an East German with sporting talent and ability was sixteen times more likely to reach the top and gain an Olympic or world gold medal than a Soviet or American citizen.

For East Germany, therefore, to quote the West German book, *Sport in der DDR*, we have seen how:

> Sport has played a vital role in breaching the blockade which, at the time of the Cold War, kept the GDR out of virtually all international relations outside the communist states. Because GDR sport attained international standards and in many areas actually set those standards, world sports organisations were unable to ignore the country.
>
> (Schmidt 1975: 12–13)

This was an important step towards helping East Germany break out of its political isolation, gain credibility for the communist government with its own people, and be recognized as an independent state. Hence the high priority that the authorities accorded the development of sport and international sports performance.

Although not as spectacular, the evolution of Cuban and Chinese sport, since 1960 and 1984 respectively, was dominated by similar considerations – of international recognition and prestige.

The communist countries, therefore, were keenly aware of the advantages that are thought to accrue from sporting, and especially Olympic, success, and so prepared their athletes accordingly. They believed that the Olympics brought more exposure and prestige and were, in the view of some communist leaders, *the* measure of a nation's viability.

To sum up, with its control of the sports system, the communist leadership was able to mobilize resources to use sport to perform what it believed to be salient political functions in foreign policy. It is, of course, impossible to measure the impact of sport on the behaviour of states – to discover whether sport can, in fact, ever affect policies, let alone minds and hearts.

All that can be said is that sport would no longer seem to be (if it ever was) the neutral, apolitical medium that some people once considered it to be. The sporting gains of communist policy towards developing and neighbouring countries are evident and tangible. There have been some successes in the 'hearts and minds' campaign among such nations, but the staunchness of friendship and solidarity remains open to question; for example, very few developing states showed solidarity with the Soviet-led boycott of the Los Angeles Olympics in 1984 or, indeed, with the Soviet armed involvement in Afghanistan. Some might argue, further, that western commercial sport had more of an impact on the popular imagination in Africa, Asia and Latin American than had communist- and Olympic-style sports. It may be that, as far as communist influence was concerned, communist policy was most effective where Marxist–Leninist assumptions were accepted, in a handful of communist countries themselves. Like the space programme, it seems more important in establishing national pride and ideological hegemony, though it appears to have had markedly less impact outside of states that were already Marxist–Leninist; and in the late 1980s and early 1990s even that bastion crumbled.

Some conclusions

The rapidity of post-totalitarian change in all areas, sport included, in eastern Europe and the one-time Soviet Union would seem to indicate that the élite sports system and its attainments, far from inspiring a national pride and patriotism, tended to provoke apathy and resentment. This appeared to be more evident in those states – Poland, GDR, Hungary, Romania, Bulgaria – which had 'revolution' and an alien sports system and values thrust upon them contrary to their indigenous traditions. A similar mood is apparent, too, in Islamic areas of the old USSR. Sports stars were seen as belonging to a private, élite fiefdom within the overall domain; they were not part of a shared national achievement, let alone heritage. That is not to say that in societies of hardship and totalitarian constraint, and in the face of western arrogance and attitudes that were sometimes tantamount to racial prejudice, the ordinary citizens obtained no vicarious pleasure in their champion's or team's performance. But, overall, the dominant attitude was not entirely different from western class attitudes to sports and heroes which are not 'theirs' (for example the ambivalent attitude by many western workers to Olympic show jumpers, yachtsmen and fencers).

On the other hand, in countries like the now defunct Czechoslovakia and Yugoslavia, as well as the Slav regions of the old Soviet Union (the Ukraine, Belorus and Russia), the patriotic pride in sporting success and heroes would appear to have been genuine. One reason for this may be that the socialist revolution of 1917 in the old Russian empire, and of 1946 and 1948 in the cases of Yugoslavia and Czechoslovakia, came out of their own experience and had some popular support. The same might be said of China, Cuba and Vietnam.

That is not to say that it was communist ideology that motivated athletes or that Marxism–Leninism was responsible for Olympic success. A more compelling reason was that the sports system grew up with and was integral to the building of a strong nation-state which generated its own motivational forces and patriotism. The same central control and planned application of resources, allied to state priorities and direction of labour, which initially achieved such remarkable success (in relatively backward states like Russia, China, Bulgaria and Romania) in constructing the infrastructure of socialist society, provided conditions that were more conducive to discovering, organizing and developing talent in specific sports than those of the more disparate and private western systems. It should be added that communist sport was oriented on *Olympic* success, and its far from privileged athletes fared less well in the fully professionalized and commercial sports of the West: soccer, basketball, boxing, rugby, motor-racing, tennis and baseball.

Today, the inheritors of the sports system that evolved during the communist years are faced with a choice of how sharply they should break with the past and adopt a pattern of sport based on market relations. 'Westernizers' in eastern Europe, with public support nourished on a reaction to the communist past, aided by those westerners eager to see the old communist states join the 'free' world, abandon socialism, central planning and social provision, seem bent on rejecting the past *in toto* and embracing its antithesis.

It is possible that sport in such states will become a hybrid of the worst of both worlds, retaining the bureaucracy of the old and adding only the exploitation and corruption of some forms of western sport. The final product may well not inspire admiration. Much the same could be said of the larger reform processes underway.

Such a radical shift of policy is bound to cause a tinge of sadness in those who have admired aspects of communist sport down the years – not only because it provided good competition with the West. The old system, it merits saying, was generally open to the talents in all sports, probably more so than in the West. It provided opportunities for women to play and succeed, if not on equal terms with men, at least on a higher plane than western women. It gave an opportunity to the many ethnic minorities and relatively small states in eastern Europe and the USSR to do well internationally and to help promote that pride and dignity that sports success in the glare of world publicity can bring. Nowhere in the world has there been, since the early 1950s, such reverence by governments for Olympism, for Coubertin, for Olympic ritual and decorum. One practical embodiment of this was the contribution to Olympic solidarity with developing nations: to the training of Third World athletes, coaches, sports officials, medical officers and scholars at colleges and training camps. Much of this aid was free. None of it was disinterested, it going to those states whose governments generally looked to socialism rather than capitalism for their future. Further, no one outside the Third World did more than the communist nations to oppose apartheid in sport and have racist South Africa banned from world sports forums and arenas.

In eastern Europe and the erstwhile USSR, the international challenge is today diluted through lack of state support; the free trade-union sports societies, as well as the ubiquitous Dinamo and armed forces clubs, have given way to private sports, health and recreation clubs; women's wrestling and boxing attract more profit than women's chess and volleyball; the various ethnic groups (Czechs and Slovaks, Croatians and Serbs, Armenians and Ukrainians) prefer their own independent teams to combined effort and success.

And right across the central and eastern European plain, as far as the Ural Mountains, sports and every other aid is at an end, the Third World students (in medicine and engineering as well as in sport) have had to go home as their support grants have run out. The ex-communist states have become competitors with other poor nations for development aid from the West.

No doubt, in time, a new sports nationalism will emerge and international rivalries will resume. For the moment, however, it is time to concentrate on more important things. In the immediate post-communist period, the one-time communist nations have decided that bread is more important than circuses.

References

Castro, F. (1974) Quoted in S. Castanes (ed.), *Fidel. Sobre el deporte* Havana: El Deporte, 37.

Childs, D. (1978) 'Sport and physical education in the GDR', in J. Riordan (ed.), *Sport under Communism* London: Hurst, 78.

Davletshina, R. (1976) 'Sport i zhenshchiny', *Teoriya i praktika fizicheskoi kultury* 3: 62.

Glassford, R.G. and Clumpner, R.A. (1973) *Physical Culture inside the People's Republic of China* (Physical culture around the world. Monograph 6, Edmonton, Canada), 13.

Hann, C. (May 1987) 'The withering of muscular socialism: physical culture, nutrition and personal responsibility in contemporary China' (unpublished paper), 3.

Honecker, E. (1976) *Report of the Central Committee to the Socialist Unity Party of Germany*, Berlin, 133.

Kultura i zhizn (1 November 1949), 11: 5.

Landar, A.M. (1972) 'Fizicheskaya kultura – sostavnaya chast kulturnoi revolyutsii na Ukraine', *Teoriya i praktika fizicheskoi kultury*, 12: 11.

Mao Zedong (1962) *Une étude de l'education physique*, Paris: Maison des sciences de l'homme (originally published in Chinese in 1917).

Nekrasov, V.P. (1985) 'Fizicheskaya kultura protiv pyanstva', *Teoriya i praktika fizicheskoi kultury*, 9: 37–9.

Rodionov, V.V. (1975) 'Sport i integratsiya', *Teoriya i praktika fizicheskoi kultury*, 9: 7.

Schmidt, O. (1975) *Sport in der Deutschen Demokratischen Republik*, Bonn, 12–13.

Further reading

Soviet Union

Riordan, J. (1977) *Sport in Soviet Society*, Cambridge: Cambridge University Press.

——(1980) *Soviet Sport. Mirror of the Olympics*, London: Blackwell.

Shneidman, N. (1979) *Soviet Sport. Road to Olympus*, Queen's/McGill.

Edelman, R. *Serious Fun. A History of Spectator Sports in the USSR*, Oxford: Oxford University Press.

Peppard, V. and Riordan, J. (1992) *Playing Politics. Soviet Sport Diplomacy to 1992*, Jai Press Inc.

China

Brownwell, S. (1995) *Training the Body for China*, Chicago, IL: University of Chicago Press.

Knuttgen, H.G., Qiwei, M. and Zhongyuan, W. (eds) (1990) *Sport in China*, Champaign, IL: Human Kinetics.

Riordan, J. and Jones, R. (eds) (1998) *Sport and Physical Education in China*, London: E & FN Spon.

Kolatch, J. (1972) *Sports, Politics and Ideology in China*, Jonathan David.

East Germany

Dieter, E., Heinrich-Vogel, R. and Winkler, G. (1981) *Die DDR Breiten- und Spitzensport*, Munich: Kopernikus Verlag.
Gilbert, D. (1980) *The Miracle Machine*, Coward, McCann and Geoghegan Inc.
Kühnst, P. (1982) *Der missbrauchte Sport. Die politische Instrumentalisierung des Sports in der SBZ und DDR 1945–1957*, Cologne: Verlag Wissenschaft und Politik.

General

Riordan, J. (1991) *Sport, Politics and Communism*, Manchester: Manchester University Press.
Riordan, J. (ed.) (1981) *Sport under Communism (USSR, Czechoslovakia, GDR, China, Cuba)*, London: C. Hurst.

4 Strength through joy

The culture of consent under fascism, Nazism and Francoism

Arnd Krüger

This chapter evaluates the role of sport for the fascist governments in Europe. Although the emphasis is on Germany, Italy and Spain, other fascist governments are also covered to explain certain distinctive features and to differentiate their kind of sport from that of contemporary democratic countries. Things physical played an important role for fascist regimes as radical Darwinism was one of its basic features (Wippermann 1983; Payne 1995). Historically, the use of sport by the Nazis seems to have been the most extensive and efficient of the fascist regimes (in spite of the fact that the so-called thousand years' empire lasted only twelve), and it is therefore dealt with as the main case, although fascist Italy served as a model for the Germans, and the Spanish fascists made the longest use of sport. Sport for the sake of national fitness and the demonstration of it was nothing new at the time of the fascist governments in Europe (Krüger 1995), but the extensive use of it for indoctrination to establish a totalitarian system was new.

Introduction

The issue for the 1932/3 winter issue of *Forum*, the journal of the famous German Academy of Physical Education and Sport in Berlin, carried a series of interviews with the most important German sports leaders of the time. The PE students wanted to know how their future profession would change if the National Socialists came to power in two months' time. Even those sports leaders who were either members of the Nazi Party or were known for their pro-fascist positions did not have a clear idea of what the immediate future would bring. The Nazi organization did not have precise notions for many fields of public life. For sports they neither had an idea nor did they have anybody with personal authority who would have been the automatic choice as leader.

What were the options for them? They had a strong party group, the Storm Troopers (SA), that did paramilitary exercises, complained that military conscription no longer existed, spent a lot of time shooting and fighting, and were very useful for the intimidation of political opponents; but was this sport? Women were only included in as much as they would cheer the men in their exercises, or marry them and bear their children.

In the *Völkische Beobachter*, the Nazi daily newspaper, the sports pages were filled with the press service of the Deutsche Turnerbund (DTB), an anti-Semitic gymnastics (Turner) organization that had broken away from the mainstream Turners before the turn of the century because only the DTB forbade Jews as members in their clubs and 90 per cent of the Turners did not. Out of the same anti-Semitic Austrian tradition much of the original Nazi thought had come. All Turners resented individual competition, as it was supposed to be leading to what they called a 'star cult', and they had team competitions only with other Germans and those foreigners who had been allies in the Great War.

Turnen was done to strengthen the individual to prepare for the next war. Women were included mainly in the rhythmic gymnastics and dance. As convinced Darwinists, the Turners were fully aware that the quality of the offspring would not only depend upon the quality of the stallion, but also that of the mare; but they resented the idea of the 'horse show'. In that respect they were often members of the SA, as the ideas of the two organizations overlapped.

The Nazis among actual sports leaders, like the president of the German Athletics Federation, IOC-member Karl von Halt, Ph. D., or Carl Krümmel, Ph.D., president of the Physical Education Teachers' Association and head sports teacher of the German military, or Hans Geissow, president of the German Swimming Federation, agreed that the Italian fascist model of state sport should be followed, 'as it was not only important that you could talk and sing about defending your fatherland, but that you were actually fit and capable to do so' (Krümmel). The Schutz Staffel (SS), élitist paramilitary organization and Hitler's personal guard, was not included in the series of interviews, and did not speak up for any direction of physical education and sport.

What were the chances that any one of the three directions could get its way? Gregor Strasser, the Nazi Party Organizational Director, had been asked in October 1932 by party members and sports fans from the county of Würtemberg whether they were permitted to start a Nazi sports federation, just as there were relatively large social-democratic, communist (Krüger and Riordan 1996), Catholic, Protestant and Jewish ones (Krüger 1994). Strasser told them that it was too late for this. The takeover of power was imminent, and 'we do not have the time to build up a proper organization. We should not have a second rate one. Therefore, we shall follow the Fascist model of state sport'. But this answer was never published (Krüger 1985).

The PE students drew their own conclusions. When the Nazis came to power at the end of the winter semester, they ripped up the famous cinder track of their stadium and planted oak trees on the track. The track for them had been the instrument of foreign (British) influence, the stopwatch a symbol of the pressure on athletes to race against each other instead of all together for the betterment of the Germanic race. The German oak, the symbol of Jahn, the *Turnvater*, stood for paramilitary training. At the beginning of the 1933 summer semester – only six weeks later – the trees were all gone. Training was intensified as athletic success was to demonstrate the superiority of the Aryan race and the fatherland.

Nazi sport

National Socialism was organized as a political party in 1919. Its main aim – apart from coming to power – was the unification of all Germans in a German Empire, purification of German blood, the provision of more *Lebensraum* (space to live) for the German people, particularly in the East. It was assumed that a Germanic, Aryan breed by itself would create a superior culture. To ensure this, non-Germanic people and their ideas had to be excluded. This 'horse-breeder' perspective (Krüger 1998) was widespread in Germany even before the Nazis came to power. It has always been the basic assumption of German citizenship that it is based on blood (*ius sanguinis*) and not on culture, as in France, or birthplace as in the United States. Therefore, Germans whose families have lived for generations abroad are entitled to a German passport. Putting more emphasis on sport, investing more money in the cultural sphere, were among the positive eugenic measures of the Nazis; expelling, eventually killing German Jews and gypsies, sterilizing and eventually killing the mentally handicapped and those that were in some other way deviant, were among the negative measures (Krüger 1999). Hitler had already described all of this in his *Mein Kampf* (*My Struggle*) which he wrote when in prison in 1923; although this was one of the most widely circulated books, it was either not read or not taken seriously.

As for sport, Hitler demanded: 'Not a day should go by in which the young man does not receive one hour of physical training in the morning and one hour in the afternoon, covering every type of sport and gymnastics' (Hitler 1925/1971: 409).

Nazism itself was not a clear-cut ideology, but an odd mixture of the beliefs of many groups that often had conflicting views. By this, it created a special kind of totalitarianism in that there was competition within the system for legitimacy and grace before the eyes of Hitler and his inner circle of power. As there had not been any defined creed for physical culture and sport, it was even doubtful what was part of it and what was not (Hoberman 1984). After coming to power, the Nazis immediately abolished the communist sports organizations. Not long after, the social-democratic organization was also dissolved, although it contained over one million members. In fact, Hitler made the *Reichssportführer* (the national sports leader) Hans von Tschammer und Osten, a regional SA leader who had been known for his brutality in beating up communist sportsmen and sportswomen. On one occasion his gang had even killed three children who were in a communist-run gym.

The Deutsche Turnerschaft (DT), the largest single Turner organization, immediately kicked out its Jewish members and offered itself as the new umbrella organization of sport in the 'true national spirit', refusing competition against all non-Germans. Although traditionally the Turners were more nationalistic than any other organization for physical exercise, the Nazis decided otherwise. They co-ordinated all sports federations, made sure that they all had a Nazi as president, now called 'führer' (leader), that the 'leadership principle' was introduced, i.e. that the boards were no longer elected but appointed from above, and that they kicked out their Jewish members. As for former members of the socialist sports organizations, they were permitted back into Nazi-dominated bourgeois sports, provided that they produced two sworn statements by two Nazis guaranteeing that they were not 'Marxists'. On the whole, this meant that the sportsmen and sportswomen and their coaches could continue, while the functionaires could not or would not.

The Turners were also 'co-ordinated'. From the nineteenth century onwards they had had the notion of being the dominating force behind organized exercise. So, they felt also that they had the right to be in charge of athletics, swimming, fencing and all other exercises with military usefulness, although separate sports federations existed for these sports. Now the Nazis reduced the Turners to a national sports governing body for gymnastics with apparatus under the umbrella of the Deutscher Reichsbund für Leibesübungen (DRL).

The flexibility of the Nazis can be seen from another example. In cycling there had been twelve national federations. The Nazis closed them all and made the president of one – who happened to be a well-connected Nazi – the führer of the new combined cycle federation. The former president of another, who was also a Nazi, did not accept that he should now be reduced to serving under a former rival, and complained publicly in the cycle journals about the random decision from 'above'. The Nazis fired the new leader and made the director of the largest hall with the best indoor cycling track the new cycle führer – but not the one who had complained.

The German nudist organizations were banned in the spring of 1933 for being lewd and un-German. The eight different national nudist federations kicked out their Jewish and socialist members, 'co-ordinated' themselves under a nudist who was a member of parliament for the Nazi Party and asked for reconsideration of the ban. As their new führer happened to be the MP for the same town as von Tschammer, the nudist federation was readmitted in October 1933 as a sports federation in the DRL (and stayed a member of the German Sport Federation after World War II until today).

This shows that Nazism was a frame within which people could move if they knew the rules and did not object publicly to the basic ideas. In 1933, the concepts for sport were being formulated. As in other fields where the Nazis did not really know how to run the country, they looked for help to Italy, as the Italian fascists had shown how a relatively small group of convinced party members could bring the whole country behind itself through force and a 'culture of consent'. To let the socialist sports people back into mainstream Nazi sports was already part of this culture. In 1935 the Catholic and the Protestant sports organizations were dissolved, but the clubs were not altered much if they wished to enter the DRL. Now everybody was underneath the same umbrella. Nobody was to be excluded.

Elite sport received particular emphasis as the Olympic Games of 1936 happened to be in Germany and the IOC kept them there in spite of international pressure to include sport in the front of cultural isolation of Nazi Germany. In the old federations very little needed to be changed. The Nazi system of co-ordination on the whole improved performance as now all talents were centralized in one group and the former socialist athletes that had not participated in bourgeois competition before could be included.

The 'Mussolini Boys' had placed second to the United States at the 1932 Los Angeles Olympics and had shown that national representation through sports and a positive image transfer was possible. The Nazis could rely on a strong German tradition that had assured a second place in the Olympic Games of 1928. In 1936 Germany placed first in the Olympics beating the United States into second with Italy third, thus showing to the German people and the world what a strong unified Germany could achieve in the world of physical culture. To stress the importance of élite sport, Germany had more international dual meets during the Nazi period than before – including during much of the war – to demonstrate a state of normality (Teichler 1991) (Table 4.1).

As for women's sport, the position of the Nazis was quite ambiguous. On the one hand, they enjoyed the athletic success of women, like world-record holder and Olympic champion Gisela Mauermeyer. After all, the Edda and other ancient Germanic sagas are full of powerful, athletic women. On the other hand, the Turner spirit that resented competition was even stronger for women and was maintained as official ideology. Strenuous competition might inflict danger on the reproductive function of women and was therefore discouraged. As in other fields of Nazism the two conflicting positions could exist side by side, one cherished more by the Minister of Propaganda and the other by Bund Deutscher Mädel (BDM, Union of German Girls), the official representation of female matters (Czech 1994).

On the day of the opening of the Olympic Summer Games in Berlin, the sports clubs lost all their youth sections of boys and girls aged 10–18.

Table 4.1 International dual meets of the German national team

Year	Total dual meets	Number of countries
1920–30	192	19
1932	27	16
1933	23	12
1934	32	12
1935	78	23
1936	39	18*
1937	62	18
1938	86	21
1939	106	19
1940	50	11
1941	50	9
1942	51	9
1943	2	2

*Additionally, Germany and 48 other countries took part in the Olympic Games of 1936.

What had happened? Even before 1933, the Nazis had a youth organiza-tion, Hitler Jugend (HJ), which now had a mandate over all German youth. No youth group was permitted to exist that was not part of the HJ for boys or the BDM or girls. The sports movement was not hit as hard as some of the church groups. For the sports movement relatively little changed, as the youth coaches in sports clubs just continued to work for the HJ or the BDM – and liked it much better on the whole as they received better pay and performed a public service. If you were working in the civil service – and many Germans were – at least one *public* service was expected from you. Although a sports club was useful, it was not yet accepted as 'public'. Now the youth coaches had to identify themselves a little more with the system, had to include party songs and ideology in the training sessions and were under a more severe supervision – the national youth championships were changed into the national Hitler Youth championships, the sports regions (for regional championships) were changed in some places to coincide with the regional subdivisions of the HJ (often not even the club vest changed as new ones could not be provided in the quantities necessary).

Only in 1938 did the Nazis go one step further: while the DRL sport organization had been close to the state before, it drew closer to the Nazi Party and then transformed into the Nationalsozialistischer Reichsbund für Leibesübungen, NSRL, an organization that was under the Nazi Party. The state sports system along Italian fascist lines had been embraced by the party. This can be seen as a symbol that the party had now taken over many of the institutions of the state, that the party had become the state in many instances. Some considered that an advantage for the sports system. By then all German citizens were required to do some sort of *public* service in any of the Nazi organizations. By making the sports clubs Nazi organizations, work in the clubs as voluntary administrator or coach (and not just for the youth section as of 1936) was accepted as party service. This way, the sports clubs could compete for the best personnel with the other three organizations that dealt with sport, the HJ, the KdF (see below) and the SA. It also meant, however, that in 1945 – after the end of the war – all German sports clubs were dissolved as they had been a part of the NSRL, an organization under the control of the Nazi Party.

The Storm Troopers also had their sports sections and did not only engage in an adventure type of military sport. In horse riding and fencing some of their athletes were as good as any élite athlete in the regular federation. Von Tschammer had reached a compromise in his person: he was the führer of exercises in both. If somebody from the SA wanted to compete internationally, he had to join a regular DRL, or later NSRL club. But for sports for all and local competition, the SA stayed autonomous and drew heavily on the membership of sports clubs.

German military sport was quite liked by many of its followers. It should not be overlooked that Bernhard Zimmermann, Ph.D., an authority on military sports from 1933 to 1937 in Germany, emigrated to Britain because of his Jewish wife, became the PE teacher of Kurt Hahn's Public School in Gordonstoun (and where he taught PE to Prince Philip), started another school in Abberdovy (Wales), and eventually his theories – which he did not have to change one bit – became the basis of the Outward Bound Movement and adventure education in Britain. These war games were, therefore, as popular with young Germans as Outward Bound has been with the British (Krüger and v. Lojewski 1998).

The last of the Nazi sports movements came directly from Italy, but could also partially rely on what had been present in Germany before: Kraft durch Freude (KdF, strength through joy) was at first called Nach der Arbeit (after work) to duplicate the Italian Opera Nazionale Dopolavoro (after work). KdF was an organization sponsored by the Minister for Social Work and paid for out of employers fees and taxes. It was intended for the work-force and contained elements of organized mass tourism, factory-sponsored sports, factory-sponsored concerts and dances, etc. Factory sports, often called 'yellow' sports by the socialist worker sports movements, had been around since the turn of the century as paternalistic factory owners wanted to provide their workers with decent recreation that would not leave them in the hands of the socialists or the trade unions in their leisure time. The factory often provided the sports grounds, coaches, subsidized travel to competitions at other factories and education for coaches. It assured the identification of workers with *their* company. So the Krupp workers called themselves 'Kruppianer', the workers of the Henschel tank factory referred to themselves as 'Henschelianer' to demonstrate unity with their company. The Nazis made use of these existing organizations, although the DRL and the SA complained because the Nazis had abolished the trade unions and replaced them by organizations that contained all the workers of the same company (no longer organized according to their separate trades like in the Trade Union Council) and the employers as well in the Deutsche Arbeitsfront (DAF). There was quite a lot of money around for the activities of the KdF and they could, therefore, hire decent coaches and make participation in the KdF attractive to many workers. Although ideologically they had completely different roots, many of the qualified personnel of the worker sports movement could survive in the KdF, where their skills were required to deal with a sports-for-all situation, that was much closer to the worker sports tradition than to the regular bourgeois sports traditions, with emphasis on élite sports. If KdF members wanted to compete internationally, they had to join the DRL or later the NSRL. Von Tschammer was also made nominal head of this conflicting sporting body to assure a certain unity (Fasbender 1997). KdF is best remembered today because of its emphasis on mass tourism. Their international cruises were the first holidays they had away from home for many workers. Their leisure-time activities constituted an important part of the Nazi 'culture of consent' that ensured vast public support.

Of course, there were more national organizations that were involved in sports: the students had their own organization and continued to participate in the World Student Games (Oelrich 1997), the farmers were not members of the DAF, therefore not the KdF, and had their own sports. The Schutz Staffel (SS), although their activities were similar to the SA, were independent from them and therefore also had their own sports, and finally the Wehrmacht (armed forces) and the police had their own sports as they stayed aloof from all of the others.

After the 1936 Olympics an unofficial competition started between the branches of the military, the police, SA and SS to show who had the most athletes in the 1940 Olympic team. They selected top-calibre athletes willing to train on a full salary for four years. In 1939 the war ended these efforts and replaced sport as an ersatz war by bleak reality (Bernett 1980).

Sport had high esteem. Physical education teachers often served as deputy directors of their schools – and often were the most ardent Nazis in the school system. They had been sacked during the world economic crisis and the Nazis had not only given them their jobs back but had also provided them with a position in the school system better than ever before or after.

Sport continued to be as important during the war as before. It demonstrated a state of normality and kept young people fit for the war effort. National championships and international sporting competition with German participation took place as late as 1944 – and started again in 1946. The success of national teams in international competition helped to create a sense of unity. Although neither Hitler nor Goebbels were actual sports people, they sensed the enthusiasm that went with the success of national teams in such sports as football and invested heavily. But also the joy of everyday sports for all in a relaxed atmosphere provided by the sports clubs or factory groups, helped to create a culture of consent. This notion was also emphasized in the major manifestations of sports, like the 1933 national Turnfest, the 1934 national Combat Games and the 1938 national Turnfest, each drawing masses of participants and spectators – just like the annual party reunion in Nuremberg. It showed that the sports movement could mobilize masses of participants and not just spectators (Krüger 1997; Lissina 1997).

What changed in German sport in those twelve years of Nazi power? According to Dr Carl Diem, secretary-general of the 1936 Olympics and later chief of foreign sports relations for the Nazi government (advisor after the war to the German government and rector of the Cologne Sports College), apart from gestures – like the Nazi salute – nothing changed because of Nazi power and the situation was only different because of the war, which – according to Diem – was forced upon innocent Germany. Of course, he meant bourgeois sport only – and for some clubs he was probably right. The sports movement was quite conservative and competitive sport has been called a 'proto-fascist' phenomenon (Brohm 1986) because of its celebration of strength and the construction of a value system based almost entirely on physical traits. Detesting weakness was a fascist trait that has been around Europe well into the Reagan and Thatcher era (Ofstad 1989).

For bourgeois sports clubs Nazism was a means of modernization. The areas for which a sports governing body was responsible became identical with political boundaries. This meant that each sports body had a political body with a responsibility for the same area. This form of co-ordination has been kept until today as it is the basis for the political strength of sports organizations in their search for public subsidies.

Of course, Jewish and worker sports organizations were closed, their members often persecuted and murdered, but not because of their sport. Jewish sport survived in a separate organization until 1938 and even gained in strength after 1933 as the bourgeois organizations expelled their Jewish members; but under Zionist influence many of their members emigrated between 1933 and 1938 (Bernett 1978; Krüger 1994). The bourgeois sports organizations ignored as well as they could the atrocities committed in their midst and worried instead about how they could get more and better subsidies from the civic authorities. As late as February 1945, the sports clubs asked for their coaches to be reimbursed for the 1944/5 season (Krüger 1991a).

The sports fans got what they wanted: glory for their colours, which had changed from black–red–gold, via black–red–white, to the swastika. Although the Nazis officially resented professionalism in sport, professional boxing and cycling flourished, attracting many spectators as late as autumn 1944. Sport provided good cheap entertainment, an island of friendship, trust and understanding in the midst of distrust, secret police activities, and blatant propaganda (Krüger 1993). Even in the midst of the bombing, football fans discussed who would become German champion, whether the traditional Schalke or the Vienna style of football was better (Stecewicz 1996). Football stars had good chances of serving only on the home front, and football rules were changed in such a way that transfer from one club to another became a lot easier. International matches were played as late as 1944.

Although Hitler and his inner circle of cronies were not athletic, many of the men who had taken part in the putsch with Hitler in 1923 and who were in high esteem in the party were athletic. The Nazis as a male-dominated cult of youth and strength, who believed in genetic and racial endowment, on the survival of the fittest, used the sports movement for their purpose of national unity. The improvement of conditions for the sports clubs and for physical education in the school system will always be identified with Nazism – when looking at such a supposedly positive gesture, it should not be overlooked that the main purpose was to prepare youth for the war to come, and to convince the population that the German nation was the strongest in the world when unified under Nazi rule. A culture of consent is not bad in itself, but the way the Nazis instrumentalized it for war preparation and to prepare the population to fight it to the bitter end, was.

People in the sports system tended to say that sports and politics should be kept apart and that they as athletes had very little to do with the war machinery, but the culture also served to include and exclude parts of the German population. Excluded were the handicapped, Jews, gypsies, Jehovah's Witnesses and political dissidents. The Nazis brought technological and organizational progress to Germany at the highest level for the benefit of the war machinery – and the sports system profited from the spin-offs. But technological and organizational progress also meant mass murder of those excluded in camps such as Auschwitz.

Fascist Italy

Although the use of sport as a symbol of vigour and for the sake of national representation had been already discussed prior to the Great War in Britain, Germany, France, and some other countries, it was Italy that revived the notion afterwards (Krüger 1995). Benito Mussolini was personally athletic and made use of sport to bring Italians together, modernize the nation, and improve the physical side of Italy in a Darwinist sense. For this he needed the young sports movement to get his ideas across. The *Gazetta dello Sport,* Italy's foremost sports paper, owned and published by IOC member Earl Bonacossa, was instrumental in pushing fascism and sport. But sports papers flourished on the whole in fascist

Italy as the government wanted to make sure that its athletic success would influence everyone to become prouder of Italy, identify with the nation and the regime and become athletic themselves.

When Mussolini came to power in 1922, one of the first acts was to decrease the influence of the trade unions. To assure this, trade-union-related organizations such as the worker sports movement were also closed down (Krüger and Riordan 1996). As the fascists wanted to make use, however, of sports for the sake of modernization, the Opera Nationale Dopolavoro (OND) was founded to ensure that company sports and other after-work activity on a company level could be maintained. Much of this was not quite as athletic as Mussolini would have preferred, but at least such sporting activities, like Boccia, brought high participation rates. This old men's town square activity, with much less physical activity than lawn bowling, has been traditionally a favourite activity around the Mediterranean as participants do not have to be athletic (Krüger 1986). In 1925 the Fascist Party took complete control of the different sports associations with the election of a committed fascist, Lando Ferretti, as president of the Italian Olympic Committee (CONI), which was not modified in its structure. The government did not change the organization of bourgeois competitive sports (Bianda *et al.* 1983), but instead occupied all major positions and even succeeded in placing Augusto Turati, fencing partner of Mussolini and secretary-general of the Fascist Party, in the IOC. He fitted so well into the IOC that IOC Executive Committee member, American General Charles H. Sherrill, even wrote a laudatory biography of Mussolini and publicly expressed the hope that a comparable figure would rise in American politics (Krüger 1978). The fascists either placed new leaders in the sports organizations or many of the old ones accepted fascism as their dominant creed, changed statutes as they wished and created a state-run élite sports system.

After worker sports, now the Catholic sports organizations (FASCI and YMCA) were banned, while the bourgois clubs and local associations, combined in the Italian Olympic Committee (CONI), were taken forcibly by petty party officials who made sporting organizations subordinate to the regime. It should be noted, however, that fascism at the time was quite popular, and that little if any force was necessary to gain a majority in these associations.

Basic physical education was first reformed in 1923 as young men's (to a far lesser extent girls') physical and moral health was an essential part of fascist ideology. The fascist minister Giovanni Gentile took it out of the control of the Ministry of Education and transferred it into an independent organ, the Ente Nazionale Educazione Fisica (ENEF). Physical education was considered so special for the new fascist moral order that it should not stay under the influence of so many of the old civil servants in the Ministry who had little if any interest in sport. Because of the increase in the role of physical education in the school system the period has been called 'the golden age of physical education' (Teja 1998). The ENEF proved to be incompetent and all responsibility for physical education was soon passed to the newly founded Opera Nazionale Balilla (ONB), the Italian equivalent to the Hitler Youth. Founded in 1926, the ONB soon started to take responsibility for the physical education and sport of all primary and secondary school children inside and outside the school system; this created a number of difficulties as the teachers resented being controlled by an external agency which strengthened tremendously the position of the pupils and the parents. They now had their own organization to complain to in case teachers were not going along with the new political system. Thus, teachers were supervised by the students rather than the other way around. The ONB was placed under the aegis of the Ministry of National Education in 1929. It had great financial means at its disposal and used them to emphasize the practice of physical education and sport among pupils and students of both sexes. Children and youth were divided into age groups: *Balilla* (boys) and *Piccole Italiane* (girls) (8 to 14 years) and *Avanguardisti* (boys) and *Giovani Italiane* (girls) (14 to 18 years); they wore a uniform and were organized into squadrons to develop a sense of military readiness. From the beginning the ONB was directed by Renato Ricci and placed directly under Mussolini. This mixing up of old ministerial government structures and the new Fascist Party structures was typical of the regime. This way, a totalitarian system was achieved in which the various branches competed with each other. It was therefore extremely difficult – even under such lenient conditions as in Italy – to avoid fascist rule.

The aim was to get young people from the earliest age into fascist activities and thinking. To ensure this, the ONB controlled eventually all activities in secondary and higher education through the school and university system. For those who did not go to school, those who had left school, primarily the working class, the Fascists created the Opera Nazionale Dopolavoro (OND) for intellectuals and manual labourers, the Gruppi Universitari Fascisti (GUF) for students, and the Fasci Giovanili di Combattimento (FGC) for young people who were not students. The difficult relationship between the overlapping organisms of sport was put into order with the *Carta dello sport* (enacted in 1929) which provided order, but at the same time competition between the various sporting bodies. This ensured that all sport could be reached by fascist bodies of some sort, that no sport was being done without the party and state getting involved. This helped to make the Fascist Party more than just a political party: it was a movement that created a culture of consent and helped tremendously in the modernization process.

The other aim of the fascists was to demonstrate that Italy was improving physically and morally under the new regime. International success in major sporting events was therefore important to confirm that the new Italy was a world power. Football, cycling and other sports in which Italy was proficient were followed passionately and, in 1936, it was reported that 40 million spectators watched 30,000 sports events in one year (Banti 1936). Ferretti (1928), the fascist sports leader, was very enthusiastic about such numbers and assumed that sport spectatorship would fire up Italian citizens to become honourable citizens and heroic soldiers. But this remained mere theory for the majority of Italians, as they were culturally unprepared for the sporting life. They did not join CONI, but instead preferred the OND in which any physical activity (bathing, boccia, billiards, hiking, etc.) was accepted as 'sport'. Thus, Dopolavoro gained many new members while CONI just kept its old ones. In 1930, CONI had only 60,000 members, 0.75 per cent of the population; and even that figure contained hunters, as CONI embraced all voluntary activity for which one needed a licence. All the other enrolments in ONB, OND, GUF, FGC and MVSN were more or less compulsory, so it is difficult to know how many members were really doing which activity.

The fascists had the ideological difficulty that, on the one hand, they wanted many fit men for wars of the future and fit women to bear fit children (Frasca 1983), and, on the other hand, they wanted international success which could best be achieved by (semi-)professional athletes. For the professionals they needed plenty of spectators to pay for the sport. The regime also offered financial rewards and special privileges to all its champions, who were seen as special emissaries of Mussolini. From the 1932 Olympics in Los Angeles the 'Mussolini Boys' returned in triumph, placing second to the USA, ahead of the rest of the world. In soccer, Italian national sport number one, Italy won the world championships in 1934 and 1938. It can well be argued that this was the high point of enthusiasm for the fascist regime in Italy (Murray 1994). It could show that it was the world's best – before it got involved in an expansionist war and lost.

The practical and ideological difficulties of the fascist system can be seen in the example of football. We can spot the dilemma between competition for some and good health for many, between the importance of championships and high visibility on one side, and collectivism and mass participation on the other, professionalism for some and amateurism for all, sport and leisure-time activities as being private, and the responsibility of the state for the well-being of the population. To solve the dilemma, Augusto Turati started to introduce the game of volata in 1928. This was an invented tradition, a game that was supposed to be the ancient Roman football (Hobsbawm and Ranger 1983), a game close to rugby, team handball and soccer. With the help of the new game, Roman tradition was supposed to be fostered and military readiness furthered, more through ball handling than football. Besides, it was Italian and not British, which was an asset in itself in the view of the fascist leadership. It became the game of the OND and had already over 2,000 teams playing for the Trofeo Turati in 1930. When Turati fell from favour and was eventually exiled in 1933, the game soon lost its popularity and was apparently no longer played in 1936 (Impiglia 1997). The game shows, however, that the fascists could enforce new rules within the OND (they did not dare within CONI), but on the whole they tried to mould the existing rules to meet their aims rather than to set up new ones.

While Turati stood for an élitist fascism, Achille Starace (Secretary of the PNF from 1932 to 39) forced employees of the fascist State into the PNF and militarized the party – and thereby the basic structure of sports organizations. Uniforms of all kinds, ritual and symbolism started to play a much greater role. He has been called 'a high priest of the Cult of the Duce' (Brooker 1991: 158). Starace not only showed off his own athletic abilities, but forced the sub-leaders of the PNF into sports as well. Under his leadership a democratization of access to many forms of sport took place. He satisfied the needs of a Depression-weary public for simple diversions, such as sport, but also parades and party ceremonies. By this the consumption of commodities was de-emphasized and the consumption of leisure itself was stressed (de Grazia 1981). Starace is probably best remembered for introducing the 'fascist Saturday' in 1935. Work stopped at 1 p.m. on Saturday and the afternoon was free for parades and sport. Although this was used at first to fire up the population for the war against Ethiopia, it was soon to become the basis for much more sport and sport spectatorship.

The Duce himself was built up as a living example of an active sportsman: a skier, rider, fencer, motorcyclist, aviator, speedboat-racer, swimmer, shooter – superman himself. Of all heads of state in this century possibly only Teddy Roosevelt was of similar stature as athlete and hero (Lucas 1982/3) and Mussolini did not fail to encourage competition himself, he publicly performed athletic feats and made sure that he was photographed as often and as much as possible doing sport. He was more a man of action than of ideology. With his mystification of the state and the glory of the Roman past he fitted well into the international sports movement that shared much of the same ideas (Gentile 1975).

Italy was quite efficient in nationalizing the sport system. It served as a role model to many European countries. Although Germany was eventually more efficient in terms of medals won, it should be noted that the Italian basis for athletics was far less developed, so their progress was probably the greatest. The cross influence between Germany and Italy was quite extensive from the nineteenth century onward and was even more intensified in the fascist period (Krüger 1991b). Italy also shows how easily the bourgeois sports movement accepted the fascist form of sport. Not only did it accommodate the fascists in international sports all along, but the fascist law to reorganize top-level sports of Italy in 1942 is still today the basis of the regulations of much of Italian sport and particularly CONI (Porro 1997). What changed in the fascist era? The direct influence of the state and the party was much greater, so that after 1943 a movement to give sport back to the sportsmen (not so much the sportswomen) was started, as many decisions had been determined more on the basis of the Fascist Party or the state than by the sport officials themselves (Alcanterini 1997). Sport was instrumentalized but relatively little changed within the sports movement, so that it was readily accepted as a role model.

Franco's Spain

Although Barcelona had applied to stage the Olympic Games of 1936 and eventually prepared to stage the Workers' Olympics that same year, Spain can hardly be seen on the sporting world map at the time. When General Francisco Franco Bahamonde came to power with the help of the Spanish Civil War (1936–9), it was questionable whether his political regime was really 'fascist' in the Italian or the German sense of the word, or whether it was a traditional military dictatorship along the lines that have been typical for South America. Franco was anything but an athlete, he was considered more to be of moral than of physical strength. He was interested in traditional Spanish values, best demonstrated by such activities as bull fighting and hunting (which he did himself excessively). What is more, Franco stayed in power for thirty-nine years, more than Hitler and Mussolini put together. What made him so successful and what did that have to do with sport?

Franco was able to achieve a wide coalition government of fascist, Catholic conservative, Carlist, and monarchist groups. He also succeeded in adapting his system to the cultural and economic necessities of the times, creating a sufficient amount of terror with the help of the *Guardia Civil* and the secret police, and distraction. While sport in Italy was part of the 'culture of consent' (de Grazia 1981), in Spain this was considered the 'culture of evasion' (Carr 1979):

> 'Football had a dimension above actual sport. It was the best catalyst of Spanish nationalism . . . . The victories in football against England in 1950 or the Soviet Union in 1964 served as mile stones of first order to the official propaganda . . . . Football, bull fighting and radio plays were part of the culture of evasion and created an artificial silence around the real problems of a poor country'. (Carr 1979: 158f.)

His reign is therefore divided into the political years (1936–47), the football years (1947–67), the transition years (1967–75) (Gonzales Aja 1998). Although Franco was heavily supported by Hitler and Mussolini in the Civil War and would not have won without European fascist support, Spain remained basically neutral during the world war. Spain did not enter the war against France or Britain in 1939. Only when Germany declared war against the Soviet Union in 1941, did Spain join. But Spain again stayed neutral in the war against the United States (1942), showing off Franco's stout anti-communism. Similarly, the Spanish policy towards European Jewry was as independent as could be: Spain reclaimed its own Jewry (although it had been exiled from Spain in the sixteenth century) from all the countries that Germany had occupied – but none of the others. On the other hand, Spain did not seal off its borders as Germany had demanded and provided transit visas to refugees from many European countries, Jews and Gentiles, as long as they were not communists. This pro-fascist, but independent, policy was the basis for the post-war years. Although the newly founded United Nations did not permit Spanish membership in 1945 and the western powers demanded the ousting of Franco as the last fascist ruler (1947), Franco gained acceptance when the Cold War started. He could say to the world 'I told you so' and was admitted to the UN in 1950 and included into the western military alliance of NATO in 1953 when Spain leased airforce bases to the US. A Spanish government in exile existed in Mexico from 1945 to 50, but the Franco dictatorship, supported at first only by other Spanish-speaking dictators in Latin American states and the Philippines eventually won limited world approval.

The sports world had always accepted Spain. Spain had participated from the Olympic Games of 1900 onward, had only six athletes at the 1932 Olympics owing to the economic crisis and none in Berlin 1936 owing to the Civil War. Even at the time of the international ban, the IOC invited Spain to the 1948 Olympics in London, where the Spanish team was represented by sixty-five athletes. Although the USSR had demanded that 'fascist' Spain be ousted before it would join the IOC and participate in the 1952 Olympics, Avery Brundage made the point that the USSR could not make such demands as a non-member. Once the USSR had joined, it put the expulsion of Spain again on the agenda – and lost. The IOC stood by its member. Spain sent twenty-seven athletes to the 1952 Olympics, six to the Equestrian Olympics in Stockholm in the summer of 1956 – but boycotted the Melbourne Olympics in the winter of 1956. As a convinced anti-communist country Spain thus protested at the Soviet invasion of Hungary and abstained from participation together with such democratic countries as Switzerland and the Netherlands. In spite of Olympic enthusiasm, Spain won only one Olympic gold, two silver and two bronze medals in all of the Franco years.

In 1941 Franco created the National Sports Delegation (DND) to co-ordinate all athletic efforts and provide the basis for better national representation. It was under the Falange, the fascist movement of Spain and not the government. This followed the German example of the time and tried to combine the demand for physical readiness on the one hand and the prestige that came with being involved with international sport on the other. Just as in Nazi Germany, the president of the DND was by definition also the president of the Spanish National Olympic Committee and had the power to appoint all presidents and board members of all national sports federations. The first president was

Gen. Moscardó, a Civil War hero, who just like von Tschammer in Germany had the task of instilling the fascist spirit into every sport. He abolished the traditional national vest and replaced it with the blue shirt of the Falange, made sure the Spanish teams would bring out the fascist salute, and influenced the training of physical education teachers in a fascist way. After his death in 1955 the Falangist youth leader took the office to show that it was attempted to move all of the youth more towards sport. In 1966 he was dismissed as Spain had not been very successful internationally. His successor was Juan Antonio Samaranch who was considered to be a loyal Falangist and also stood for athletic success and international connections. With the taking of office of a new minister in 1970, Samaranch was dismissed and replaced by another Falangist politician. As the DND was considered a fascist political body, with limited feedback to the actual sporting scene, it was not very successful (Gonzales Aja 1998). The only real international successes were those of the football club Real Madrid.

What made Spain stake so much on football? First of all, it should be kept in mind that – while Hitler and Mussolini invested heavily in élite sport – Franco did not. Therefore, it is obvious that only money-generating sports could be viable at a high international level. The biggest success of Spain in the Olympic Games prior to the Franco years had been the silver medal in the 1920 Olympics. Spain had been victorious over Denmark, Italy and Holland, only losing to gold medal winner Belgium. The Spanish furore had excited the fans at home and abroad alike. Spanish football had been at the crossroads of all football styles of the world, always up to date in its technique and style. There had been a lot of enthusiasm for football during the Civil War, although a national championship could not be played owing to lack of transport and communication over the boundaries of the respective 'zones'. As soon as the Civil War was over, football served to show that Spain was again one nation. FC Barcelona, symbol of Catalan separatism, and Atletico Bilbao, likewise the emblem for Basque independence, played in the Primera Division, placing third and ninth in the 1939/40 season. The Spanish champion was the Atletico Aviación (airforce) club of Madrid; it later dropped the Aviación, which had shown that the military was still supreme in Spain.

Football served a double function: it demonstrated Spanish unity, so important for the nationalists after the Civil War and it created the culture of evasion, the chance to talk about something other than the war, economic problems, lack of freedom, police brutality. This can be seen in the censored press. The journals of the separatist peoples of Spain had not only to give up publishing in Basque or Catalan, but they also had to report more on football than on political matters (in the case of the *Diario Vasco* 17 per cent sport, 3 per cent national politics) (Fernandez Santander 1990: 242). At first, there was little idea about international success. The internal aims of a pretty much isolated Spain were predominant. It may be assumed that Spain stumbled into international success in football rather than that there was a master plan for all sport, as in Nazi Germany or fascist Italy.

The situation changed in 1945 when international isolation had to be broken. What Germany achieved with the help of the international sports federations and the Olympic Games of 1936, Spain started in March 1945 with its first post-war international against Portugal, likewise a semi-fascist country under the dictatorial rule of Salazar. Spanish long-range planning was clear in that even before the war ended Spain searched for international matches. Two days before Germany signed its capitulation in May 1945, Spain played its second match against Portugal. In 1947 more international matches against Portugal and now also against Ireland followed suit; Switzerland (also the first post-war adversary of Nazi Germany in football) followed in 1948. When Spain defeated France 5 : 1 in 1949 it had re-established itself as a football power. The DND was useful in providing rapidly citizenship for foreign football stars who came to play in Spain such as Di Stefano (Columbia) and Kubala (Hungary). South American players of Spanish origin could regain Spanish citizenship easily which helped to improve the standard of play tremendously as Spanish football was professional and well paid by most standards. When the European Champions Cup was introduced for club teams that had become national champions, Real Madrid won the first five years, 1955–60. The Spanish national team was equally successful. Of the extraordinary many 148 matches Spain won 71, drew 40 and only lost 37. Franco enjoyed watching Real Madrid more than any other sport and handed them the highest Spanish order for their international success – as ambassadors of the new Spain. As television really started to become big in Spain after 1956, the Real Madrid years also served to introduce television on a grand scale and bring Spanish victories to every household.

Another sport which has always been important in Spain is roller hockey. Spain applied to become a member of the international federation for that sport in October 1945, and thus again broke through the isolation barrier shortly after the formation of a Spanish government in exile and only a few months before France sealed off the border with Spain. A certain Juan Antonio Samaranch was the second Spanish representative at the international congress on roller hockey in Montreaux (Switzerland). Samaranch, a former goalkeeper, was the coach of Español Barcelona and the best-known sportswriter for this sport under the pen-name 'Stick'. Samaranch made the acquaintance of the IOC chancellor Mayer who had also been a goalkeeper. The friendship between the two eventually helped Samaranch to become the IOC member for Spain (see Chapter 1). In 1946, the meeting served to set up international matches for Spain and thus help break the cultural and political isolation of Spain. In the following year, the Spanish national team finished second in the world championships in the same sport. This success has been identified in the Spanish press with Samaranch. In 1951, Spain staged the world championships in Barcelona. Samaranch was fully in control. He was the manager of the Spanish team, and head organizer, personally providing the funding for the preparation – and he won on all counts. Spain won its first world title ever, the championships turned out to be a financial success and Samaranch was accredited with being the unofficial number one in Spanish sports outside football. This was eventually the basis on which he became president of the DND and by this the highest Falange functionary in sport.

For Spanish sport, just as for business and many other fields, the transition from the Franco years to the time after was easy. It was well prepared. Spain had gradually changed from a totalitarian dictatorship to a modern democratic state. While the other fascist dictatorships were ended by the war, the Spanish one ended when Franco died. In his testament he had provided for the change to a constitutional monarchy. The new King Juan Carlos had participated in the Olympic Games and thus sport improved its position in Spain as the new head of state and the royal family were of a similar athletic calibre as Mussolini had been. So the democratic Spain is now investing much more heavily in sport than Franco ever had.

Conclusion

Nothing is more successful than success. When the Axis powers were doing so well in sport, the other fascist regimes in Europe copied their efforts and started to invest in sport at all levels, particularly after the Olympic Games of 1936. The athletic success of such countries as Yugoslavia (Radan 1986) and Hungary (Kutassi 1986) after the war has its basis in these efforts. After the beginning of the war and the occupation of most of France, the remaining France under Maréchal Pétin put much emphasis on élite sports to demonstrate its vitality (Gay-Lescot 1991). Many of the fascist states co-operated more and more during the war. In 1942 a European Sports Federation was on its way with von Tschammer as president (Carl Diem as secretary-general) and vice-presidents from Hungary and Italy. The other members were to come from Bulgaria, Finland, Holland, Croatia, Norway, Rumania, Slovakia, and Spain. Belgium was split into the two independent federations of Walonia and Flanders. This new organization was to co-ordinate fascist sport and counteract the Anglo-American domination in many international sports federations. Although Germany had Belgian IOC President Baillet-Latour more or less as hostage, the IOC did not give in to German pressure to support fascism on all issues. The organization was not only to organize European championships but also to help to co-ordinate paramilitary sports. Only when Germany was about to lose the war and the Eastern front crumbled after the Soviet victory at Stalingrad in the winter of 1942/3, were the plans cancelled as there were more pressing things to do than to organize a fascist sports international (Teichler 1991).

Much of what the fascists were planning in sports had been present in European sport before the fascist regimes came to power, and much stayed with us for many years after the downfall of fascism. Only the cultural revolution of 1968 started to create some changes: the preselection of athletes, sports schools for young people, anthropometric measurements for the selection of athletes, and doping practices on the élite sport side, co-ordinated sport structures and its functionaries, adventure education, the cult of the body. Fascist sport could base itself on the same principles of the European past as the democratic sports tradition, it did not have to make too many changes. You could still base yourself on the classical Greek tradition, the only change you needed to make was that it was no longer Athens one was striving for but Sparta (Krüger and Ramba 1991).

References

Alcanterini, R. (1997) 'Lo sport agli sportive (1943–1955)', in A. Krüger and A. Teja (eds) *La Commune Heredità dello Sport in Europa*. Rome: CONI, 311–12.

Alegi, G. (1997) 'Italy's future is in the sky', in A. Krüger and A. Teja (eds) *La Commune Heredità dello Sport in Europa*. Rome: CONI, 407–12.

Banti, A. (1936) 'L'importanza dello spettacolo sportivo', in *Lo sport fascista* 9(1), 31.

Bernett, H. J. (1978) *Der jüdische Sport im nationalsozialistischen Deutschland. 1933–1938*, Schorndorf: Hofmann.

—— (1980) 'Das Scheitern der Olympischen Spiele von 1940', in *Stadion* 6(1), 251–90.

Bianda, R. and Leone, G. *et al.* (1983) *Atleti in Camicia nera. Lo sport nell' Italia di Mussolini*, Rome: Volpe.

Boiz, J and Espada, A. (1991) *El deporte del poder. Vida y milagro de Juan Antonio Samaranch*, Madrid: Temas de Hoy.

Brohm, J. M. (1986) 'Zum Verhältnis von Olympismus und Nationalsozialismus', in G. Gebauer (ed.) *Olympia-Berlin. Gewalt und Mythos in den Olympischen Spielen von Berlin 1936*, Berlin: Freie Universität, 190–205.

Brooker, P. (1991) *The Faces of Fraternalism. Nazi Germany, Fascist Italy, and Imperial Japan*, Oxford: Clarendon Press.

Cagigal, J. M. (1975), *El deporte en la sociedad actual*. Madrid: Española.

Carr, R. (with J.P. Fusi) (1979) *España: de la dictadura à la democracia*, Barcelona: Planeta.

Crolley, L. (1997) 'Real Madrid y Barcelona. The State against a nation. The changing role of football in Spain', in A. Krüger and A. Teja (eds) *La Commune Heredità dello Sport in Europa*. Rome: CONI, 450–6.

Czech, M. (1994) *Frauen und Sport im nationalsozialistischen Deutschland. Eine Untersuchung zur weiblichen Sportrealität in einem patriarchalen Herrschaftssystem*. Berlin: Tischler.

De Grazia, V. (1981) *The Culture of Consent. Mass Organizations of Leisure in Fascist Italy*, Cambridge: Cambridge University Press.

Diaz, E. (1991) *Intellektuelle unter Franco. Eine Geschichte des spanischen Denkens. 1939–1975*, Frankfurt: Vervuert.

Fabricio, F. (1976) *Sport e Fascismo. La politica sportiva del regime. 1924–1936* Florence: Guaraldi.

Fasbender, S. (1997) *Zwischen Arbeitersport und Arbeitssport. Werksport and Rhein und Ruhr. 1921–1938*, Göttingen: Cuvillier.

Fernandez Santander, C. (1990) *El futbol durante la guerra civil y el franquismo*, Madrid: San Martin.

Ferrara, P. (1992) *L'Italia in palestra. Storia, documeni e immagini della gimnastica dal 1833–1973*, Rome: La Meridiana.

Ferretti, L. (1928) *Il libro dello sport.* Rome: Littorio.

Frasca, Isidori R. (1983) *. . . e il duce le volle sportive.* Bologna: Patron.

Gay-Lescot, J. L. (1991) *Sport et éducation sous Vichy, 1940–1944.* Lyons: Presses Universitaires de Lyon.

Gentile, E. (1975) *Le origini dell' ideologia fascista.* Rome: Laterza.

Gonzales Aja, T. (1998) 'Spanish sports policy in Republican and Fascist Spain', in J. Riordan and P. Arnaud (eds) *Sport and International Politics.* E & FN Spon: London.

Gonzales Aja, T. and Teja, A. (1997) 'Mussolini and Franco sportsmen: two contrasting conceptions of sport', in A. Krüger and A. Teja (eds) *La Commune Heredità dello Sport in Europa*, Rome: CONI, 413–19.

Gori, G. (1996) *L'atleta e la nazione. Saggi di storia dello sport.* Rimini: Panozzo.

Griffin, R. (1995) *Oxford Readers: Fascism.* Oxford: Oxford University Press.

Grunberger, R. (1995) *The 12-Year Reich. A Social History of Nazi Germany, 1933–1945.* New York: Da Capo.

Hitler, A. (1925/1971), *Mein Kampf* (English, *My Struggle*) Boston: Houghton Mifflin.

Hoberman, J. (1984) *Sport and Political Ideology.* Austin: University of Texas Press.

Hobsbawm, E. and Ranger, T. (1983) *The Invention of Tradition.* Cambridge: Cambridge University Press.

Impiglia, M. (1997) 'The volata game. When fascism forbade Italians to play football', in A. Krüger and A. Teja (eds) *La Commune Heredità dello Sport in Europa.* Rome: CONI, 420–6.

Krüger, A. (1972) *Die Olympischen Spiele 1936 und die Weltmeinung. Ihre außenpolitische Bedeutung unter besonderer Berücksightigung der USA*, Berlin: Bartels & Wernitz.

—— (1978) '"Fair play for American athletes." A study in anti-Semitism', *Canadian Journal of the History of Sport and Physical Education* 9(1), 42–57.

—— (1980) 'Neo-Olympismus zwischen Nationalismus und Internationalismus', in H. Ueberhorst (ed.) *Geschichte der Leibesübungen*, vol. 3/1. Berlin: Bartels & Wernitz, 522–68.

—— (1985) '"Heute gehört uns Deutschland und morgen . . ."'? Das Ringen um den Sinn der Gleichschaltung im Sport in der ersten Jahreshälfte 1933', in W. Buss and A. Krüger (eds) *Sportgeschichte: Traditionspflege und Wertewandel. Festschrift zum 75. Geburtstag von Prof. Dr. W. Henze*, Duderstadt: Mecke, 175–96.

—— (1986) 'The influence of the state sport of fascist Italy on Nazi Germany. 1928–1936', in J. A. Mangan and R. Small (eds), *Sport – Culture – Society.* London: E & FN Spon, 145–65.

—— (1991a) ' "Leibesübungen jetzt erst recht!" Sport im Zweiten Weltkrieg', in A. Krüger and H. Langenfeld (eds), *Sport in Hannover*. Göttingen: Die Werkstatt, 185–88.

—— (1991b) 'Fasci e croci uncinate', in *Lancillotto e Nausica. Critica e storia dello sport* 8(1/2), 88–101.

—— (1993) 'Germany and sport in World War II', *Can. Journal of the History of Sport* 24(1), 52–62.

—— (1994) ' "Wenn die Olympiade vorbei, schlagen wir die Juden zu Brei." Das Verhältnis der Juden zu den Olympischen Spielen von 1936', in *Menora 5. Jahrbuch für deutsch-jüdische Geschichte 1994*. Munich: Piper, 331–48.

—— (1995) ' "Buying victories is positively degrading." The European origins of government pursuit of national prestige through sports'. *International Journal of the History of Sport* 12(2), 201–18.

—— (1997) 'The Olympic Games of 1936 as Fifth German Combat Games', in R. Naul (ed.), *Contemporary Studies in the National Olympic Games Movement*. Frankfurt: P. Lang, 153–75.

—— (1998) 'A horse breeder's perspective: scientific racism in Germany, 1870–1933', in N. Finzsch and D. Schirmer (eds) *Identity and Intolerance: Nationalism, Racism and Xenophobia in Germany and the United States*. Cambridge: CUP, 371–96.

—— (1999) ' " . . . the breeding of absolutely healthy bodies." Shaping supermen the Nazi way', *Int. Journal of the History of Sport* (in print).

Krüger, A. and v. Lojewski, F. (1998) 'Ausgewählte Aspekte des Wehrsports in Niedersachsen in der Weimarer Zeit', in H. Langenfeld and S. Nielsen (eds) *Beiträge zur Sportgeschichte Niedersachsens. Teil 2: Weimarer Republik*. Hoya: NISH, 124–48.

Krüger, A. and Ramba, D. (1991) 'Sparta or Athens? The Reception of Greek Antiquity in Nazi Germany', in R. Renson, M. Lämmer, J. Riordan, D. Chassiotis (eds): *The Olympic Games Through the Ages: Greek Antiquity and its Impact on Modern Sport*. Athens: Hellenic Sports Research Institute, 345–56.

Krüger, A. and Riordan, J. (eds) (1996) *The Story of Worker Sport*. Champaign, IL: Human Kinetics.

Kutassi, L. (1986) 'Sportpolitik in Ungarn zur Zeit des Horthy-Regimes. 1919–1944', in M. Olsen (ed.) *Sport and Politics. 1918–39/40*. Oslo: Universitetsforlaget, 180–6.

Lissina, H. E. (1997) *Nationale Sportfeste im nationalsozialistischen Deutschland*, Mannheim: Palatium.

Lucas, J. A. (1982/3) 'Theodore Roosevelt and Baron Pierre de Coubertin: Entangling Olympic Games Involvement. 1901–1918' *Stadion* 8/9(1), 137–50.

Murray, B. (1994), *Football. A History of the World's Game*. Aldershot, Hants: Scholar Press.

Oelrich, H. (1997) ' "Who has the youth has the future." International youth sports activities of the "Axis Berlin Rome" from 1940 on and the founding of the "European Youth Association" in 1942', in A. Krüger and A. Teja (eds) *La Commune Heredità dello Sport in Europa*. Rome: CONI, 427–39.

Ofstad, H. (1989) *Our Contempt for Weakness. Nazi Norms and Values – and our own*. Gothenburg: Almquist & Wiksell.

Payne, S. G. (1995) *A History of Fascism. 1914–45*. London: UCL.

Pivato, S. (1994) *L'era dello sport*. Florence: Giunti.

Pollack, B. (1987) *The Paradox of Spanish Foreign Policy. Spain's International Relations from Franco to Democracy.* London, Pinter.

Porro, N. (1997) 'The Sports System and Nationalization in Italy', in A. Krüger and A. Teja (eds) *La Commune Heredità dello Sport in Europa.* Rome: CONI, 370–4.

Radan, Z. (1986) 'Sport und Politik in Jugoslavien, 1918–1941', in M. Olsen (ed.), *Sport and Politics. 1918–39/40.* Oslo: Universitetsforlaget, 187–96.

Shaw, D. (1987) *Futbal y franquismo.* Madrid, Alianza.

Silva, U. (1975) *Arte e Ideologia del Fascismo.* Valencia, Torres.

Stecewicz, L. (1996) *Sport und Diktatur. Erinnerungen eines oesterreichischen Journalisten.* Vienna: Turia & Kant.

Teichler, H. J. (1991) *Internationale Sportpolitik im Dritten Reich.* Schorndorf: Hofmann.

Teja, A. (1998) 'Italian Sport and International Relations under Fascism', in J. Riordan and P. Arnaud (eds), *Sport and International Politics.* E & FN Spon: London.

Tusell, J. (1988) *La dictadura de Franco.* Madrid: Alianza.

Wippermann, W. (1983) *Europäischer Faschismus im Vergleich. 1922–1982.* Frankfurt: Suhrkamp.

5　Religion and sport

Swantje Scharenberg

Introduction

Cassius Clay and George Foreman, both one-time Olympic and World champions in both amateur and professional boxing, became eloquent lay preachers. Clay changed his name to Muhammad Ali in order to demonstrate his new association with the Muslim religion and discard his 'slave' name. Foreman became a Christian minister in his own church. Both boxers changed their value system from sporting to religious, and their careers illustrate the complex intermeshing of religious and sporting values and norms. Boxing, nonetheless, is regarded by many as a brutal sport whose actions are sanctioned by the rules of the sport; its values appear to contradict those common in society.

According to Max Weber's sociology of religion, the value system of modern capitalist European society is based on religious ideas. He describes religion as a catalyst in the process of nation-building which operates as long as society's economic situation is stable. Politics, based as it is on the interests of the economy, develops its own system of values, and religion can no longer exert a public influence; it is used only to guide individual existence.

Sport has its own value system, and for many it is a way of life throughout the world. It is governed by rules and events that follow a certain pattern in time and space; this transforms actions into rites. Originating in different culture-specific systems of rules and value hierarchies, sporting culture has been generalized to fit the concept of 'the global village'. As a consequence, the sporting system of new cultural norms results in cultural and even political alienation: single achievements and common achievements are assessed differently in various cultures; activity or contemplation do not play the same role everywhere in the world, and sport associated with self-awareness or rivalry can be at variance with an education system following certain cultural patterns.

This chapter follows Max Weber's theory of religion in society to explain the effect of monotheistic religions on selected developments in twentieth-century sport. Starting with the ideas of the founder of the modern Olympic movement, Baron Pierre de Coubertin, who founded the idea of *religio athletae*, we find ourselves in an era when religion was an important system of values which underpinned the capitalist societies of Europe.

For comparison, we then look at North America and ask whether a similar religious function gave meaning to sport in the same period when Coubertin was developing the Olympic Games.

The Deutsche Jugendkraft, the German Catholic youth organization founded in 1920, is then taken as an example of the impact of politics on a religion-based sports youth organization under Nazi rule.

Limitations on the ecumenical role that sport can play will be examined by reference to developments in Northern Ireland.

Finally, discrimination against athletes and sport from a religious standpoint will be looked at in Islamic societies.

The Olympic 'religion'

Baron Pierre de Coubertin regarded sport as a religion, with its own church, dogma and culture, but above all with religious *feelings* (Coubertin 1897: 114). He 'had politics on his mind. The decline of the French spirit after the Franco-Prussian War was the primary motivating factor in his work to rebuild the Games' (Lapchick 1979: 251). In his religious attitudes he was deeply influenced by the Dominican Father Henri-Martin Didon (1840–1900), who was highly regarded in France at the time. Didon had researched the motives behind German political and economic success during the 1880s and was open-minded on social problems in general. In that, he was far ahead of his time. Together with Coubertin he worked on plans to introduce sport and physical education into education generally. Not only with his speech on the 'Character-building qualities of sport', delivered to the Olympic Congress at Le Havre in 1897, but with his motto *Citius, Altius, Fortius*, which was adopted at the founding congress in 1894 as the motto of the Olympic movement, Didon shaped the character of the new event and of Coubertin himself.

Religion was the centrepiece of Coubertin's *pédagogie sportive* and of the modern Olympic movement. He employed the term *religio athletae* to emphasize sport as a matter of conscience for the athlete (Hörrmann 1968; Krüger 1993). His ideology of spiritual and moral comportment was modelled on antiquity. Because he succeeded in linking Greek philosophy with the political outlook of members of the educated classes (Alkemeyer 1996: 179), his system of values was of definite interest to the educated classes. Participation in the Olympic Games, whether as athlete or as spectator, was thought to be the basis of behavioural attributes like chivalry, fair play and respect for one's opponent, as well as an exemplary lifestyle. All these values were easy to transfer from sport to other parts of the political and social environment; yet they worked as a kind of philosophy of life (Krüger 1981: 189).

Later on, during a radio broadcast in 1935 (*The Philosophical Basis of Modern Olympism. Message Given through Radio Broadcasting*), Coubertin stressed the importance of the *religio athletae* for Olympism, while equating religion and Olympism. Olympism was not a system for him, but an ecumenical and, above all, a spiritual attitude of mind. During the games, there were supposed to be no national rivalries, but peace in the competition arenas, which were regarded as sanctuaries, rather like churches. The athlete should shape his body through sport and glorify his country, his masculinity and his flag through this action. Coubertin regarded the individual athlete, who had learned positive character traits through sport, as a priest and servant of the religion of muscularity (Hörrmann 1968: 12).

Cult and rituals were immanent in the production of the games so as to create the tradition of *religio athletae*. This should be an educational value in the athlete's head which would enhance moral development. The Olympic Games should not be seen just as an event:

> At Olympia, vulgar competition was transformed and in a sense sanctified by contact with national sentiment superbly excited .... There states and cities came together in the persons of their young men who, imbued with a sense of the moral grandeur of the Games, went to them in a spirit of near religious reverence.
>
> (Coubertin 1928: 5f.)

Religion was here again used as a catalyst, as a model for structuring and (re)inventing a sporting competition with a high and long-lasting degree of effectiveness. The political use of this approach can be seen in the link between sporting success and a proper conception of the world – the transition from stadium to state. The feedback of sport to common convictions strengthens the sense of duty (Hörrmann 1968: 21).

Coubertin's major religious ideas were, however, not understood by athletes and therefore did not survive (Coubertin 1987: 239). All the same, the *religio athletae* was redefined with considerable mass effect into a heroic anthropology, impressively presented during the 1936 'Nazi' Olympics in Berlin (Alkemeyer 1996: 453). This was possible because 'interests (material and idealistic), not ideas, dominate the actions of human beings' (Weber 1920). According to Weber, a changing conception of the world is important to structure one's own way of life.

The Olympic Games survived because the concept based on different ideas (ethics based on religion or values of sport, like integration of athletes and spectators in the global village) could be employed and re-evaluated for different interests as national (Tornas 1994), political (for example boycott) and economic instruments with an international effect. The obvious symbols of the games have remained as a kind of liturgy, but the importance of the ideas espoused by Coubertin diminished soon after the games were reinvented (Guttmann 1978: 25; 1992: 148).

The American YMCA

The Young Men's Christian Association (YMCA) was founded in England by George Williams and then spread throughout the United States in the 1850s. In 1860, a convention was published which favoured athletics and gymnastics as 'a safeguard against the allurement of objectional places of resort' (Betts 1974: 108). Particularly the YMCA in Boston and New York (1869) employed sport 'as the best means of attracting worldly young men' (Pence 1947: 17) and, therefore as a driving force to spread their ideas of education. At the end of the 1880s, nearly a quarter of all YMCA groups were supporting sport, most of them being equipped with gymnasiums. *Harper's Weekly* noted (1890), 'It is the muscular form of Christianity that seems to take on best among young men' (Betts 1974: 108).

The rounded personality, however, was still the centre of attention. Luther Halsey expressed this idea through a triangle of body, mind and spirit, which was adopted as the YMCA slogan in 1895. The Young Women's Christian Association (YWCA) did not have its own sports facilities when it organized the first games for women in Boston in 1882. But from then on sport became important in the YWCA too.

Economic changes at the end of the nineteenth century, accompanied by the dream of material wealth, were followed by a population migration from rural to urban areas. Given the limited space for recreation,

> the nature of popular sport also shifted from sport connected to one's livelihood . . . to sport disconnected from one's livelihood. . . . The growth of sport is a symbolic break with the past, and at the same time a new medium through which to explore old values.
>
> (Knott 1994: 31)

The Christian gymnasium was and still is used as a bastion against the moral decline of youth. Basketball (1892) and volleyball (1895) were introduced as Christian games by YMCA members 'to meet the need for indoor sport on winter evenings' (Betts 1974: 77). James Naismith wanted 'to invent a game which should be suitable for the particular conditions obtaining in the Young Men's Christian Association' (Hopkins 1951: 260). Basketball was planned from a bureaucratic ivory tower and rules were set before the sport was ever played. Two peach baskets were used as goals in the first game.

But Naismith achieved what he desired. He wanted to invent a team game that worked as a laboratory in which to do research on moral attributes. The other condition was that the coach had to be a Christian. Twelve attributes were associated with basketball: the ability to meet new conditions with efficiency, agility, accuracy, alertness and a ready response to stimulus, co-operation, skill, reflex judgement, speed, self-confidence, self-sacrifice, self-control and sportsmanship (Naismith 1941: 184ff.)

The public acceptance of basketball was initially less spectacular than expected. 'Basketball was accepted by the high schools before colleges took it up as an organised sport. I believe that the younger boys who played in the YMCA gymnasiums took the game with them into the high schools. It was only after these boys graduated from high school and entered college that basketball really began to take hold in that institution' (Naismith 1941: 105).

The prerequisites of Christian values that Naismith demanded were not important any more once basketball started to spread throughout the world and gained public attention after World War I as an export of US sporting culture.

The religion-based YMCA, with its focus on sport and its many followers, took on another, more general, responsibility of national proportions. It offered urban dwellers military training. Since 1903 when Brooklyn Central 'Y' started collaboration with the 14th Regiment, the YMCA spread programmes into communities, Sunday schools and industries to foster physical education. The Association's experience and popularity were used politically during World War I:

> The army drew heavily on the personnel and resources of the YMCA, and 300 athletic directors took charge of the sports programme, operating 836 athletic fields. The YMCA sent scores of these directors overseas and spent between one and two million dollars on athletic equipment. . . . Under the directorship of Elwood S. Brown, the YMCA carried the burden of athletic activities in France until General Order 241 made athletics and mass games a matter of military schedule.
>
> (Betts 1974: 137)

Even during demobilization, the programme for mass organized sport initiated by the YMCA continued, but switched to foreign sports aid on the basis of internationalism. The gospel of sport was thereby embodied in several friendly contests between athletes of the Allies.

The YMCA was a politically suitable organization for the purpose of winning the war. The simple idea to use sport for selling religion (Deford 1976: 64f.) in a more ecumenical way did not work out completely. The interests of sport obscured religious ideas and the power of sporting bodies was successfully employed for political purposes on the basis of national sporting enthusiasm.

Sport linked to religious ideas can also be a threat to political interests, and the ideas therefore have to be either ignored, suppressed, redefined or abolished, as the example of the *Deutsche Jugendkraft* from its foundation up to the Nazi period shows below.

The Deutsche Jugendkraft

The Deutsche Jugendkraft (German Youth League) was a Roman Catholic sports organization, founded in 1920 and based on the religious ideas of the nineteenth century. In the nineteenth century, sports clubs and especially the gymnastic *Turnvereine* were regarded by the Church as dangerous because of their charismatic effect on young people. Particularly the Roman Catholic Church, supported by Pope Pius X, wanted to set an educational framework to compete against such organizations and the ideas they espoused; it therefore promoted the importance of artistic and physical abilities and power as a social foundation for young people. Poor living conditions and hard work were said by the Church to be ruining young people's health. That is why it developed special programmes for school-leavers. Part of this 'youth welfare programme' included gymnastics, games and nature rambling.

The other main reason for the programme was to publicize the Church; sport was an attractive means of self advertisement and the overall sporting enthusiasm of youth was too strong to ignore.

The Deutsche Jugendkraft (DJK), which developed mainly in Catholic areas of Germany, promoted rational health and physical exercise in order to develop will power. From the very beginning, only boys and men were allowed to join (a separate and, up to 1970, independent women's organization was founded in 1928). The DJK became a member of the Deutscher Reichsausschuss für Leibesübungen (DRA – the German State Department for Physical Exercise), which was the sports umbrella organization.

Both the organization and the clubs were structured in a hierarchical way. The organizer of every single stage of the association was invariably a clergyman.

The reasons for young people joining the clubs were largely the poor living conditions and a desire for an outlet in playgrounds or sports fields, as well as genuine Catholic beliefs. Members had to subscribe to the church doctrine, attend church service on Sundays and take the sacrament.

The monthly journal distributed to members published the organization's basic principles: unity of human values and aims – such as peace, awareness, duty, will power, determination, uniformity, single-mindedness and modesty. Protection from evil influences was mot important, leading to the supreme aim: synthesis of religious belief, Church and sport.

In 1925, the leaders accepted basic principles which required division of the sexes, decent modest clothing (which did not evince a sense of shame), the avoidance of one-sided optimum performance (because that was a threat to health and Christian habits), fulfilment of religious duties, rejection of rhythmic schools, and modesty at all public functions.

In line with these aims, the organization offered pre-military education for young people. But with the political changes which took place in Nazi Germany in the early 1930s, all Church-related youth organizations suffered a fierce onslaught from the regime. The state wanted to be the sole controller of youth physical training. The result was open conflict between the claims of the regime and those of the Church; both wanted to exploit sport for their own purposes.

However, individual freedom and, with it, religion invariably suffer under dictatorship; in addition, the DJK suffered from a lack of supporters. Young people wanted to engage in physical recreation, but their mental bond with the DJK was not that strong.

While forcing members to join its sports association up to 1934, the DJK then officially lost its specific task of seeking to be a community of Catholic youth. On 23 July 1935, the publication of the DJK periodical was banned; shortly afterwards, the DJK itself was disbanded, outlawed and had all its assets confiscated.

The religious organization with its strong Christian value system lost the battle for sport even before it was outlawed politically. The unpredictable value system of sport and the traditional, predictable value system of religion differed too much to work in unity.

After World War II, the DJK was re-established with a reformed value system. With fair play, chivalry and fraternal co-operation, the organizers chose more general values, while putting more emphasis on fun and joy of play, as children of God. Since then they have worked with changing concepts and have adapted superficially to the trends in daily politics and society.

According to their contemporary ethical background, the leaders focus on Sport For All and foster sports disciplines which are less popular. Yet the impact of the Church on sport seems to be diminishing despite co-operation with the various sports federations (Pfister 1981: 256). As a controlling body of society (Lotz 1981: 23), the DJK has found a niche outside the mainstream of sport and politics (Deford 1976). Today, the DJK and its clubs have only a local influence (Rösch 1995), but they follow general socio-political development without moving into a strong position. They seem to have learned from history how to be tolerated and survive.

Where politics is based on different religious beliefs, as in Northern Ireland, sport can be, on the one hand, a political tool that expresses religious division or, on the other, a bridge over sectarian and constitutional boundaries – or it can be both, as we see below.

Limitations to the ecumenical role of sport: Northern Ireland

Northern Ireland is a state where inter-community conflict and national sporting success gain international recognition at one and the same time.

While sport demonstrates religious unity and therefore shows evidence of normality, the religiously based political conflict continues apace. The 'wider community imposes political meaning on all sporting activity in Northern Ireland' (Sugden and Bairner 1986: 117). Sporting events even offer a stage for religiously based assassinations in order to gain public recognition (Mason 1989: 173). Sport has been used as a moral equivalent of war.

The conflict which grew between British domination and Gaelic culture was expressed at the end of the nineteenth century, especially in sport. Two different sporting traditions, each associated with a certain national and religious value system, confronted one another. 'The Irish Republican Brotherhood (IRB) was concerned that sport in Ireland was becoming the prerogative of Anglophiles and promoted the idea of using athletics to boost Irish nationalism' (Sugden and Bairner 1986: 92). In 1884, during a period of national reassertion, the Gaelic Athletic Association (GAA) was founded. Its aim was to foster Irish traditions, especially games and sports, through the safeguarding of Irish identity and working against Anglicization which was having an increasing impact on culture, the economy and the polity.

Originally set up as a sports organization, the GAA used the ideas of sport for its own interests in the mounting political nation-building process. The GAA was seen as a cornerstone for the revival of Gaelic culture. According to a free and independent Ireland, three patrons were chosen: the leader of constitutional nationalism, the Archbishop and the Land Leaguer. Although they all pursued the same idea, their interests differed. The question of the controlling influence – either of the IRB or the Catholic Church – led to conflict, which was only resolved by accepting the GAA as factionally neutral in order to keep it alive.

Even after the partition of 1921, the sports organization operated under two distinct political systems: the Catholic Irish Free State of twenty-six counties and the more Protestant and strongly Unionist six Ulster counties in the north-east of the country under British jurisdiction.

> Indeed, one of the enduring qualities of the Association is that despite mirroring all shades of Republican political opinion and giving rhetorical support to the concept of a united Ireland, it has proved capable of subsuming nationalist divisions when they appear in the context of Gaelic sport.
>
> (Sugden and Bairner 1986: 95)

All the same, it was still a symbol of Gaelic separateness.

One example of the Anglophobic attitude was the ban of 1886 (which lasted until 1971) on members joining any other sports than those fostered by the GAA. The strong link between the Protestant way of life and the Anglophile obsession had to be broken down and weakened. The GAA worked against a colonial structure as well as the religious and social context of sports in Britain (Williams 1989: 321). The division of sport under the aspect of religion was made according to the roots of the sport, either traditional Irish or British, and this perpetuated national differences.

The ban on cricket and rugby worked especially in rural areas, but both sports were spread through schools attended by Protestants.

> Rooted as it is in a differentiated school system which divides Catholic from Protestant and working class from middle and upper class, rugby is but one of a range of social activities through which young gentlemen are able to carry forward into adulthood what is presented to them as a respectable social, religious and political apartheid.
>
> (Sugden and Bairner 1986. 103)

While the umbrella organization, GAA, described itself as neutral, it used sport as a vehicle to carry the politics of a united Ireland into the public domain. After eighty-five years of banning certain sports for religious reasons, the GAA is responsible for the reflection and maintenance of class and status identity through sport. Therefore, it has set religious limitations on the ecumenical role of sport which are traditionally still in place even today.

In the struggle between the two states, Ireland and Great Britain, with their strong (state) religion, sport itself seized power and worked as a symbol of the *status quo*.

Sport in Islamic society

With its increasing international importance since the 1980s, Islam seems to be growing into a major force not only in countries of Arab Muslim culture, but all over the world through the cultural export of emigrants. True, there is no unified Islam, either in reality or in dogma. Today's religious cults are being adapted to the democratic structure of ways of thinking, as far as one can integrate these into Islam (Tibi 1979: 68). Yet, there is the fundamentalist way of living: the religion, which has become highly politicized, propagates the original ideas of Islam by rejecting all European and modern developments, including sport.

In most countries of the Arab Muslim cultural region with clear-cut social and political systems, life is still determined by looking back to the values and norms rooted in classical Islam (Yaldai 1987: 7). Islam offers a clearly structured system of doctrines, which is a rough alignment of the ideology of Islam with the existing world. The monotheistic religion, to be lived in total humility to the will of God, demands subjugation, devotion and obedience.

According to early Islam, a system of methodical control of one's entire life, worldly affairs such as wealth, power and glory were to be encouraged, and this offered a suitable explanation for the meaning of sport and warfare (Naciri 1973: 652f.; Sfeir 1989: 189). 'In later Islam, the motivations were fatalism, mysticism and resignation – all of which are alien to the true spirit of athletic achievement' (Sfeir 1989: 190).

The traditional ideology of Islam has to be interpreted as providing social as well as individual functions. While there are obvious demands in terms of public behaviour – for example, praying, fasting and covering parts of the body (men: navel to knees, women: the whole body except face and hands), those requirements on education have certain implications to the individual. 'No less analogous to public ritual expression is the private search for religious meaning through rites, whether the specific activity of the Muslim's daily domestic practices or the runner's solitary ten-miler at dawn' (Prebish 1993: 65). Praying five times a day can be interpreted as a kind of physical exercise because it has certain rules, like strong breathing, arm movements and bowing, and repeated motions can positively influence people's health (Jordan 1931: 41; Riedel 1942: 46).

A physical and psychological burden for any Muslim (one might even say stamina training for the body) is the one-month period of fasting, one of the five cornerstones of the faith, when eating is allowed only after sunset. Children start this rite at the age of twelve and are therefore less active. As a consequence, there are no sport or PE classes during Ramadan in fundamentalist areas. Even students take the fasting for granted and do not attend lectures, for example, at the Sports University of Teheran. Swimming is forbidden during the daytime in this one month because the mouth must not come into contact with water; otherwise the fasting does not count (Yaldai 1987: 65). 'Even today it puts an obstacle in the path of modern sport, at least in the conservative-fundamentalist states of Islam (eg Iran, Libya)' (Yaldai 1987: 65).

The clothing regulations are another obstacle in the way of modern sport, especially for women (Stevenson 1989: 43; Sfeir 1989: 195). This invariably restricts women's participation in sport. There are top female athletes in Islamic countries, for example Algeria's gold medallist of the 1992 Barcelona Olympics Hassiba Boulmerka (1,500 m) and Salima Souakri, who came third in the judo world championships. The achievements of these women have been seized upon by politicians and commentators as evidence of normality and allegedly give grounds for optimism. But the success of these outstanding women athletes only disguises the real situation in their home country. Even today, national championships involving women are threatened by terror and violence, reasons for several female athletes to abandon a sporting career. As Leila Sfeir (1985) notes, Islam encourages physical activity for everyone, but local cultural patterns and government policies restrict women's participation (Sfeir 1985; Stevenson 1989).

Sport is part of public life, and women have to keep their beauty solely for their husbands instead of 'flaunting' it before other men. Even if women are only together with other women, they have to obey the rule of concealing their bodies so as to avoid vulgar remarks. If they dare to be spectators at a sporting event, they take the first step away from the traditional role of a woman in conservative Islamic society. If they take part in sport, it is almost impossible for them to wear trousers, a skirt or a veil (Higab), their normal attire.

In Islam the body is as important as the soul. This holistic approach fosters an anthropology without differences between the state and religion, and politics is a way of putting this ideology into practice. In reality, this often leads to a suppression of sport. In Yemeni schools, for example, women's physical education is restricted to urban high schools and university (Stevenson 1989: 42f.). In Egypt, there are not enough sports facilities for female students or secluded places like indoor gymnasiums where schoolgirls can practise sport, and many schools still neglect PE (Sfeir 1989: 199). Another example has been the attitude of fundamentalist students at the Sports University of Teheran after the Islamic revolution in Iran. They called the swimming pool – even though there were no coeducational lessons in swimming – a centre of whoring, sexual licentiousness and shame; they put pressure on the minister of education to close down the pool (Yaldai 1987: 76). This all stemmed from the delicate issue of the naked body, which is a matter of privacy in fundamentalist Islam. It is even improper for fellow athletes to see others getting changed or having a shower.

A Sfeir concludes, 'A crisis in the Islamic world is indicated by resistance to everything new, including modern sport' (Sfeir 1989: 186). While sport associated with western values offers a system of modern organization, it is criticized by Islamic fundamentalists as having a depoliticizing effect and turning people's minds away from temporal matters (Douglas 1989: 167, 180).

Conclusions

The impact of religion on sport varies from country to country, from religion to religion. On the whole, religion with its traditional background offers a definite structure of ideas, while sport is an unpredictable factor which can be formed or instrumentalized by politics. Politics needs to be based on a structure, and religion helps as a catalyst for that. On the other hand, some believe that sport expresses the principles of industrial society far better than society itself (Krockow 1971).

By itself, in Huxley's famous dictum, sport is not enough to maintain ethical principles that offer a pattern for social behaviour, as the boxing example at the start of this chapter indicates. Modern sport is used as a political instrument and as a means of interpreting the processes of secularism. It reflects progress in politics and society as well as in the natural sciences. High productivity is a consequence of heightened political and social demands and a rational view of the world (Seppänen 1981), values which can be located in sport. 'While sport may epitomise or even rein-force a set of values peculiar to class, a culture, or both, those values are not grounded in sport itself, but derive from the socio-cultural context within which sport is played' (Chandler 1992: 58).

Agreement on competitive sport in the global village does not offer concepts for single events or for single states; it cannot replace traditional ethical values. The development and redefining of Coubertin's *religio athletae* to fit a situation where the meaning of the ritual background is lost shows true interest in sport expressed by the community and politics. 'It is action that matters' (Korsgaard 1990: 116).

Action was also employed by the North American YMCA to spread sports and concepts all over the world. The invention of two new games – volleyball and basketball – based on the USA's social situation and their acceptance in many different countries indicate the potential ecumenical character of sport.

Moral obedience rather than ritual order was fostered by the German Deutsche Jugendkraft. It used participation in sport as a challenging occupation so as to reduce the possibility of a crisis rocking society's foundations, and as an instrument to remove moral deficiencies in society. However, religion as a function of stabilization is useful only until politics takes over and uses well-established patterns for its own purposes.

Northern Ireland does not easily fit the pattern of diminishing religious influence. The ongoing conflict between Catholics and Protestants may, in terms of sport, be reduced to contention between Anglophile and Anglophobe attitudes, both reflected in different sports disciplines. Sport has become a religious game reflected in politics and is used thereby as a moral equivalent of war.

The changes in religious attitudes in fundamentalist Islamic states has had, as we have seen, a profound influence on the acceptability of sport, especially for women.

Religious values, then, often determine politics and participation in sport; such sports participation may be restricted both by religious belief and social control, and also by a lack of sporting facilities and political negligence of non-religious physical activity. The twentieth century has witnessed plenty of examples of all of these.

References

Alkemeyer, T. (1996) *Körper, Kult und Politik*, Frankfurt: Campus Verlag.

Bairner, A. and Sugden, J. (1986) 'Observe the sons of Ulster: football and poli-tics in Northern Ireland', in *Off the ball* (ed. A. Tomlinson and G. Whannel), London: Pluto, 146–57.

Betts, J. R. (1974) *America's Sporting Heritage: 1850–1950*, Reading/Massachusetts: Addison-Wesley Publishing Company.

Bright, B. (1970) *Come help change the world*, Old Tappan NJ.

Burke, K. (1970) *The Rhetoric of Religion: Studies in Logology*, Berkeley, CA: University of California Press.

Chandler, J. M. (1992) 'Sport is not a religion', in *Sport and religion* (ed. S. J. Hoffman), Champaign, IL: Human Kinetics, 55–61.

Coubertin, P. de (1897) *Olympische Erinnerungen*, Berlin: Sportverlag Berlin.

—— (1928) 'Religio Athletae', *Bulletin du Bureau Int. de Pédagogie Sportive*, 1, 5–6.

Deford, Frank (1976) 'Reaching for the Stars', *Sports Illustrated*, May 3, 60.

Douglas, S. A. (1989) 'Sport in Malaysia', in *Sport in Asia and Africa. A comparative Handbook* (ed. E. A. Wagner), New York/Westport/London: Greenwood Press, 165–82.

Durkheim, E. (1981) *Die elementaren Formen des religiösen Lebens*, Frankfurt: Suhrkamp Verlag.

Edwards, H. (1973) *Sociology of sport*. Homewood, IL: Dorsey Press.

Eliade, M. (1959) *The Sacred and the Profane. The Nature of Religion*, New York: Harcourt, Brace & World.

Enz, F. and Paas, M. (1991) *Brückenschlag Kirche und Sport*, Neuss: Neusser Druckerei und Verlag GmbH.

Geldbach, E. (1975) *Sport und Protestantismus*, Wuppertal: Theologischer Verlag R. Brockhaus.

Guttmann, A. (1978) *From Ritual to Record: The Nature of Modern Sports*. New York: Columbia University Press.

—— (1992) 'From ritual to record', in *Sport and religion* (ed. S. J. Hoffman), Champaign, IL: Human Kinetics, 143–51.

Hakenmüller, M. (1996) 'Gebete begleiten den Sport und das moderne Olympia', *Olympisches Feuer* 1, 30–2.

Hezbri, N. (1978) *Islamische Tradition und moderner Sport – dargestellt am Beispiel Tunesiens*, Cologne: Dipl. Arb. DSHS.

Higgs, R. J. (1992) 'Muscular christianity, holy play and spiritual exercises: confusion about Christ in sports and religion', in *Sport and religion* (ed. S. J. Hoffman), Champaign, IL: Human Kinetics, 89–103.

Hille, G. (1994) 'The Church and Lillehammer '94', in *Olympic church guide: Olympic Vision* (ed. K. Brakstad), Lillehammer, 3.

Hoffman, S. J. (ed.) (1992) *Sport and religion*, Champaigne, IL: Human Kinetics Publishers, inc.

Hoffman, S. J. (1992) 'Evangelicalism and the revitalization of religious ritual in sport', in *Sport and religion*, (ed. ibdem), Champaign, IL: Human Kinetics, 111–25.

Hopkins, C. H. (1951) *History of the Y.M.C.A. in North America*, New York.

Hörrmann, M. (1968) *Religion der Athleten*, Stuttgart/Berlin: Kreuz-Verlag.

Howell, R. A. and Howell, M. L. (1992) *The Genesis of Sport in Queensland*, St. Lucia: University of Queensland Press.

John, M. and Schulze-Marmeling, D. (1993) 'Haut's die Juden! Antisemitismus im Europäischen Fußball', in *Fußball und Rassismus*, Göttingen: Verlag Die Werkstatt, 133–58.

Jordan, R. (1931) 'La Allah ila Allah. Hygiene und Körperübungen im Kultdienst des Islam', *Die Leibesübungen*, 50: 41–3.

Knott, Richard D. (1994) *The Sport Hero as Portrayed in Popular Journalism*, Ann Arbor, MI: UMI Dissertation Services.

Korsgaard, Ove (1990) 'Sport as a practice of religion: the record as ritual', in *Ritual and Record. Sports Records and Quantification in Pre-Modern Societies* (eds J. M. Carter and A. Krüger), Westport, CT: Greenwood Press, 115–22.

Krockow, C. G. von (1971) *Sport und Industriegesellschaft*, Munich: R. Pieper & Co.

Krüger, A. (1981) 'Ursprung und Bedeutung von Coubertins Religio Athletae', in Proceedings of the IX International HISPA Congress: *Sport and Religion. The History of Sport and the Physical Education in the Iberian Cultures,* Lisbon, 183–92.

—— (1993) 'The origins of Pierre de Coubertin's Religio Athletae', in *Olympika. The International Journal of Olympic Studies* Vol. II. London/Canada, 91–102.

Kuchler, W. (1969) *Sportethos. Eine moraltheologische Untersuchung des im Lebensbereich Sport lebendigen Ethos als Beitrag zu einer Phänomenologie der Ethosformen*, Munich: Johann Ambrosius Barth.

Lapchick, R. E. (1979) 'Race, politics and sport: South Africa, 1978', in *The Dimensions of Sport Sociology* (ed. M. L. Krotee), West Point, NY: Leisure Press, 250–5.

Lotz, F. (1981) 'Das Verhältnis von Kirche und Sport in der Bundesrepublik Deutschland 1949–1980', in Proceedings of the IX International HISPA Congress: *Sport and Religion. The History of Sport and the Physical Education in the Iberian Cultures*, Lisbon, 17–26.

Maslow, A. (1968) *Toward a psychology of being* (2nd ed.), New York: Van Nostrand Reinhold.

Mason, T. (1989) 'Football', in *Sport in Britain. A social history* (ed. Tony Mason), Cambridge: Cambridge University Press, 146–86.

Naciri, M. (1973) 'Die Einstellung des Islam zum Sport', in *Sport in unserer Welt – Chancen und Probleme. Referate, Ergebnisse, Materialien. Wissenschaftlicher Kongreß München vom 21.-25. August 1972* (ed. Ommo Grupe), Berlin/Heidelberg/New York: Springer-Verlag.

Naismith, J. (1941) *Basketball. Its Origin and Development*, New York.

Pence, O. E. (1947) *The Y.M.C.A. and Social Need. A Study of Institutional Adaption*. New York.

Pfister, G. (1981) 'Frauensport aus katholischer Sicht', in Proceedings of the IX International HISPA Congress: *Sport and Religion. The History of Sport and the Physical Education in the Iberian Cultures*, Lisbon, 249–57.

Prebish, C. S. (1984) 'Heavenly Goalie, Divine Father: sport and religion', in *The Antioch Review* 42 (Summer): 306–18.

—— (1993) Religion: Approaches and Assumptions, in *Religion and Sport – The Meeting of Sacred and Profane*, (ed. ibidem), Westport, CT: Greenwood Press, 3–18.

Riedel, H. (1942) *Leibesübungen und körperliche Erziehung in der osmanischen und kamalistischen Türkei,* Würzburg.

Rösch, H.-E. (1995) *Sport um der Menschen willen. 75 Jahre DJK–Sportverband 'Deutsche Jugendkraft' 1920–1995*, Aachen: Meyer & Meyer.

Rotenberk, L. (1992) 'Pray ball', in *Sport and religion*, (ed. S. J. Hoffman), Champaign, IL: Human Kinetics, 177–81.

Schluchter, W. (1988) *Religion und Lebensführung Bd. 1. Studien zu Max Webers Kultur- und Werttheorie*, Frankfurt: Suhrkamp Verlag.

Seppänen, P. (1981) 'Olympic success: a cross-cultural perspective', in *Handbook of social science of sport* (ed. G. R. F. Lüschen and G. H. Sage) Champaign, IL: Stipes Publishing, 93–116.

Sfeir, L (1985) 'The status of Muslim women in sport: conflict between cultural tradition and modernization' *International Review for Sociology of Sport* 10(4): 283–306.

—— (1989) 'Sport in Egypt: cultural reflection and contradiction of a society', in *Sport in Asia and Africa. A comparative Handbook* (ed. E. A. Wagner), New York/Westport/London: Greenwood Press, 185–214.

Stevenson, T. B. (1989) 'Sport in the Yemen Arab Republic' in *Sport in Asia and Africa. A comparative Handbook* (ed. E. A. Wagner), New York/Westport/London: Greenwood Press, 27–49.

Sugden, J. and Bairner, A. (1986) 'Northern Ireland. Sport in a divided society', in *The Politics of Sport* (ed. L. Allison), Manchester: Manchester University Press, 90–117.

Sugden, J. and Bairner, A. (1993) *Sport, Sectarianism and Society in a Divided Ireland*, Leicester: Leicester University Press.

Tibi, B. (1979) *Internationale Politik und Entwicklungsländer-Forschung*, Frankfurt.

Tornas, S. (1994) 'Embrace Olympic Aid!' in *Olympic Church Guide: Olympic Vision* (ed. K. Brakstad), Lillehammer, 8–90.

Weber, M (1920) *Gesammelte Aufsätze zur Religionssoziologie Bd I*, Tübingen: Mohr-Verlag.

Weis, K. (1995) 'Sport und Religion. Sport als soziale Institution im Dreieck zwischen Zivilreligion, Ersatzreligion und körperlich erlebter Religion', in *Soziologie des Sports: Theorieansätze, Forschungsergebnisse und Forschungsperspektiven* (eds J. Winkler and K. Weis), Opladen: Westdeutscher Verlag, 127–50.

Williams, G. (1989) 'Rugby Union', in *Sport in Britain. A social history* (ed. T. Mason), Cambridge: Cambridge University Press, 308–48.

Yaldai, S. (1987) *Islam und Sport. Religiöse Tradition und moderne Einflüsse*, Düsseldorf: Düsseldorfer Sportwissenschaftliche Studien Heft 2.

6 The worker sports movement

James Riordan

Introduction

A year after the 1924 Paris Olympic Games, some 150,000 workers attended the first Worker Olympics, held in Frankfurt, Germany. Six years later, a year before the Los Angeles 'official' Olympic Games in which 1,408 athletes competed, over 100,000 worker athletes from twenty-six countries took part in the second Worker Olympics in Vienna; they were open to all, irrespective of ability, and watched by more than a quarter of a million people. Five years later, in opposition to the 1936 'Nazi' Olympics in Berlin, an even grander Worker Olympics was planned for Barcelona (it never took place owing to the fascist putsch and execution of the would-be organizers of the games).

In numbers of competitors and spectators, in pageant, culture and some-times even sporting record, the Worker Olympics easily surpassed the rival 'bourgeois' Olympic Games.

And yet it is the latter that is commemorated in hosts of books in every town library, on radio and film, glorifying the exploits of Nurmi and Owens, Abrahams and Liddell; they are romanticized in films like David Putnam's *Chariots of Fire*. The Worker Olympics and the worker sports movement are cast into oblivion – except in the work of only a handful of sports historians.

Yet for millions of workers in the period between the two world wars, sport was an integral part of the labour movement, and worker sports clubs and associations existed in almost every country of Europe, in Canada and the USA, in Asia and South America. By 1930, worker sport united well over four million people, making it by far the largest working-class cultural movement.

Principal aims of worker sport

At the zenith of its existence, worker oppositional sport combined the notion of healthy sport with socialist fellowship, solidarity and working-class culture.

The aims differed from country to country, yet all were agreed on the basic principles: that it would give working people the chance to take part in healthy recreation and to do so in a comradely atmosphere. Worker sport was to differ from bourgeois sport in being open to all workers, women as well as men, black as well as white. Moreover, it was to provide a socialist alternative to bourgeois competitive sport, to commercialism, chauvinism, the obsession with stars and records. It was to replace capitalist by socialist co-operative values and thus lay the foundation for a true working-class culture. Hence the initial emphasis upon less competitive physical activities, such as gymnastics, tumbling, acrobatics, pyramid-forming, mass artistic displays, hiking, swimming and cycling.

The founders of the worker sports movement believed that sport could be revolutionary, that it was no less salient to workers than their political, trade-union and co-operative movements. Sport was to play a paramount role in the struggle against capitalist nationalism and militarism which pervaded the 'politically neutral' bourgeois sports organizations and, through them, corrupted young workers. So the formation of separate worker sports organizations was one way of shielding youth from bourgeois values. While capitalism fostered mistrust among workers of different nations, the worker sports clubs would band together internationally to create peace and solidarity. They would turn physical culture into a new international language capable of breaking down all barriers.

In any case, bourgeois society largely excluded workers from public life and from amateur sports clubs and competitions. Consequently, if workers were to play and compete at all locally, nationally or internationally, they had to establish their own sports associations and contests. Such organizations were part of a far-reaching political, trade-union and cultural movement, forming a network of worker-based organizations that could accompany workers literally 'from the cradle to the grave'. The bourgeois state did all it could to obstruct this movement by introducing new laws, constantly moving the bureaucratic and administrative 'goalposts' and at times resorting to brute force. Yet it was unable to destroy the rapidly growing worker movement – at least until the advent to power of Adolf Hitler.

It has to be remembered that worker sport was not taking place anywhere in a vacuum; it was influenced by similar forces and faced similar problems. Like other branches of the labour movement – trade unions, social-democratic or labour parties, the co-operative movement, youth organizations like the Woodcraft Folk, Young Pioneers or Young Communist League – worker sport rose and fell almost everywhere simultaneously, reaching a peak in the 1920s and a trough in the late 1930s, fading away virtually to nothing after World War II. National peculiarities invariably added brakes and accelerators – from the German and Austrian tragedies under Hitler to a relatively peaceful demise in North America, Britain and Scandinavia, as well as the persistence of worker sport in Israel and Finland.

Emergence of a worker sports movement

A worker sports movement began to take shape initially in Germany in the 1890s, with the foundation of the Worker Gymnastics Association in conscious opposition to the nationalistic German Gymnastics Society – the *Turnen*. This was followed by the Solidarity Worker Cycling Club and the Friends of Nature Rambling Association, both in 1895, the Worker Swimming Association in 1897, the Free Sailing Association in 1901, the Worker Track and Field Athletics Association in 1906, the Worker Chess Association in 1912 and the Free Shooting Association in 1926. Germany thus was the hub of the worker sports movement, with over 350,000 worker athletes in various worker clubs even before World War I.

Elsewhere, a Worker Rambling Association was set up by Austrian workers in Vienna in 1895; in the same year a British Worker Cycling Club was organized around the socialist *Clarion* newspaper. In 1898, a Socialist Wheelmen's Club came into being in the USA, and French workers started to create clubs and the umbrella Socialist Sports Athletic Federation from 1907. By 1913, there were enough members internationally for the worker sports federations of five European nations – Belgium, Britain, France, Germany and Italy – to come together at Ghent on the initiative of the Belgian socialist Gaston Bridoux to establish the Socialist Physical Culture International.

By the time the various worker federations regrouped after World War I, two new tendencies were emerging, both of which were to cause division and controversy. The first was the growing movement away from non-competitive recreation to competitive sports. So when the Ghent International was re-formed in 1920 at Lucerne, it was renamed the International Association for Sport and Physical Culture, amended five years later to the Socialist Worker Sport International (SWSI). The evolving nomenclature reflected national developments: in Germany, the Worker Gymnastics Association became the Worker Gymnastics and Sports Society; in Austria, a Worker Soccer Association came into being; and the *New York Call*, periodical of the American Socialist Party, began to sponsor a baseball league.

This shift towards team sports and competition was a response to popular pressure within the working class, particularly young people. It certainly helped to boost support for the worker sports movement.

In Germany, membership of the Worker Gymnastics and Sports Society in the late 1920s was 1.2 million, covering a dozen different sports; the Society was able to open the most modern sports club in all Germany, the DM1.25 million *Bundesschule* in Leipzig (subsequently the nucleus of the German Democratic Republic's *Deutsche Hochschule für Körperkultur*). One of its affiliates, that for cycling, not only had 320,000 members – the largest cycling organization in the world – it also ran a co-operative cycle works.

Elsewhere, the various Austrian worker sports groups combined into a single association in 1919 (VAS, later the Austrian Worker Sports and Cultural Association – WSCA), which grew from 100,000 to 250,000 by 1931. Its swimming club gave free swimming lessons to over 10,000 working people in 1930, and to as many as 29,000 in 1932.

Membership of the Czechoslovak worker sports movement increased to over 200,000 between the wars, and in 1921, 1927 and 1934, the Czechoslovak Worker Gymnastics Association put on festivals in Prague in which as many as 35,000 took part and 100,000 attended.

In Britain, the British Workers' Sports Federation showed a steady growth after its formation in 1923, and the Clarion Cycling Club put on the National Workers' Sports Association (NWSA) championships in 1930, the same year as the Workers' Wimbledon Tennis Championships were held. As evidence of its commitment to organized sports, the NWSA entered a team, the London Labour Football Club, in a London soccer league. And in 1934, the NWSA played host to worker athletes from Austria, Belgium, Czechoslovakia, Palestine and Switerland at its Dorchester Sports Festival.

In Canada, although the Workers' Sports Association was not established until 1928, several immigrant groups had engaged in worker sports well before then, especially the Finns and the Ukrainians. But it was mainly the Canadian Young Communist League, taking its lead from the Young Communist International, that sought to pull all the various strands of worker sport together and build up the worker sports movement. In 1928 it set up the Workers' Sports Association Confederation (WSAC) which, four years later, claimed a membership of 4,000 and, in 1933, as many as 5,000 in 100 clubs, of which 40 were Finnish.

The second post-war tendency after the shift from non-competitive 'physical culture' to competitive sports was the mounting division between socialists and communists over leadership and aims of the worker sports movement. A number of worker sports organizations broke away from the Lucerne Sport International (LSI – a branch of the Bureau of the Socialist International) after the formation of the communist International Association of Red Sports and Gymnastics Associations (better known as Red Sport International – RSI) in Moscow in 1921, as a branch of the Communist International or Comintern. Relations between the two worker sports internationals were hostile right from the start, the RSI accusing its 'reformist' rival of diverting workers from the class struggle through its policy of political neutrality in sport. True, the socialists were not trying to make their sports movement into an active revolutionary force; instead, it was to be a strong, independent movement within capitalist society ready, come the revolution, to implement a fully developed system of physical culture. The RSI, however, wished to build a sports international that would be a political vehicle of the class struggle; it did not want merely to produce a better sports system for workers in a

capitalist world. The LSI countered that the RSI only aspired to undermine, infiltrate and take it over. So it banned all RSI members from its
activities and all contacts with the USSR.

The two worker sports internationals therefore developed separately
and, as with the parent political movements, spent much time and energy
fighting each other rather than the common foe. By the time they eventually came together, in 1936, it was virtually too late to save the worker
sports movement from fascist repression. The German WGSA had been
one of the first targets of the Nazis in 1933, the Austrian WSCA was suppressed a year later, and the Czechoslovak association two years after that.

The Worker Olympics

While the worker sports movement did not take issue with much of the
Coubertin idealism concerning the modern Olympic Games, it did oppose
the games themselves and counterposed them with its own Olympiads
on the following grounds.

First, the bourgeois Olympics encouraged competition along national
lines, whereas the worker Olympiad stressed internationalism, worker solidarity and peace. While the International Olympic Committee debarred
German and Austrian athletes from the 1920 and 1924 Games, for example,
the 1925 Worker Olympics were held precisely in Germany under the
slogan 'NO MORE WAR!'

Second, while the IOC Games restricted entry on the grounds of sporting
ability, the worker games invited all comers, putting the accent on mass
participation as well as extending events to include poetry and song, plays,
artistic displays, political lectures and pageantry.

Third, the IOC Games were criticized for being confined chiefly to the
sons of the rich and privileged (through the amateur rules and the aris-
tocratic-cum-bourgeois-dominated national Olympic committees, as well
as the IOC itself). Coubertin had always opposed women's participation,
and many Olympic leaders readily accepted the cultural superiority of
whites over blacks; the longest-serving IOC presidents Baillet-Latour and
Avery Brundage, both collaborated with the Nazi regime and were
unabashedly anti-semitic.

By contrast, the worker Olympics were explicitly against all chauvinism,
racism, sexism and social exclusivity; they were truly amateur, organized
for the edification and enjoyment of working men and women, and demonstrated the fundamental unity of all working people irrespective of colour,
creed, sex or national origin.

Fourth, the labour movement did not believe that the Olympic spirit
of true amateurism and international understanding could be attained in
a movement dominated by aristocrats and bourgeois leaders. It was therefore determined to retain its cultural and political integrity within the
workers' own Olympic movement.

So the worker sports movement organized a series of its own international festivals between 1921 and 1937.

Prague 1921

The festival in Prague was hosted by the Czechoslovak Worker Gymnastics Association from 26 to 29 June 1921 and advertised as the first unofficial Worker Olympics. It has to be remembered that the event was only three years after the foundation of the nation of Czechoslovakia, and was intended to celebrate that fact. The festival attracted athletes from twelve countries: Austria, Belgium, Britain, Bulgaria, Czechoslovakia, Finland, Germany, Poland, Switzerland, the USA, the USSR and Yugoslavia. In addition to sport, the festival featured mass artistic displays, choral recitals, political plays and pageants, culminating in the singing of revolutionary songs.

Frankfurt 1925 and Schreiberhau 1925

The first official Worker Olympics were arranged by the 1.3 million-strong Lucerne Sport International in Germany, seven years after the end of World War I. The games were billed as a festival of peace. The summer games, held in Frankfurt-am-Main, attracted contestants from nineteen countries and over 150,000 spectators, while the winter games, held in Schreiberhau (now Riesengebirge) had athletes from twelve nations.

Both winter and summer events included traditional competitive sports like skiing, skating, track and field, gymnastics and wrestling, although the organizers stated their intention of avoiding the quest for records and the idolization of individual 'stars'. All the same, they did not discount top performances and the world record for the women's 100-metre relay was broken. But the accent was on mass participation and socialist fellowship. For example, every athlete took part in the opening and closing artistic display; the atmosphere was festive and unashamedly political. The opening ceremony and victory rituals dispensed with national flags and anthems, featuring instead red flags and revolutionary hymns like the *Internationale*.

The centre-piece of the festival was a mass artistic display accompanied by mass choirs, and featuring the multi-person pyramids and tableaux symbolizing working-class solidarity and power in the class struggle. It culminated in the dramatic presentation *Kampf um die Erde* (*Struggle for the World*), using mass speaking and acting choruses who portrayed sport as a source of strength for the creation of a new world.

Despite the success of the Frankfurt games, they were marred by continuing rivalry between socialists and communists and were confined to LSI affiliates, excluding all worker associations belonging to the communist RSI, as well as groups and athletes who had had contacts with RSI (including those who had been to the Soviet Union or played host to Soviet athletes). Besides Soviet athletes, they therefore excluded as many as quarter of a million Germans and 100,000 Czechoslovaks, some of whom staged counter-demonstrations during the Frankfurt games.

Moscow 1928

As a counter to both the socialist games of Frankfurt and to the bourgeois Olympics of Amsterdam in 1928, the communist sports movement put on the First Worker Spartakiad in Moscow. It was launched on 12 August by a parade of 30,000 banner- and torch-carrying women and men, marching in colourful formation through Moscow's Red Square to Dinamo Stadium (the largest Soviet stadium at the time). Despite the boycott by both socialist and bourgeois sports associations, some 600 worker athletes from fourteen countries were said to have taken part. The foreign athletes came from Algeria, Argentina, Austria, Britain (twenty-six participants), Czechoslovakia, Estonia, Finland, France (thirty-two participants), Germany, Latvia, Norway, Sweden, Switzerland and Uruguay.

The comprehensive sports programme of twenty-one sports (the Amsterdam Olympics comprised only seventeen) covered track and field, gymnastics, swimming, diving, rowing, wrestling, boxing, weightlifting, fencing, cycling, soccer, basketball, shooting. Although standards fell below those at the Amsterdam Olympics, Soviet sources claim that in virtually all events the Spartakiad winners surpassed the records set at the Frankfurt Worker Olympics. But the emphasis was not wholly on sport; the festival included a variety of pageants and displays, carnivals, mass games, motor-cycle and motor-car rallies, demonstrations of folk games, folk music and dancing. In addition, there were poetry readings and mock battles between 'workers of the world' and the 'world bourgeoisie' in which everyone participated, there being no passive spectators for this 'sports theatre' finale.

The winter counterpart to the Spartakiad took place in Moscow in late 1928, with 636 participants in skiing, speed skating (women and men), biathlon and special ski contests for postal workers, rural dwellers and border guards.

Vienna 1931

Although the social democrats had held a Worker Sports Festival at Nuremberg, Germany, in 1928 (with limited success), their next venture was to represent the pinnacle of the worker sports movement. The LSI, as sponsor, now had over 2 million members, including 350,000 women (almost a sixth of the total) and arranged a festival in winter at Mürzzuschlag and in summer at Vienna that far outdid in spectators, participants and pageantry the 1932 'bourgeois' Olympics at Lake Placid and Los Angeles.

As the invitation by the Austrian hosts to the Vienna Olympics announced in German, French, Czech and Esperanto, the programme was to include a children's sports festival, a meeting of the Red Falcon (Sokol) youth group, 220 events in all sports disciplines, Olympic championships, national competitions, friendly matches, city games, a combination run and swim through Vienna, artistic displays, dramatic performances, fireworks, a festive parade and mass exercises.

Some 80,000 worker athletes from twenty-three countries came to 'Red Vienna', and on the opening day as many as a quarter of a million spectators watched 100,000 men and women parade through the streets to the new stadium constructed by the Viennese socialist government. As many as 65,000 later watched the soccer finals and 12,000 the cycling finals. This time the sports programme and ceremony were more in line with the 'bourgeois' Olympics. An Olympic flame was borne into the stadium (brought from Mount Olympus); each delegation marched into the stadium as a separate nation, though under a red flag; and the sports programme roughly paralleled that of the 'bourgeois' Olympics – though still being open to all, irrespective of ability.

By design the Vienna Olympiad coincided with the opening of the Fourth Congress of the Socialist International, and it was pointedly noted that, whereas the political International assembled no more than a few hundred delegates, the sport International brought together the masses themselves. Indeed, there was no other element of the labour movement in which popular participation was more manifest. Congresses might pass resolutions about proletarian solidarity and revolution energy, but worker sport provided practical manifestation of those ideas.

Barcelona 1936 and Antwerp 1937

Alarmed at the mounting popularity and strength of the worker sports movement, capitalist governments stepped up their repressive actions. When communist workers tried to organize a Second Spartakiad in Berlin in 1932, they first ran into visa problems (all Soviet and some other athletes were refused visas to enter Germany) and then, when several hundred worker athletes had managed to reach Berlin, the games were banned.

Under attack from fascism, the socialists and communists at last came together in a popular front, and jointly organized a third Worker Olympics, scheduled for Barcelona in Republican Spain from 19 to 26 July 1936. They were to be in opposition to the bourgeois 'Nazi' Olympics held in Berlin a week later. The Catalonia Committee for Worker Sport received promises of attendance from over 1,000 French worker athletes (the socialist government of Leon Blum gave equal funds to the Barcelona and the Berlin teams), 150 Swiss, 100 Soviet, 60 Belgian, 12 US, 6 Canadian, etc.

The Spanish Olympic Committee declared that it would boycott Berlin and take part in Barcelona.

But the third Worker Olympics never took place. On the morning of the scheduled opening ceremony, the Spanish fascists under Franco staged their military putsch. Some worker athletes remained in Spain to fight in the International Brigade during the Spanish Civil War, and many who returned home (like the Canadians, including the national high-jump champion Eva Dawes) were banned from sport by their national federations – whilst those athletes who had given the Nazi salute to Hitler in the Berlin opening ceremony returned as national heroes.

After the abortive Barcelona games, the communist and socialist coalition rescheduled the third Worker Olympics for Antwerp in 1937. While the Antwerp games were not as large as those in Vienna, or as the intended Barcelona games would have been, they did present an imposing display of worker solidarity. Despite the difficulties put in their way by increasingly hostile and fascist regimes, special trains carried an estimated 27,000 worker athletes from 17 countries (including the Soviet Union) to Antwerp – an astonishing achievement in the Europe of 1937. Some 50,000 people filled the stadium on the final day, and the traditional pageant through the city attracted over 200,000.

Following this success, a fourth Worker Olympics was planned for Helsinki in 1943, but war brought down the curtain on an inspiring period of worker Olympic festivals.

Concluding words

The worker sports movement survived World War II, although the radically changed circumstances of the post-war world inevitably brought about a transformation of the movement. The new role was one of selective co-operation and amalgamation with national sports clubs and federations.

Immediately after the war, the socialist worker sports association in western Europe set up the International Worker Sports Committee (IWSC) in London in 1946. Despite a peak of 2.2 million members in fourteen countries in the late 1940s, however, the IWSC never attained the significance the prewar movement had had, with the exception of the worker sports movement in Finland, France, Austria and Israel.

The Finnish Worker Sports Association (TUL), while co-operating with the national sports association (SVUL), retained its own identity and had a membership of 450,000 in 1990 (half the SVUL membership). It promotes mass gymnastics and artistic displays, family exercise programmes, cultural events and particularly women's sporting activities. Its worker sports festivals held in Helsinki's Olympic stadium attract as many as 50,000 spectators.

The French Worker Sport and Gymnastics Federation (FSGT) had over 100,000 members in 1990; it co-ordinates the activities of worker sports clubs throughout the country, organizes conferences and sponsors worker sports events like the annual cross-country and cycling contests associated with the communist newspaper *L'Humanité*, as well as the annual *Fête de l'Humanité*, in whose sports activities some 6,000 people took part in 1981.

The Austrian Worker Sports and Cultural Association (ASKÖ) has similarly retained its identity and plays an important part in Austrian sport. In Israel, Hapoel (The Worker) is still the country's largest and strongest sports association. It is the only exception, outside the remaining socialist states, where a worker sports organization controls its country's sport.

There are several reasons why the worker sports movement diminished in popularity, and why it never captured the majority of the working class. One handicap was that worker sports almost always duplicated the bourgeois sports, clubs, federations and Olympics. As long as the older organizations remained socially exclusive ('amateur') preserves of the bourgeoisie and aristocracy, this was not particularly significant. But once the workers succeeded in democratizing sport, and once industrial firms, the Church and governments came to realize the potential of sport for social control, this presented a major problem. Worker sports clubs rarely had the 'name', facilities or funds to compete with bourgeois teams, and were often denied access to public funds and amenities.

Another problem was the media. Coverage of worker sport was usually confined to the socialist press and was ignored by the bourgeois media altogether. In so far as only a minority of workers read the socialist press, it is not surprising that only a minority of workers joined the worker sports movement or were prepared to turn their backs on the glamorous bour-geois clubs for the low-status worker sports organizations. In any case, it was common for bourgeois clubs to recruit the best worker-athletes, just as they did with the best athletes from Africa, Asia and Latin America, by attractive financial inducements.

Efforts were certainly made to enhance the attractiveness of worker sport, but they were hampered by a number of problems: the explicitly political nature of worker sport, the uncertain and at times insensitive attitude to organized sport and competition by labour leaders, and the tactical differences over the role of sport in society – not to mention the socialist–communist wrangling. What many worker sports leaders seemed to have failed to understand was that a sports organization might be more politically effective by being less explicitly political.

Recent developments have opened up a great number of possibilities for working men and women in certain sports. There are, for example, far more opportunities for organized sports participation today than before World War II; the best athletes now are more highly skilled and have a better chance to nurture their talent to the full for the benefit of both individual and the community. Gifted working-class, non-white or women athletes can with dedication reach the top of their sport, and we now have sports spectacles of unprecedented scale, grandeur and public exposure from which working people gain considerable enjoyment. At the same time, it has meant increasing subjection to society's dominant values in sport and capitulation to a form of sport which is by no means controlled by workers themselves.

The worker sports movement needed to expand if it was to fulfil its cultural and political mission. But the needs of growth presented complex problems. Organized sport, like the working class itself, is a product of modern industrial society, and in a bourgeois world a large proportion of working men and women are steeped in and subscribe to the dominant social values.

All the same, the worker sports movement did try to provide an alternative experience based on workers' own culture and inspired by visions of a new socialist culture. To this end it organized the best sporting programmes it could, regardless of the level, whether a Sunday bike ride or a Worker Olympic festival, founded on genuinely socialist values. Its story is as much a part of the history of sport and of the labour movement as is Coubertin's Olympic Games or the trade unions.

Further reading

Major works

Krüger, A. and Riordan, J. (eds) (1985) *Der internationale Arbeitersport*, Cologne: Pahl-Rugenstein.
—— (1996) *The Story of Worker Sport*, Champaign, IL: Human Kinetics.

Germany

Arbeiter-Turn-Zeitung (ATZ) (1893–1933). A full set is available on microfilm in the archives of the Institut für Sportwissenschaften of the Georg-August-Universität Göttingen.

Auerbach, A. (1925) *Kampf um die Erde. Weihespiel zur internationalen Arbeiter-Olympiade*, Frankfurt: Union.

Beduhn, R. (1982) *Die Roten Radler. Illustrierte Geschichte des Arbeiter-radfahrerbundes 'Solidarität'*, Münster: Lit.

Buck, A. (1927) *Die Arbeitersportbewegung und ihre Beziehungen zur Partei und zu den Gewerkschaften*, Leipzig: ATSB.

Denecke, V. (1990) *Die Arbeitersportgemeinschaft. Eine kulturhistorische Studie uber die Braunschweiger Arbeitersportbewegung in den zwanziger Jahren*, Duderstadt, Mecke.

Dierker, H. (1990) *Arbeitersport im Spannungsfeld der Zwanziger Jahre. Alltagser-fahrungen auf internationaler, deutscher und Berliner Ebene*, Essen: Klartext.

Fischer, J. and Mainers H. P. (1973) *Proletarische Körperkultur und Gesellschaft. Zur Geschichte des Arbeitersports*, Giessen: Achenbach.

Krüger, A. (1975) *Sport und Politik. Vom Turnvater Jahn zum Staatsamateur*, Hannover: Fackeltrager.

Nitsch, F. (1985) *90 Jahre Arbeitersport. Bundestreffen des Freundeskreises ehemaliger Arbeitersportler*, Munster: Lit.

Nitsch, F. and Peiffer, L. (eds) (1995) *Die roten Turnbrüder. 100 Jahre Arbeitersport*, Marburg: Schuren.

Teichler, H. J. and Hauk, G. (eds) (1987) *Illustrierte Geschichte des Arbeitersports*, Berlin: Dietz.

Ueberhorst, H. (1973) *Frisch, Frei, Stark und Treu. Die Arbeitersportbewegung in Deutschland. 1893–1933*, Dusseldorf: Droste.

France

Arnaud, P. (ed.) (1994) *Les origines du sport ouvrier en Europe*, Paris.

Holt, R. (1981) *Sport and Society in Modern France*, London.

Marie, P. (1934) *Pour le sport ouvrier*, Paris.

Moustard, R. (1983) *Le sport populaire*, Paris.

The Soviet Union

Chudinov, I. D. (ed.) (1959) *Osnovnye postanovleniya, prikazy i instruktsii po voprosam fizicheskoi kultury i sporta 1917–1957*, Moscow.

Kozmina, V. P. (1967) 'Mezhdunarodnoye rabocheye sportivnoe dvizhenie posle Velikoi Oktyabrskoi sotsialisticheskoi revolyutsii', in F. I. Samoukov and V. V. Stolbov (eds) *Ocherki po fizicheskoi kultury*, Moscow.

Riordan, J. (1977) *Sport in Soviet Society*, Cambridge University Press.

—— (1991) *Sport, Politics and Communism*, Manchester University Press.

Semashko, N. A. (1926) *Puti sovetskoi fizkultury*, Moscow.

Finland

Hentilä, S. (1987) *Suomen työläisurheilun historia*. Vol. I (1919–44) (Helsinki, 1982); Vol. II (1944–59) (Helsinki, 1984); Vol. III (1959–79), Helsinki.

Laine, L. and Markkola P. (eds) (1989) *Tuntematon työläisnainen*, Tampere.

Strunz, W. (1983) *Zur Soziologie und Sozialgeschichte des Finnischen Arbeitersports. 1919–1959*, Münster.

Austria

Arbeiterkultur in Österreich 1918–1945. ITH-Tagungsbericht, vol. 16, Vienna.

Gastgeb, H. (1952) *Vom Wirthaus zum Stadion. 60 Jahre Arbeitersport in Österreich*, Vienna.

Krammer, R. (1981) *Arbeitersport in Osterreich. Ein Beitrag zur Geschichte der Arbeiterkultur in Österreich bis 1938*, Vienna.

—— (1981) *Mit uns zieht die Neue Zeit. Arbeiterkultur in Österreich 1918–1934*, Vienna.

Great Britain

Condon, M. (1933) *The case for organised Sunday football*, London.

Groom, T. (1944) *The fifty year story of the club: National Clarion Cycling Club 1894–1944*, Halifax: Jubilee souvenir.

Holt, R. (ed.) (1990) *Sport and the working class in modern Britain*, Manchester University Press.

Jones, S. (1991) *Sport, politics and the working class: organised labour and sport in inter-war Britain*, Manchester University Press.

Rothman, B. (1982) *The 1932 Kinder Trespass*, Timperley.

Sinfield, G. (1927) *The Workers' Sports Movement*, London.

Israel

Gill, E. (1977) *Sipuro shel Hapoel*, Tel Aviv.

Simri, U. (1971) *Ha'chinuch ha'gufani ve'hasport be'Eretz Israel, 1917–1927*, Netanya.

Simri, U. and Paz, I. (1978) *30 shnot sport be'Israel*, Tel Aviv.

Part II

7 Women in sport and society

Annette Müller

Introduction

The twentieth century has seen far-reaching developments which have sharply changed society in modern industrialized countries, affecting the way in which people have come to understand their surroundings. Changing attitudes to sport, and to the way in which people take part in sport, cannot be examined in isolation from the society in which they occur, since sport is not an isolated part of life. Rather, it is an integral part of life in society (Bierhoff-Alfermann 1983: 20). We can conclude that social phenomena are reflected in the social subsystem which we know as sport. This is why many of the problems of women's sport are clearly not problems which are specific to sport – instead, they are rooted in social traditions and situations. Nonetheless, many problems either arise, manifest themselves or are passed on through the medium of sport. Women and girls enjoy equal rights in sport to a much lesser degree than the legal basis of democratic society might lead one to suppose.

> 'There are many concerns relating to the quantity and quality of opportunities available to women in sport ... the socioeconomic status of women in general is low; women are paid less than their male counterparts in like occupations, which denies them equal buying power and/or access to certain sports.'
>
> (Bailey 1993: 300)

It is clear that specific social, societal and structural factors have disadvantaged women and have meant that their participation in sport has been dogged by problems (Peyton 1989: 10).

> 'Research in a variety of countries has shown how women 'service' men's and children's leisure and lack any sense of 'entitlement' to enjoy their own leisure. Men, on the other hand, dominate local recreational resources and activities, and often deliberately exclude women.'
>
> (Hall 1996: 19)

Although more and more women are beginning to take part in sport, discrimination is evident not least in the fact that they are underrepresented in important areas of sport – which, in turn, has a significant influence on how far women can influence the 'world of sport' themselves. For example, the functionaries who represent sport in public are largely male, and it is they who determine sport's structure and goals (Klein 1989: 26). Therefore, 'the conflict between gender and culture exists only in the realm of the feminine because cultural practices, like sport and leisure, are defined by masculine standards' (Hall 1996: 19).

The low representation of women in positions of leadership means both that women's spheres of experience are excluded and that women have less opportunity to influence decision-making processes. An understanding of games and sport, which represents the interests and values of many women, is still regarded with scepticism. Consequently, women face restrictions in practice and training, and the kinds of sport available in sports clubs are still insufficiently oriented towards the interests of women and girls. Of course, allegedly female interests require a critical second glance, since processes of socialization are undoubtedly responsible for the fact that women and girls turn predominantly to types of sport which are considered female. 'Socialization is more than just a routine or natural process whereby individuals learn skills, traits, values, attitudes, norms, and knowledge associated with a particular social or gender role' (Hall 1996: 23).

Greendorfer demonstrates 'that female interest and involvement in sport is not a chance occurrence that depends on legislation or on innate skill and motor talent. Rather, it is an outcome of a complex and systematic process called socialization' (Greendorfer 1993: 3). In integrating individuals into society by transmitting cultural values and traditions from one generation to the next the process of socialization plays a key role. It is important to recognize the extent to which this dynamic social process relates to gender roles and how gender roles influence the likelihood of who will and who will not become involved in sport and physical activity. Although some believe that today females enjoy limitless opportunities to participate in sport, others would argue that women's physical activity continues to be controlled by an ideological system of gender roles and values that dictate what a woman can and cannot do with her physicality. Gender role socialization itself maintains the gender inequalities that exist in the social order, because 'biological' sex determines opportunity and experience.

Thus, many socialization practices represent a type of systematic discrimination based on unfounded beliefs about gender (Greendorfer 1993: 5). 'Since men's aggression, strength, and competitiveness were believed to be biologically based, athletics seemed a natural activity for boys' (Sabo 1994: 203). These differentiations find justification in the dictates of an official culture which maintains that aggressiveness, brutality, force and risk-taking are physiologically masculine, whereas aesthetics, grace, light-footedness and a sense of rhythm are specifically feminine (Midol-Beauchamps 1981: 111). It is obvious that these arbitrarily defined boundaries between 'male' and 'female' activities are cultural constructs. The basis for this kind of female socialization lies in 'residual patriarchal ideologies concerning the "inferiority" of feminine practices.... Socializing women into selective roles in active leisure serves to legitimate the dominant ideology of patriarchy, that is, the system of power relations based on male domination' (MacNeill 1994: 275). This means, first, that a great many women cannot identify with the current masculine understanding of sport or with the roles allotted to them in the sport system; it also means, however, that an alternative understanding of sport, developed by women, is considered of little value. Academic writers have not yet seized the opportunity to change this situation.

The unequal treatment of women in sport is not only evident from the fact that women continue to be excluded from most positions of power and influence in both the educational and amateur sports systems, but also from the fact that the opportunities for skilled women athletes to pursue careers in professional sport remain severely restricted. Moreover, 'within sport studies, feminist scholars have often found themselves marginalized and ghettoized . . . (and) there has been resistance to the new perspectives developed by feminist scholars' (Messner and Sabo 1990: 3). In addition, 'disparities are evident in comparison of the earnings of individual men and women athletes' (Theberge and Birrell 1994: 336), various kinds of sport are still not open to women competitors, and money, material and personnel are distributed in a way that disadvantages women.

> 'In most countries, despite a decade of 'progress', males still have access to more than twice the number of opportunities and public resources available for sport. The Olympic Games still hold more than twice as many events for men than for women.'
>
> (Kidd 1990: 36)

Although it is certainly important to document the distributive problem of unequal allocation of resources, it is crucial to understand the nature of the social relationship between females and males, now as in the past, that determines gender inequality. Ann Hall asks the following questions, which are of great importance for sport and sport science. These questions focus on the relationship between the sexes and on the meaning of sport for the construction of gender relationships:

> 'How . . . did sport come to embody and recreate male power and domination? What are the connections between women's sporting practice and the broader ensemble of patriarchal relations? Does women's sport have the potential to take on a set of oppositional

meanings within a patriarchal ideology, and could it become a site of resistance to a specifically patriarchal social order? What is the relationship between power and physicality in countering the long-standing hegemonic control men have had over women's bodies?'

(Hall 1990: 225)

According to Whitson, men and women inhabit and experience their bodies in profoundly different ways (Whitson 1994: 353). While women's beauty norms require a weak, tender build in order to reflect women's supposedly natural tendency to be sensitive, tender and softhearted (Schmausser 1991: 26), the male body is meant to embody physical power and strength – which, of course, denotes social power as well. Even if beauty norms do repress men as well as women (Minker 1993: 14), it is clear that the ideal male body is a symbol of activity and independence, while the female ideal has been degraded to a passive object of desire, which is at least to some extent simply a chattel for men (Ridder 1986: 314).

But dispossession and reconstruction of the female body does not only occur when women internalize and try to imitate the models of femininity which men have designed. The problem also arises when women try or are compelled to try to adopt the dominant public behavioural patterns and the concomitant physical posture (Abraham 1992: 168f.). Existing power structures are made clear – and are reinforced – by the demands which men place upon the female body and by the fulfilment of those demands through women's behaviour. Despite the progress of women's liberation, the male image of women has changed very little. Women are still reduced to the sum total of their erotic parts; 'womanly' behaviour is still seen as attractive. Since women are subject to standards of beauty which are much harsher than those imposed on men, and since they are still heavily judged by their appearance and their physical attractiveness (Schmidt 1991: 79), the growing importance of sport in the lives of many women should be assessed critically.

'Although data on rising rates of involvement among women are encouraging, optimism should be tempered by a consideration of the feminization of physical activity present in some types of fitness activities. Exercise and training programs that emphasize weight control, appearance, and sex appeal are contemporary incarnations of the myth of female frailty in women's athletics.'

(Theberge and Birrell 1994: 334)

Thus, the question arises whether sport really offers women a chance to experience freedom, or whether they are forced into predefined sporting roles because sport is increasingly implicated in the social construction of womanhood. For, even if more and more women are taking part in sport, it is a socio-cultural area which is still dominated by men.

Media Interpretation

The media play a significant part in defining gender-specific standards of beauty and behaviour. Certain images of men and women are hailed by the media; deviations from the norm are derided. Gender stereotypes become evident from the way in which athletes of both genders are represented. Willis emphasizes that the coverage of athletics frequently 'concerns not their sports identity but their gender identity' (Willis 1994: 42). One important way in which the media can exercise influence is by giving coverage to athletic role models. This kind of gender-specific approach influences our conception of the value of sport and physical activity and the opportunities that may be available to people in the world of sport. It is especially distressing that the media presents both male dominance in sport and sharply defined gender roles as natural, rather than subjecting these phenomena to critical examination. It is true that 'there have been some incentives to publish articles and illustrations of women's sport which promote a radical image, but these have been outside the mainstream media outlets' (Hargreaves 1994: 196).

Male dominance in the media is evident from the fact that the content and form of sports coverage are aimed at the interests of a male audience. The journalists who cover sport, and whose audience is first and foremost supposed to be male, are themselves men. Consequently, women and girls watch stadium sports to a much lesser extent than do men, and they pay less attention to sports news in the media (Klein 1989: 20). The presentation of sport to the outside world – in the media, in publicity work, and in commercial aspects of sport – is essentially masculine (Langer 1986: 7). To what extent does sport, in its current state, generate structures which oppress women? There is certainly no doubt of the importance of the media in moulding opinion – including opinions on sport. Hence, many forms of discrimination which women experience in sport are rooted in ideological patterns which are broadcast to a very great extent by the media.

It is hardly surprising that the treatment of women in the media has been one of the major topics of analysis and criticism about women in sport. 'Television both shapes and reflects the attitudes of our society' (Wilson, 1994: 249). Taking this assumption as a starting-point, Duncan *et al.* (1994) investigated quantitative and qualitative aspects of televised coverage of women's sport. They discovered that women's sport is still vastly underrepresented:

'The quality of the production of women's sporting events differs substantially from that of men's events .... For men, sophisticated productions focus on superlative camera work, slow-motion and split-screen images, instant replays, multiple-angled views, and elaborate on-screen graphics. The production of women's games, however, is less technically sophisticated, less dramatic, tends to use flowery commentary and ambivalent visual images, and often contains errors

in reporting. Furthermore, television's representation of male hegemony in sport is reinforced during men's competitions by the regular
attention given to women in the stands, who serve as comical targets
and objects of sexual innuendo as the camera zooms in on various
parts of their anatomy.'

(Cohen 1993: 174f.)

Male domination of the journalism profession – and especially of sports
journalism – might perhaps offer one explanation for the underrepresen-
tation of women's sport in the media. It does undoubtedly influence sport
journalism, but Theberge and Cronk correctly point out that 'increasing
the number of women in sport journalism will not of itself eliminate sexism
in the sports news. Sexism in the sport media is not primarily a function
of the prejudices of individual journalists, male or female' (Theberge and
Cronk 1994: 296). Rather, the reasons lie in the fact that the coverage
given to sports is continually shaped by routine practices that construct
the news. Moreover, the most formidable barrier standing in the way of
improved media coverage of women's sport lies not within the realm
of the media, but in the sports world itself. On the basis of their investigation of North American newspapers, Theberge and Cronk conclude that

'despite the recent rise in the number of females participating in sport,
and the perhaps less dramatic rise in the social acceptance and appreciation of women's sports, there has been little improvement in the
quality and amount of coverage of women in ... sport media.'

(Theberge and Cronk 1994: 289)

They suggest that the media construct an imaginary general public or
readership that is assumed to be more interested in men's sport than in
sports played by women, which, they say, is why the media are still predominantly interested in male sport.

This reinforces the dominant ideology which claims that male sport is
more important and more interesting than female sport. The dominant
philosophy in journalism – influenced, of course, by market forces – is
that the media should cover the events and issues which attract the greatest
public interest. Women and minority groups are automatically disadvantaged by this practice. The argument that there is no interest in women's
sport 'is a justification for holding on to power and privilege and repro-
ducing stereotypes. And it is flawed, because sports often enough only
become popular audience events after being shown on television'
(Hargreaves 1994: 196). The feminist struggle for media change concentrates on several goals – lobbying for more space and time, an improvement
in the quality of coverage, increasing the number of sports journalists who
are women, tackling the ways in which women's sport is constructed by
the media, and breaking down gender stereotypes.

Sport does offer women a chance for liberation which is bound up with body image, self-concept and the embodiment of feminist perspectives; it also offers a path to self-awareness. It can be used to change existing social inequality and to break down existing power structures. None the less, sport is still one of the main areas where gender and other power relationships are constructed, and where women (on the basis of gender) and others (because of membership in a given group) are oppressed. Thus, sport is an influential actor on the socio-political stage: it encompasses much more than physical activity, relaxation, enjoyment of activity and mass entertainment. The way in which these political, cultural and structural components of sport influence the individual and determine his or her personal relationship to sport depends largely on that individual's personal disposition. Age, personality, ethnicity, education, profession, class, family circumstances, health, upbringing, religious denomination, social environment, sexuality and so on exercise a considerable influence on how sport is played and experienced, how sport appears to women, the meaning that it has for them, how they are and were moulded by sport and whether and how they participate actively in determining the form of their sports surroundings. Given these differing influences, attempts at understanding various aspects of women's sport and investigations of the question of which barriers prevent women from achieving full equality in sport are fascinating endeavours. One of the many reasons why such endeavours are important is that sport, in its various structural manifestations and individual interpretations, has become an important social phenomenon in industrialized states (Kröner 1990: 8).

Feminist sports theories

Although the history of women's sport stretches far back into history, a phenomenon which began in the early 1970s is of especial interest. The direct result of practical and theoretical feminist work, it led to women taking part in sport today in far greater numbers, and it meant that they had many more opportunities in sport than had ever been the case before. Of course, it is crucial to refer to feminism, which must be examined in any attempt to understand women's sport. Feminist approaches to research have a great deal of political relevance, since feminist research is always conducted with a view to facilitating social change. The various feminist theories (for example psychoanalytical, radical, liberal, Marxist, social and poststructuralist theories) all try in their own way to understand how 'conventional gender relations have been built, reproduced and contested' (Hargreaves 1994: 3). They offer different ways of seeing ourselves as women and suggest different strategies for changing existing power relationships between men and women in society. Changing these relationships is necessarily a complex task, since power relationships of this kind determine all aspects of life (family, child-rearing, work, politics, culture and leisure) and these areas of life are all interrelated. To understand 'why women tolerate social relations which subordinate their interests to those of men and the mechanisms whereby women and men adopt particular discursive positions as representative of their interests' (Weedon 1987: 12), and to change the existing situation as effectively as possible, most feminists assume an integral relationship between theory and practice.

While the term 'feminism' does not denote a single, unified theory, every type of feminism deals with the central question of what it means to be a woman in a male-dominated society, with how femininity and sexuality are defined for women and with the issue of how women might begin to redefine them for themselves. It is important, therefore, to adopt theoretical premises from which domination can be criticized and new possibilities envisaged. These kinds of theory must consider women as individuals, but they must also see women as a social group. Considering the perspective of women as individuals can make sense of women's awareness of the conflicts and contradictions in women's everyday lives. However, possibilities for social change are more likely to be generated when women are regarded as a homogenous social group. The deeper understanding of women which feminist discourse has achieved is certain to lead to an enhanced understanding of women for society as a whole, but also for sport – and for the role played by sport in society.

A significant aspect of feminist sports scholarship is that it puts women in the centre of the investigative field and hence provides 'an important challenge to the way in which male standards have become generalized standards in sport theory' (Hargreaves 1994: 3). Admittedly, one might object that purely feminist research is a blinkered approach. But a feminist approach is necessary to bring unjust states of affairs to light, to provide answers to long-neglected questions and to liberate women from a lifetime spent in the wings. The way in which feminist research views itself, and, in particular, the assumption that gender is constructed by the sociocultural environment, has led to further, extremely significant research into social, psychological and political topics. This research has generated investigative contexts which allow the complexity of the topics addressed to be dealt with adequately.

Contemporary feminism has its roots in the Women's Liberation Movement, a political movement which has been an active force for change since at least the late 1960s. In the intervening years, feminists have increasingly begun to re-examine the traditional research into women and women's issues, since that research had 'not tackled critical conceptual and methodological issues; rather the tendency has been to accept the assumption and use the constructs of a male-defined and male-dominated scholarship' (Parratt 1994: 5). These male perspectives meant, for example, that sport scholarship had only very limited insight into women's experiences; it also meant that almost no understanding of the importance of women's experience was achieved. Recently, more and more women have begun to describe their experiences in sport. These reports indicate that women are trying to establish a discourse which deals with subjects which were not traditionally discussed. This kind of communication can, for example, show that many women experienced similar types of discrimination which derive from specific definitions of femaleness and femininity. Moreover, exchanging experiences is one way to recognize how different experiences can be, and to see which alternative behaviour patterns and interpretations are and were possible.

> [M]any feminists assume that women's experience, unmediated by further theory, is the source of true knowledge and the basis for feminist politics. This belief rests on the liberal humanist assumption that subjectivity is the coherent authentic source of the interpretation of meaning of 'reality'.
>
> (Weedon 1987: 8).

The issue of the importance of the relationship between theory and experience has central significance for feminist discourse. Many radical feminists reject theoretical approaches, since they see them as embodying a masculine form of discourse 'which maintains male dominance by co-opting women and suppressing the feminine. These arguments link dominant western forms of rationality with male power and control over women and nature, a power which is associated with violence, oppression and destruction' (Weedon 1987: 7). The fact that until recently most theories were indeed developed by men has undoubtedly influenced the status which women accorded theoretical writing. None the less, one should be careful not to attach too much importance to that fact. It is, I think, more important to recognize the political potential of a given theory and to judge according to its usefulness – for example, by looking at whether it adequately describes causes and structures, and offers alternatives which might change them.

Moreover, recognizing a connection between biological gender and a specific type of discourse maintains an existing stereotype – namely, that men are better at abstract thinking and are more rational, whereas women tend towards a style of recognition which is based on individual experience. Certainly, theories must recognize and take account of the political meaning of experience; none the less, anecdotal accounts of personal experiences can only be a first step towards recognizing the specific experience which women have had, and the power relationships which are responsible for that. Thus, many feminists try, despite their view of existing social theory and knowledge as patriarchal, to develop theoretical alternatives. To do this, they take advantage of existing theories. The theory sought would need the potential to describe and account for patriarchal power structures. This would require an adequate description of the place of men and women in the system within which we live; moreover, the theory would have to encompass the political goal of working for change.

Like its historical predecessors, recent feminist theory has developed through a critique of the patriarchal values and interests informing existing social theories. Feminist history, which should be understood as an answer to the absence of women both as researchers and as objects of research, is a powerful model for reshaping women's sport history and 'women's contribution to their status in, and their oppression by a male-defined society' (Parratt 1994: 6). It is men who tend to benefit in such a society, since women's interests are and have been subordinated to theirs. '[M]ost of the historical research on women's sport has been set in a liberal feminist framework. From this perspective, the history of women's sport has been seen as a gradual, progressive unfolding of increased opportunities for participation' (Parratt 1994: 11).

The focus of research is no longer on describing the place and value of women in sport, the difficulties which women had to overcome and the way in which traditional world-views and cultural inheritance had made it possible for men to use sport to celebrate their physicality, while 'women . . . had to battle against cultural, pseudoscientific and religious ideologies that identify being female with frailty and associate female athleticism with sexual "deviance"' (Parratt 1994: 8). Rather, the important question posed is how sport 'has been implicated in the social construction and maintenance of gender relations?' (Parratt 1994): 11). On the assumption that social, legal, public and human discrimination does not follow from a difference of nature, but from a difference of culture, and that psychological, relational and attitudinal differences in life are the products of a culture of discrimination (Cagical 1981: 101), feminist research has critically examined 'traditional ideas about several conceptual and methodological issues: periodization, the definition of basic concepts and research categories' (Parratt 1994: 6) and established that women's history cannot be forced into categories and values which are based on male experience and have been defined by men. In general, sport historians have begun to look more critically at the role which sport has played in the construction of a constellation of social inequalities, without concentrating exclusively on those between women and men.

Sports psychology and sports sociology are disciplines which have generated the major paradigms and debates which have influenced feminist research into sport. In the 1960s, sports scholarship – itself a field which is developing increasingly narrowly focused sub-specialities – relied heavily on sports psychology and sports sociology. These disciplines both relied on theories and research methods which had been established in psychology and sociology for some time.

Although sports psychology has focused on human behaviour in sport-like situations for a long time, 'we still know very little about the female athlete from a psychological perspective' (Costa and Guthrie 1994: 232).

We know still less about women of colour and women with different levels of ability in sport. Socio-psychological research into gender roles and identity not only demanded a thorough re-examination, but was potentially harmful because it perpetuated the stereotypes which feminists were attempting to destroy. For example, psychology – like other cultural institutions in a patriarchal system – came to social discourse from a male perspective.

'In modern society, psychology has the power not only to construct normative theories about gender relations, but also to affect how children are raised to conform to these normative theories. Feminist psychology has exposed the male bias in normative views of gender relations and has undertaken the reconstruction of gender relations to improve the material and social conditions of women in culture.'
(Duquin 1994: 286)

The 'sex differences' approach favoured by psychologists in understanding the psychology of gender has come under attack, as has the privileged place given male values and behaviour patterns. Feminist psychology attaches strong significance to women's voice, and to the way in which women experience and interpret reality. The female viewpoint, feminist scholars argue, offers a way of viewing relations of dominance which counterbalances that traditionally favoured by psychology as a discipline. Moreover, feminists argue that women's subjective experience must be recognized as valid if gender and power relations in society are to change. It is still necessary, however, to adopt a psycho-social perspective, since complex concepts such as 'society' or 'sport' can best be understood in the context of interactive models. Even more significantly, sport psychologists 'infuse their work with the insights derived from feminist scholarship. Such suggestions are critical in expanding our understanding of the psychological dimensions of women's sporting and exercise realities and potentials' (Costa and Guthrie 1994: 232). Both feminist psychoanalytical discourse on moral development and poststructuralist ideas on the social construction of self-identity provided valuable starting points for feminist psychology.

Sports sociology generally assumes that sport is an important social institution and cultural practice, which is why it investigates 'its relationship to other social institutions such as the political economy, media, education, and religion' (Costa and Guthrie 1994: 233). Two distinct strands of sports sociology should be distinguished. Traditional sports sociology tends 'to view current social conditions as essentially non-problematic' (Costa and Guthrie 1994: 233). Other sociologists, whose approach is more critical, see the social environment of sport as problematic, because it is entrenched in a stratified social system. This approach puts the system itself in question; further, it tries to develop ways in which existing power relationships might be abolished. Writers from the field of feminist cultural studies, who take a similar approach, use socio-economic and political factors to construct a picture of the world of sporting women. Thus, while traditional sports sociology assumes that sport mirrors society and passively reflects social relationships, cultural studies analysts see sport as

> 'a dynamic cultural product that is actively created and recreated and thus can be changed by humans … cultural studies analysts examine how play, games, and sports reproduce the dominant culture and in what ways they become transformed as persons and groups actively respond in the sporting context to the conditions of their social existence.'
>
> (Costa and Guthrie 1994: 233)

The cultural studies approach makes clear how women react to male dominance in sport; it demonstrates how sport plays an important role for women and girls, regardless of whether or not they actually participate.

Feminist research assumes, to varying degrees, that society has a patriarchal structure. The term 'patriarchal' refers to power relationships in which women's interests are subordinated to those of men. These relationships make themselves evident in different ways – in gender-specific socialization, for example, in the unequal distribution of work or in the internalized norms which define femininity and which influence women's lives. Patriarchal power derives from the meanings with which society imbues biological sexual difference. One fundamental patriarchal assumption is the belief that the biological differences between women and men make different tasks appropriate for each gender. The 'interactionist approach, whereby biological (hormonal and genetic) determinants were thought to exert at most a predisposing rather than determining influence as they interacted with psychosocial and environmental factors' (Hall 1996: 13) does not provide an adequate description of the problem, since its biological determinism and watered-down version of a biological predisposing force are simply examples of reductionistic and categorical thinking. Reductionism is an attempt to explain the properties of complex wholes in terms of the units which comprise the whole. It leads to dichotomous characterization, dividing people into simplistic social categories (male/female, black/white) which polarize and highlight differences, ignoring similarities and overlaps (Hall 1996: 18). Further, there is a tendency to see these differences as absolute. The predominance of bioloical-determinist theories today is undoubtedly a reaction to the continuing influence of psychosocial and social constructionist theory. Biological-determinist assumptions are still evident in the structure of patriarchal societies. For example, the assumption is still regularly made that women are naturally equipped to fulfil other social functions than those allotted to men – primarily, of course, the role of wife and mother.

The phrase 'wife and mother' connotes patience, emotion and self-sacrifice – all qualities which are considered typically feminine. These expectations structure and limit women's access to the labour market and to public life, including sport. Women's gender excludes them from many social and political opportunities, both in their professional lives and after hours. Generally, these opportunities have been so constructed that they are tailored to males. The structures in place in sport, for example, have been designed historically by men for men; moreover, they have typically been administered by men.

It is true, no doubt, that an understanding of roles which is based on biological difference oppresses men as well as women. But, while men also suffer from the pressure exercised by the stereotype ideal of their gender, they none the less have more power as a social group than do women. 'In a patriarchal society men decide what is proper behaviour for both sexes' (Fasting 1987: 361). In a patriarchal system, structures are clearly defined in such a way that men as a gender dominate women as a gender. To assert that patriarchal relations are structural is to say that they are an inherent part of our social practices and institutions and cannot be explained by the intentions, be they good or bad, of individuals of either gender.

Structural theory does not deny that individual women and men are often agents of oppression, but it does suggest that we need a theory which can explain how and why people oppress each other. Such a theory would have to account for the relationship between the individual and society, since people enter society as individuals. Social institutions teach them what the current and future role of the social group will look like, and accustom them to specific mechanisms which ensure that they will grow into these social roles. According to Messner and Sabo, sport is 'the most masculine of our social institutions' (Messner and Sabo 1990: 2). It is 'a product of discourses, practices, and social relations that construct the situation of women in patriarchal societies in ways that typically dis-able women in relation to men' Whitson 1994: 358). All too often, discourse, or the ideology of masculine strength and feminine weakness tends to become embodied in men who become strong and women who become weak and vulnerable. 'It is also [true] that received ideas that say women cannot do certain physical things or push themselves in certain kinds of physical training without them (e.g., in weight training or distance running) become self-fulfilling prophecies' (Whitson 1994: 358). One interpretation of the power ideology might be to view the assertion that women cannot do certain things as a method of preventing them from doing those things.

Birrell and Theberge assume that

'in a patriarchal culture, one of the primary mechanisms of power is the control of women through the control of their bodies. Such control is accomplished through an ensemble of cultural practices that includes rape, domestic violence, sexual harrassment, pornography, male-defined standards of female beauty, unattainable media images, and compulsory heterosexuality. As a physical activity, sport is also a site where the struggle over control of women through control of women's bodies can be publicly observed.'

(Birrell and Theberge 1994: 345)

Hall emphasizes that patriarchal culture 'has defined woman as other or object, more specifically body-object. What follows for women and sport is that a culture that defines sport as body-subject and woman as body-object forces an incompatibility between women and sport' (Hall 1990: 235).

Feminist sports analysts are trying, as they have tried in the past, to uncover a hidden history of female athleticism, looking at sex differences in patterns of athletic socialization and demonstrating how the dominant institutional forms of sport have neutralized men's power and privilege over women. One of the most influential sites where images of women undergo ideological construction and dissemination is the media. The media promulgate dominant patriarchal images which misrepresent, distort, trivialize, marginalize and heterosexualize women athletes – instead of presenting them as hard-working, serious and talented. Thus, the media undermine women, and privilege men through reference to the 'natural' differences between the sexes. Many people, influenced by the media, believe that the distinct roles and behaviour patterns which characterize women and men are determined by nature, not by socialization. According to Willis, the concept of what is 'natural' is 'one of the grounds of ideology because of its apparent autonomy from "biased" interpretation' (Willis 1994: 32). Understanding social relations as 'natural' is one of the most powerfully persuasive aspects of common-sense thinking, but it denies both the historical evidence and the chance to change the *status quo*.

No feminist would adopt such a position. None the less, feminism is a broad term, embracing a range of ways to understand the meanings and implications of patriarchy. For example, Jennifer Hargreaves has argued consistently that we need to understand the way in which gender relations are part of a complex process in sport – and, indeed, other cultural activities. This process is, she believes, specific to capitalist social relations; in her opinion, hegemonic theory might offer a better framework for understanding it. 'Applying the concept of hegemony to the histories of sport enables them to be understood as a series of struggles for power between dominant and subordinate groups – the result of conflicting interests over unequal sports resources in specific social contexts' (Hargreaves 1994: 23).

The term 'hegemony' was introduced by the Italian political theorist Antonio Gramsci in the 1930s. Hegemonic theory posits that privileged social groups manage – apparently consensually – to establish their own cultural practices as the most valued and legitimate, whereas subordinates (for example women, indigenous peoples and people of colour) struggle against the absorption of their alternative practices and activities into the dominant culture – here, the dominant sporting culture. 'The mass media, schools, religious organizations, public ceremonies, sport, and other seemingly apolitical or unbiased sources are often vehicles for maintaining hegemony' (Grant and Darley 1993: 253). Resistance and struggle are important to hegemony, and the process is necessarily ongoing, since alternative cultural forms and practices always pose a threat to those forms and practices which are dominant (Hall 1996: 26). 'Sport may be a cultural sphere that is dominated by the values and relations of the dominant class' (Messner and Sabo 1990: 8), but sport can also be an arena of resistance for the subordinates, because meanings in sport can be reshaped and redefined to meet their needs.

Central to the concept of hegemony is a sense of culture as a way of life which is imbued with systems of meanings and values which are actively created by individuals and groups in different social settings. Culture is not seen as the 'whole of society' – it is understood as being distinct from the political and economic process, but, with them, it comprises the totality of social relations. Hegemony postulates a dialectical relationship between individuals and society, accounting for ways in which individuals are both determined and determining. It allows for cultural experiences, including sports, to be understood simultaneously as worthwhile and as exploitative.

> 'Male hegemony has probably been more complete in sport than in most other social institutions and still is, in numerous instances, remarkably resilient and resistant to change. In all countries in the West, sporting attitudes, values and images are products of a long and relentless history of male domination, linked to ideas about the body which have provided a theme of continuity until the present day.'
>
> (Hargreaves 1994: 116)

Bryson emphasizes that in different countries 'certain sports are more centrally implicated in hegemonic maintenance than others' (Bryson 1994: 59). The male hegemony in sport has never been static or absolute: it is a process in a constant state of flux, incorporating both reactionary and liberating aspects of gender relations. Hegemonic theory recognizes the advantages which men enjoy, especially where women are concerned, but it also recognizes that men cannot win total control. Some men – and some women – support, accommodate, or collude in existing patterns of discrimination in sports which are specific to capitalism and to male domination; other men and women oppose them and struggle to change the *status quo*. 'Male hegemony is not simple male vs. female opposition, which is how it is often presented, but complex and changing' (Hargreaves 1994: 23).

Feminists aim to change the patriarchal reality and to end women's oppression. 'In challenging any system of oppression, it is essential to understand and explain how it works, and that necessitates the development of theoretical frameworks. There are many forms of feminist theory, and they can be categorized in various ways' (Parratt 1994: 10). The feminist movement has traditionally accommodated multiple perspectives, so that its nature tends to be comprehensive, rather than representative of any single, unified position. Nor do feminists always identify solely with a single theoretical strand of feminist theory, although their projects may be characterized by a given approach. All versions of feminism reject conservative thinking, however.

Conservative, liberal and radical thinking

Conservatism holds the family to be the natural unit of the social order. The family is understood to meet individual emotional, sexual and practical needs, and it is primarily responsible for the reproduction and socialization of children. 'Power relations in the family, in which men usually have more power than women and women more power than children, are seen as part of a God-given natural order which guarantees the sexual division of labour within the family' (Weedon 1987: 38). It is seen as natural for women to be responsible for domestic labour and childcare; it is seen as natural for men to be involved in the spheres of work and politics. Both partners are understood as having equal worth, but this equality finds its expression in difference. 'To be a wife and mother is seen as women's primary role and the source of full self-realization. The natural structure of femininity will ensure that women can achieve fulfilment through these tasks' (Weedon 1987: 38). Conservatism assumes that women's place in society is biologically predetermined, and that freedom for women effectively means accepting and understanding biological necessity (Boutilier and SanGiovanni 1994: 8). Accordingly, conservatism denies that women are oppressed.

Radical and socialist feminist theories, by contrast, view the family as the instrument *par excellence* of women's oppression through male control of female sexuality and procreative powers and through male control of economic power. Feminists believe that women's continued deference to the interests of men and children is not natural, but is a result of oppression which has been exercised through the legally, economically and ideologically defined structures of the family and through the internalization of a masochistic form of femininity (Weedon 1987: 40).

The number of multi-faceted political theories covered by the term 'feminism' is increasing, because each of these political theories resurfaces (Kymlicka 1996: 200). The metaphor used by Boutilier and SanGiovanni is apt:

'[F]eminism as an overarching ideological tree has many branches, each with a special origin, leading in a different direction, with divergent policy implications for the liberation of women, and bearing a message for revamping all sexist institutions and cultural dynamics – including those found in sport.'

(Boutilier and SanGiovanni 1994: 98)

Each theory embodies a specific image of women, explains the oppression of women as individuals and as a group in a different way, and challenges us to overcome this oppression. They offer 'a vision of [woman's] participation in society that will enhance her potential for self-fulfilment and autonomy' (Boutilier and SanGiovanni 1994: 98).

Liberal feminism, which has its roots in political liberalism, has exercised a considerable influence on feminist work and scholarship. Liberal feminists 'direct most of their energy toward women's lack of equality in public life', since they see this lack as the root cause of women's oppression. Accordingly, they look for 'strategies for incorporating women into the mainstream of public life which includes politics, the workplace, and sport' (Costa and Guthrie 1994: 237). Their main demands are for 'equality' and 'equity'. Equality generally means 'equality of opportunity' for a given group; equity refers, not to the rights and opportunities of a group, but to the system as a whole. In sport, equal opportunity programmes were developed in order to increase women's overall participation in sport by providing them with equal access.

The call for equal opportunity also embraces the liberal values of liberty, justice and equality. Hence, liberal feminists see the most obvious source of injustice and infringement of liberal values in the notion that each gender has different rights, responsibilities and opportunities. Liberal feminists 'believe that when women are given equal opportunities, they will actualize their potential' (Boutilier and SanGiovanni 1994: 98). Liberal feminism aims to achieve full equality of opportunity in all spheres of life without radically transforming the present social and political system. Its adherents believe that reform conducted within the existing social structure can eliminate gender-based discrimination. Their belief in the importance of public law, for example, was behind their lawsuit to have the women's 10,000-metre track-and-field race added to the athletics schedule (Costa and Guthrie 1994: 237). Liberal feminists intend to achieve their goal, a just society, by extending political, legal and educational opportunities to women, which is why they want to reform existing socio-economic and political structures without placing them *per se* in question. Not until all women – regardless of race, ethnicity, age, sexual preference, social class, educational level or marital status – have the same rights and opportunities will they be able to 'be rewarded equally for their talents' (Boutilier and SanGiovanni 1994: 99). A just society is, according to liberal feminists, a fair meritocracy – a society in which achievement in a competitive environment determines social status and power. Costa and Guthrie explain that, 'although the rules are monitored for fairness, the game itself, which establishes the necessity of winners and losers, is rarely challenged' (Costa and Guthrie 1994: 237). Applied to sport, this would mean that, while there would be an effort to achieve equal opportunities for women (by increasing the training facilities available to them, for example), nothing would be done to try to change the structures of superiority and inferiority which are already present in sport. Indeed, many women have attempted, in sport and physical education, to work within existing structures – which stipulate, for example, that subjective experiences are less important than objective measurements of what is higher, faster or stronger.

The liberal feminist assumption that laws preventing gender-based discrimination would allow women to participate as men's equals in public life has become questionable, since it has become clear that the issues are far more complex than allowed for by the liberal feminist model. 'It is clear, then, that . . . to increase individual opportunities for women within sport (or other masculine-dominated institution) will not automatically result in increased freedom, equality and social empowerment for women' (Messner and Sabo 1990: 5). Nevertheless, liberal feminists have a great deal to celebrate, since it has been chiefly through their efforts that the legal status of women has been so much improved. Moreover, they are responsible for expanding sporting opportunities for women, and for fostering an environment that is more supportive of women developing their physicality.

Radical feminists, on the other hand, are very critical of the liberal emphasis on individual equal rights and their generally uncritical stance towards the existing social structure. Their concerns are shared by socialist and Marxist feminists. Their criticism was perhaps inevitable, since their approaches aim at transforming the structures of patriarchal capitalism rather than reforming them. They believe that the liberal approach will frequently lead to women in sport and physical education adopting the patriarchal ideology and practices of the traditional male model of sport while attempting to work within the current governing structures of sport. Radical feminists advocate the destruction of patriarchal ideologies and the abandonment of hierarchical, patriarchal institutions and relationships – not 'equal opportunity' for women within these oppressive structures. Admittedly, there exist problems within women's sport which liberal feminist strategies leave unaddressed. None the less, liberal feminists' actions continue to advance women, both within sport and in society as a whole.

Marxist sports sociology is not a unified theory; it comprises a variety of approaches whose differences have produced controversy. All Marxist feminist approaches criticize the nature of capitalist sports. Some are determinist, arguing that the economic and ideological effects of sports are crucial in all situations; others interpret Marxism as a humanist theory, asserting that it does not rule out the potential for resistance. Current developments have focused on questions of autonomy and domination, and on the relationship between creative and liberating forces in sports and cultural hegemony.

Marxist feminism concentrates on economics. Its adherents deny that it is possible for anyone – especially women – to achieve equal opportunity in a class-based society. In their opinion, a just society can only be achieved through the elimination of class distinction and oppression. Marxist feminists believe that liberation will come chiefly from women's full entry into the work-force, because they view women's oppression in a capitalist context, asserting that it is rooted in women's exclusion from the public realm of economic production. Bearing this in mind, it seems reasonable to infer that Marxist feminism would derive the right of women to participate in sport from the universal right to work. Marxist feminism's narrow focus on paid labour necessarily brings only one aspect of the specific relationship between gender and the mode of production to light. Most seriously, it ignores the significance of unpaid domestic labour.

Whereas economistic Marxists view sport as a microcosm which reflects the socio-economic macrocosm, structuralist Marxism argues that sports possess their own specific characteristics and are hence relatively independent of other aspects of culture which, too, have their own unique dynamics. One significant implication of theories of social reproduction is that social structures inevitably ensure that the dominant culture, class and power relations are reproduced, so that there is a 'structural causality' in the way in which society as a whole functions. While sports are said to have their own effective sphere of influence, so that they are relatively independent of other substructural levels, they are, in the final analysis, determined by their economic base and by other ideologies (such as competitiveness, chauvinism, nationalism and sexism), so that existing patterns of domination are reproduced.

A closer analysis of the relationship between sport and sexuality reveals 'that sexuality is mediated in sports; that sexual repression is necessary for the survival of capitalism; and that the machismo ethos of sports, by bonding men together, is a fundamental expression of male power and domination over women' (Hargreaves 1994: 17). In sports, it is claimed, people internalize meanings and rules, so that culture is automatically reproduced in a way which serves capitalist interests. Sports are seen, not as an area of free expression, opposition or complexity, but chiefly as an area of conformity. In this system, both men and women are passive agents who are induced through sports to accept conventional gender divisions. In common with economic Marxists, reproductionists imply that the relationship between sexuality and capitalism is static. They fail to subject the inequality of the male–female power relationship to critical examination. Moreover, they fail to take account of the female experience, asserting instead that class is the root cause of the oppression of both men and women in sport. Problems of gender, they believe, are secondary to problems of class.

Economistic and reproduction theories emphasize the manipulative nature of sport, failing to consider the extent to which individuals may choose freely to pursue activities which are both liberating and creative. Cultural Marxist theorists have analysed the complexities of the relationship between freedom and constraint in sport in terms of hegemony. Hegemony has been used to explain continuities and discontinuities in sport: dominant meanings and interests, inherited from past traditions, require defence, while new meanings and interests are constantly developed and fought for. Hegemonic configurations of power are seen as part of a process of continual change which incorporates negotiation and accommodation and is a lived system of constitutive and constituting meanings and values (Hargreaves 1994: 22).

As we have seen, Marxist feminists analyse class rather than gender. Radical feminists, by contrast, believe that all forms of oppression are rooted in women's oppression, and that women's oppression is grounded in the social definition of female bodies and sexuality. Although they differ considerably among themselves, radical feminists agree that the oppression of women is the most ancient and most universal form of oppression; it is, they believe, also the most difficult form to eradicate. Some radical feminists 'see the original oppression of women by men in the patriarchal family as a prototype of other forms of oppression that exist in sexual relationships, class and race relations, and in political and economic institutions' (Messner and Sabo 1990: 3). Radical feminism which emerged in the late 1960s frequently views patriarchy as the primary form of domination, because it has existed in most societies and political-economic systems. Other radical feminists

> 'see the root of women's oppression in biology itself, where enforced child-bearing functions limit women's autonomy by keeping them physically dependent on men . . . others locate the source of women's oppression in compulsory heterosexuality and call for a women-identified existence . . . other radical feminists call for a total and continuing exploration of new forms of being-in-the-world. They ask for no less than a complete reevaluation of such taken-for-granted ideas as culture, society and human nature.'
>
> (Boutilier and SanGiovanni 1994: 99)

While liberals focus on legal, educational and economic reform within a patriarchal-capitalist model and Marxists place class at the centre of oppression, radical feminists focus exclusively on the subordination of women. Radical feminism embraces a plurality of approaches to gender difference. Some radical feminists view gender as socially constructed. Others, 'who are "essentialists", emphasize fundamental biological differences between women and men; they celebrate women's nature as a source of special strength, knowledge, and creative power' (Costa and Guthrie 1994: 242). These differences in perspective do not obscure a clear feminist challenge to the androcentric understanding of human nature, however. Moreover, radical feminists, like Marxist feminists, reject dualistic notions of body and mind and believe that the body has major implications for social theory. They believe that masculine and feminine stereotypes were developed and maintained in order to subordinate groups. Since physicality is an inherent part of sport, sport assumes considerable significance for this theory. The patriarchal ideology, which gives women gender-specific definition, is the source of limits of what women may do in and beyond sport. Whenever women overstep definitional boundaries, they find themselves subject to criticism and deprived of legitimacy. 'The longstanding mythology surrounding the female athlete as less feminine and lesbian is a perfect example of an attempt to constrain women's physical potential' (Costa and Guthrie 1994: 243).

Sexual preference aside, however, one long-term goal for many radical feminists is the development of a culture which is supportive of women. Many women engaged in female projects of this kind advocate separatism, as either a long-term or transitional goal, in order to create spaces for women which are free from male intrusion. In contrast to liberal feminists, radical feminists do not attempt to secure a place for women in a male-dominated arena; rather, many radicals believe that women's potential can only be developed in a gynocentric, women-only space. Although radical feminists have shed light on the power of patriarchy in women's lives and have helped to raise consciousness, and although many alternative projects for women have been developed, one of the major criticisms is that radical feminists frequently universalize women's oppression under patriarchy without considering its socio-historical context. To do so is to ignore the fact that women may also belong to a dominant group which oppresses people who have, for example, another skin colour, less education or who belong to a lower socio-economic group. 'Feminist analyses of sport and leisure . . . failed to incorporate other issues like class, race, the state, ethnicity and consumerism' (Hall 1996: 33).

Separatist proposals have also attracted criticism. While critics accept that a limited or transitional degree of separatism may be beneficial in developing in-group pride and understanding, continual separatism, they say, minimizes possibilities for social transformation because it is based on exclusion rather than inclusion. Separatism 'has limited utility for changing prevailing conceptions about gender and sport. It also fails to address the ways men are oppressed in sport' (Grant and Darley 1993: 258).

Socialist feminism is an attempt to bridge the gap between Marxist and radical approaches, merging the best of both while avoiding the problems of each.

Unlike liberals, they stress the greater struggle of women of colour, ethnic groups, and economic classes in gaining equal opportunity; unlike Marxists, they do not assume that a classless society will also eliminate male privilege; unlike radicals, they refuse to consider economic oppression as secondary in importance to women's oppression.

(Boutilier and SanGiovanni 1994: 100)

Socialist feminists agree that women's oppression has its roots in both capitalism and male dominance; they argue, further, that sexism and economic inequity deserve recognition as fundamental and equally significant forms of oppression – neither, they believe, is more important than the other. The oppression of women is, then, a problem with dual causes, both of which much be addressed. Both class- and sex-based privileges must be eradicated. Socialist feminists are committed to the Marxist tenet that human nature is created, and historically changed, by interactions among factors arising from human biology and the socio-physical environment. The differences between women and men, according to socialist feminists, are not biologically predetermined. Rather, they are socially constructed, and can be changed. Freedom, then, will not result from isolated individual action without a complete restructuring of society: it is, instead, 'a revolutionary demand and involves a complete reconstruction of the existing social order' (Costa and Guthrie 1994: 247).

Where sport is concerned, socialist feminists view their task as the creation of a sports environment in which women's experience, needs and interests would dictate the structure and function of their sporting and exercise experience, and in which women would have equal access to the means of production (in other words, to training, technological assistance and facilities) and equal opportunity to participate at the élite level; at the same time, it would require establishing a purely egalitarian society which would make free expression possible both in competitive and in non-competitive settings. Socialist feminists would acknowledge that extensive financial support would be required for female athletes. Socialist feminism is a newer strand of feminist theory than its liberal, Marxist and radical counterparts, but socialist feminists have made a disciplined effort to develop a theory which is comprehensive and compelling, taking account of every oppressive aspect of patriarchy and capitalism. In this respect, their theory can be called multidimensional.

Although socialist feminists have recognized the important linkages among class, gender, and race, they have not yet achieved their goal of developing a theory that fully explicates the interlocking nature of such variables. Nor have their attempts to synthesize Marxism and the insights gained from radical feminism been totally successful.

(Costa and Guthrie 1994: 248)

Poststructuralism

The term 'poststructuralist' has more than one meaning. It denotes a range of theoretical positions developed by or with reference to the work of Derrida, Lacan, Kristeva, Althusser and Foucault. Poststructuralist theory is subject to many political and theoretical influences; in turn, it exercises influence in many spheres. Important factors in its development were the work of Freud and later psychoanalytic theory, which influenced the way in which subjectivity was understood, and which helped to determine which were the important questions to ask and answer in poststructuralism.

Poststructuralism has several forms, all of which have important differences, but not all of which are necessarily productive for feminism. Poststructuralist feminist theory focuses on forms of social organization and the social meanings and values which guarantee or contest partiarchal structures of society. 'The feminist poststructuralism . . . takes much more from the Marxist discourse . . . for example, the material nature of ideology, or in poststructuralist terms discourse, the importance of economic relations of production, the class structure of society and the integral relationship between theory and practice' (Weedon 1987: 31).

Language is the common factor in the analysis of social organization, social meanings, power and individual consciousness. Effectively, poststructuralist theory is about the ways in which power, subjectivity, social organization and language are interrelated. Language is the locus of definition for actual and potential forms of social organization, and for the prediction of their probable socio-political consequences. It is also the locus of construction of subjectivity – the place where ourselves are constructed. Poststructuralism looks at the ways in which the language and semiotics of a given culture (the social sciences, for example, or religion, media, written texts, art, or sport) define and legitimize what is true or false, normal or abnormal and good or bad.

> A major emphasis in poststructuralist theory is power: the power to name, define, and give meaning to reality. Analysis of language and symbols reveals that everything of symbolic value communicates a perspective or position. Language not only defines legitimate categories of thought but also communicates hierarchies of status. As a result, some people, ideas, and things have more worth in society than others. Words often connote value. For example, in sports, adjectives like fast, hard, and male have more status than slow, soft and female.
>
> (Duquin 1994: 298)

Language presents us with a historically determined range of modalities for imbuing reality with meaning. It offers various discursive positions (including the modes we know as masculinity and femininity), through which we can consciously live our lives. Women's magazines, for example, reveal various subject positions, many of which compete: the career woman, the romantic heroine, the successful wife and mother and the irresistible sexual object. Poststructuralism assumes, further, that subjectivity is not genetically determined, but is socially produced in a wide range of discursive practices (economic, social and political, for example) whose meanings are the site of a constant struggle over power. 'Unlike humanism, which implies a conscious, knowing, unified, rational subject, poststructuralism theorizes subjectivity as a site of disunity and conflict, central to the process of political change and to preserving the *status quo*' (Weedon 1987: 21).

'Deconstruction' is one of the most powerful tools in poststructuralist theory. It focuses on the ways in which the construction of social identity is historically and culturally variable; it also analyses and subverts psychological texts, techniques and forms of subjectivity or identity which have been produced by psychology as a discipline, enabling us to see how understanding of gender identity has been historically influenced by a norm which psychologists have determined. Feminist poststructuralism is productive, because its theories of language, subjectivity, social processes and institutions help us to understand the basis of existing power relations and to develop strategies for change. 'Discourse' is a structuring principle of society, its presence is evident in social institutions, modes of thought and individual subjectivity. Feminist poststructuralism uses the concept of discourse in conjunction with detailed, historically specific analysis, to explain the way in which power has been exercised on behalf of specific interests, and to analyse the opportunities for resistance. On the individual level, discourse theory offers an explanation of the origin of our experience, why experience is contradictory or incoherent and how and why it can change.

Some feminists have criticized poststructuralism's focus on language and symbols for distracting attention from the more material aspects of women's oppression. Merely changing the symbolic representation of injustice, they argue, will not stop the injustice itself. Nor will language analysis change the violence permitted by the rules and structures of sport (Duquin 1994: 300). Most sport structures exploit weakness, placing physical dominance in a position of paramount importance. Furthermore sport 'ritualizes aggression and allows it to be linked with competitive achievement and, in turn, with masculinity' (Whitson 1990: 27). Indeed, sport is often one area where participants learn to reproduce and accept male violence. Therefore, sports violence helps as a social practice not only to construct differences between various masculinities, but also to build the contemporary gender order of male domination and female subordination.

Feminists also criticize the moral levelling which takes place in poststructuralism. 'In poststructuralist theory all social construction is ideology. No single ideology is accorded privilege over any other for its greater truth value or its higher moral worth' (Duquin 1994: 300). Poststructuralism denies that it is possible to adopt a critical position outside ideology from which a judgement of superiority might be made. Hence, while feminists may use poststructuralist theory to deconstruct patriarchal language and symbolic systems, they realize that poststructuralist theory 'itself considers feminism to be as much of an ideological mythmaker as patriarchy, capitalism or Marxism' (Duquin 1994: 300).

Cultural studies

Delivering a complete codification of cultural studies is as impossible as providing an entire overview of feminist theory: the complexity of the positions which fall within its ambit prevents it. 'Cultural studies' describes the area where different disciplines (politics, for example, or sociology, literature, history, feminism, etc.) intersect, all of which analyse cultural aspects of society.

> Culture has been theorized as the site through which social relations are legitimated and mystified, the site through which the social order is constructed, categorized, experienced, regulated, and made mean-ingful and pleasurable – raising questions about the active production of identity, agency, and consent.
>
> (Cole 1994: 10f.)

Culture, then, describes the social forms through which humans live, in which they become conscious, and from which they draw subjective suste-nance. Play, games and sport, for example, are considered to be real social practices within the cultural studies paradigm; feminists cannot turn a blind eye to the fact that these are highly institutionalized aspects of the culture that help to maintain male hegemony (Hall 1987: 333).

The institution which has had the greatest significance for cultural studies is the Centre for Contemporary Cultural Studies at the University of Birmingham, which was founded in 1964 in response to the massive cultural changes of post-war Britain (Hall 1996: 35). 'In early cultural studies, culture was understood to exist within an already constituted social forma-tion, theorized almost exclusively in class terms, and as constitutive of those relations' (Cole 1994: 11). Cultural studies and cultural theory are today enjoying an international boom, especially in the United States, Britain, Australia and Canada. The key terms and concepts which informed the culture/power problem in Britain have been adopted in an interdependent cluster of elements drawn from structuralism and post-structuralism, the most influential of these being Althusserian-informed notions of ideology and the social formation, and Gramsci's theory of hegemony. 'Although it draws upon sociology, political science, philos-ophy, semiotics, history, literature, communication studies, and, more recently, feminism, it is antidisciplinary in the sense that cultural processes do not correspond to the contours of academic knowledge' (Hall 1996: 34).

The conception of cultural studies breaks with classical theories of power by reconceptualizing its location, modalities, and exercise from the state and its repressive effects to its productive effects at the everyday, bodily, local and state (theorized in dispersion) levels. The idea that the gap between theory and material culture can be bridged is an important aspect of cultural studies. Michel Foucault has explored various theoretical and political spaces, helping us to comprehend the ways in which the body is subjected to and embedded in complex cultural politics. Cultural theorists see the body as one area of cultural politics. The trend towards 'theorizing the body', and the questions and studies which that trend has engendered mark an important moment in feminist cultural studies. Accordingly, sport remains a particularly powerful ideological mechanism because it is centred on the body.

Advocates of an approach based on cultural studies and cultural criticism have also challenged traditional mainstream approaches to sport sociology, seeing a shift away from the traditional categoric and distributive research towards a clearer understanding of what constitutes more theoretically informed analyses of social relations of power in sport and leisure. The proposition that the significance of sport in (post)modern life can only be grasped through an analysis of culture now finds greater acceptance. Sport is, at least in so-called developed countries, a very visible aspect of popular culture: cultural meanings and values which are enacted through participation, competition and spectacle help to (re)make us, both as individuals and as collectives. Like other institutionalized cultural forms and practices, sport is profoundly affected by the existing structures of power and inequality which it in turn affects.

'The early work on gender . . . produced some excellent scholarship on women's leisure and girls' subcultures, which not only critiqued the consistent male bias of leisure studies and the sociology of youth but extended our knowledge about girls' and women's culture' (Hall 1996: 35). While it is true that feminism's influence on cultural studies is still very limited, there is certainly a recognition that both movements concern themselves with forms and practices of power and inequality, which they wish to change. If there exist goals in common between feminism and cultural studies, they are investigation of the role of culture in the reproduction of gender inequality, and the discovery of how an analysis of the problem of gender can contribute to an understanding of culture.

Because of the fundamental link between social power and physical force special significance is given to sport. 'It is an arena in which physical force and toughness are woven into hegemonic masculinity and the resultant ideology transmitted' (Bryson 1990: 173). The celebration of men as strong and tough in sport underscores the fact that men are in positions in which they can dominate.

Thus sport is an ideal medium for conveying messages of gender domination. Not only is sport associated with physical power and is an important, admired social activity, but it is also something to which we are exposed daily and from very young ages. Sport is an immediate mass reality and, with increasing commercialization and media exposure, the ever-present nature of this reality is likely to be magnified.

(Bryson 1990: 174)

'Feminism became more than a constellation of women's issues, it became a perspective, a philosophy, a political ideology' (Bailey 1993: 299). Feminist scholars have begun to rethink sport as an institutional element within the larger political economy and culture in which ideologies of male superiority and structures of male domination are constructed and naturalized. Feminist studies try to uncover some of the processes through which males get support in sporting practices that help to construct hegemonic masculinity, while continuing to marginalize and subordinate women. As already revealed, the power of hegemonic masculinity is never total and is often fraught with internal contradictions. Because they can be challenged, critical feminist perspectives do more than highlight and analyse these contradictions and historical developments. Rather, one purpose of critical feminist theory is to facilitate an understanding of the conditions that sustain us, an understanding that enables us to envision possibilities to change society for the better. Both men and women can be liberated by feminist ideologies from their circumscribed options. Critical feminist theory implies – in substance, aim, and process – a commitment to a moral vision and a liberating social goal. To unravel and understand oppressive dimensions in sport is the basis for transforming sport and, through it, ourselves and the wider society.

References

Abraham, A. (1992) *Frauen. Körper, Krankheit, Kunst.* (Bd. 1). Oldenburg (Bibliotheks- u. Informationssystem/Universität Oldenburg).

Bailey, N. (1993) 'Women's sport and the feminist movement: building bridges', in Cohen, G. (ed.) *Women in Sport: Issues and Controversies.* Thousand Oaks, CA: Sage, 297–304.

Bierhoff-Alfermann, D. (1983) 'Frauensport aus soziologisch-psychologischer Sicht', in *Sport für alle – aller Sport für Frauen?* DSB, editor. Frankfurt, 20–32.

Birrell, S. and Theberge, N. (1994) 'Ideological control of women in sport', in Costa, D. and Guthrie, S. (eds) *Women and sport: interdisciplinary perspectives.* Champaign, IL: Human Kinetics, 341–59.

Boutilier, N. and SanGiovanni, L. (1994) 'Politics, public policy, and Title IX: some limitations of liberal feminism', in Birell, S. and Cole, C. (eds) *Women, sport, and culture.* Champaign, IL: Human Kinetics, 97–111.

Bryson, L. (1990) 'Challenges to male hegemony in sport', in Messner, M. and Sabo, D. (eds) *Sport, Men, and the Gender Order: Critical Feminist Perspectives.* Champaign, IL: Human Kinetics, 173–84.

Bryson, L. (1994) 'Sport and the maintenance of masculine hegemony', in Birell, S. and Cole, C. (eds) *Women, Sport, and Culture.* Champaign, IL: Human Kinetics, 47–65.

Cagical, J.-M. (1981) 'Sport et identité féminine', Erraïs, B. (ed.) in *La femme d'aujourd'hui et le sport.* Paris: Editions Amphora, 101–11.

Cohen, G. (1993) 'Media Portrayal of the Female Athlete', in Cohen, G. L. (ed.) *Women in Sport: Issues and Controversies.* Thousand Oaks, CA: Sage 171-84.

Cole, C. (ed.) (1994) *Women, Sport and Culture.* Champaign, IL: Human Kinetics, 173–84.

Costa, D. and Guthrie, S. R. (1994) 'Feminist perspectives: intersections with women and sport', in: D. M. Costa and S. R. Guthrie (eds) *Women and Sport: Interdisciplinary Perspectives.* Champaign, IL: Human Kinetics, 235–53.

Duncan, M. C., Messner, M. A., Williams, L., Jensen, K. and Wilson, W. (eds) (1994) 'Gender stereotyping in televised sports', in S. Birell and C. L. Cole (eds) *Women, Sport, and Culture.* Champaign, IL: Human Kinetics, 249–73.

Duquin, M. E. (1994) 'She flies through the air with the greatest of ease: the contributions of feminist psychology', in D. M. Costa and S. R. Guthrie (eds) *Women and Sport: Interdisciplinary Perspectives.* Champaign, IL: Human Kinetics, 285–306.

Fasting, K. (1987) 'Sports and women's culture', in M. A. Hall (ed.) *Women's Studies International Forum: Special issue. The Gendering of Sport, Leisure, and Physical Education.* New York: Pergamon Press, 361–9.

Grant, C. and Darley, C. (1993) 'Equity – What Price Equality?', in Cohen, G. (ed.) *Women in Sport: Issues and Controversies.* Thousand Oaks, CA: Sage, 3–15.

Greendorfer, S. L. (1993) 'Gender Role Stereotypes and Early Childhood Socialization', in Cohen, G. L. (ed.) *Women in Sport: Issues and Controversies* Thousand Oaks, CA: Sage, 3–15.

Hall, M. A. (ed.) (1987) *Women's Studies International Forum: Special Issue. The Gendering of Sport, Leisure, and Physical Education.* New York: Pergamon Press.

Hall, M. A. (1990) 'How should we theorize gender in the context of sport?', in M. A. Messner and D. Sabo, (eds) *Sport, Men and the Gender Order: Critical Feminist Perspectives.* Champaign, IL: Human Kinetics, 223–39.

—— (1996) *Feminism and sporting bodies: essays on theory and practice.* Champaign, IL: Human Kinetics.

Hargreaves, J. (1994) *Sporting Females: Critical Issues in the History and Sociology of Women's Sports.* London: Routledge.

Kidd, B. (1990) 'The men's cultural centre: sports and the dynamic of women's oppression/men's repression', in M. A. Messner and D. F. Sabo (eds) *Sport, Men, and the Gender Order: Critical Feminist Perspectives.* Champaign, IL: Human Kinetics, 31–45.

Klein, M. L. (1989) 'Frauen und Sport in der Bundesrepublik', in C. Peyton and G. Pfister (eds) *Frauensport in Europa.* Hamburg: Czwalina, 16–37.

Kröner, S. (1990) 'Kultur- und Bildungsvereine für Körper, Bewegung und Sport von Mädchen und Frauen – Ausweg aus einem Dilemma?', in *Im Verein ist Sport am schönsten – auch für Mädchen und Frauen?* DSB, editor. Frankfurt, 7–19.

Kymlicka, W. (1996) 'Der Feminismus', in *Politische Philosophie heute – Eine Einführung.* Frankfurt/New York: Campus, 200-50.

Langer, I. (1986) 'Quote – Reizwort oder Lösung?', in *Quotierung – ein Weg zu mehr Mitbestimmung für Frauen?* DSB, editor. Frankfurt, 7–11.

MacNeill, M. (1994) 'Active women, media representations, and ideology', in S. Birell and C. L. Cole (eds) *Women, Sport, and Culture.* Champaign, IL: Human Kinetics, 273–89.

Messner M. A. and Sabo D. F. (eds) (1990) *Sport, Men, and the Gender Order: Critical Feminist Perspectives.* Champaign, IL: Human Kinetics.

Midol-Beauchamps, N. (1981) 'La mixité en cours d'éducation physique: une possibilité de faire évolver l'image féminine', in Erraïs, B. (ed.) *La femme d'aujourd'hui et le sport.* Paris: Editions Amphora, 111–119.

Minker, M. (1993) 'Die Macht der Männer und die Schönheit der Frauen', in *Psychologie heute special. Thema: Frauen-Schönheit.* (No. 4) 1993, 14–22.

Parratt, C. M. (1994) 'From the history of women in sport to women's sport history', in D. M. Costa and S. R. Guthrie (eds) *Women and Sport: Interdisciplinary Perspectives.* Champaign, IL: Human Kinetics, 5–15.

Peyton, C. (1989) 'Zur Diskussion des Frauensports in Europa', in C. Peyton and G. Pfister (eds) *Frauensport in Europa.* Hamburg: Czwalina, 5–16.

Ridder, M. de (1986) 'Der Körper als Ware', in H. Petzold (ed.) *Leiblichkeit – philosophische, gesellschaftliche und therapeutische Perspektiven.* Paderborn: Junfermann, 313–23.

Sabo, D. F. (1994) 'Different stakes: men's pursuit in sports', in M. A. Messner, and D. F. Sabo (eds) *Sex, Violence and Power in Sports.* USA: Crossing Press, 202–14.

Schmausser, B. (1991) *Blaustrumpf und Kurtisane.* Stuttgart: Kreuz-Verlag.

Schmidt, D. (1991) ' "Schöner – Schlanker – Straffer." Überlegungen zu Gesundheit und Fitness', in Palzkill, B., Scheffel, H., Sobiech, G. (eds) *Bewegungs(t)räume.* München: Frauenoffensive, 62–75.

Theberge, N. and Birrell, S. (1994) 'Structural constraints facing women in sport', in D. M. Costa and S. R. Guthrie (eds) *Women and Sport: Interdisciplinary Perspectives.* Champaign, IL: Human Kinetics, 331–339.

Theberge, N. and Cronk, A. (1994) 'Work routines in newspaper sports departments and the coverage of women's sports', in S. Birell and L. Cole (eds) *Women, Sport, and Culture.* Champaign, IL: Human Kinetics, 289–99.

Weedon, C. (1987) *Feminist Practice and Poststructuralist Theory.* Oxford: Basil Blackwell.

Whitson, D. (1990) 'Sport in the social construction of masculinity', in M. A. Messner and D. F. Sabo (eds) *Sport, Men, and the Gender Order: Critical Feminist Perspectives.* Champaign, IL: Human Kinetics, 19–31.

—— (1994) 'The embodiment of gender: discipline, domination, and empowerment', in S. Birell and C. L. Cole (eds) *Women, Sport, and Culture.* Champaign, IL: Human Kinetics, 353–71.

Willis, P. (1994) 'Women in sport in ideology', in S. Birell and C. L. Cole (eds) *Women, Sport, and Culture.* Champaign, IL: Human Kinetics, 31–47.

Wilson 1994: Duncan, Margaret C., Messner, Michael A., Williams, Linda, Jensen, Kerry, Wilson, Wayne, editor, Gender Stereotyping in Televised Sports. In: Susan Birell, editor, Cheryl L. Cole, editor, *Women, Sport, and Culture.* USA (Human Kinetics), 249–273.

8   The rise of black athletes in the USA

Othello Harris

Nearly every day, if you read the newspaper, listen to the radio or watch television in America, you will encounter something about an African American athlete. Today, African American athletes generate enormous amounts of attention from the mass media. Indeed, many journalists seem to exist only to cover African American athletes, especially those who write about professional football, boxing or basketball.

Elite African American athletes today are often considered celebrities, valued citizens, and even heroes.[1] Their sport performances and other activities shape, and are shaped by, what we think and believe about them as individuals and African Americans as a group. How did they come to occupy these prestigious positions?

The position today's black athletes enjoy is, in part, due to the accomplishments of their black athletic predecessors. The pioneers of African American involvement in sport have a long history, going back to the early seventeenth century. But in this chapter we concentrate mainly on the twentieth century.

Pioneer boxers

Africans were among the first people, other than Native Americans, to arrive in America. They came first in the early sixteenth century as explorers assisting the Spanish and Portuguese on explorations to what is now the United States – particularly the south-west part of the United States – and on expeditions to what is now Mexico and Peru (Franklin and Moss 1988; Pinkney 1969; Masotti *et al.* 1970). Later, in 1619, they came, much like whites, as indentured servants to the Jamestown, Virginia colony (Franklin and Moss 1988). They were expected to work as servants for a determined number of years. After the completion of their indentured servitude they were to be free persons, again, like whites. The perpetual slavery of Africans was not recognized in the colonies until 1661, but this condition of permanent servitude came to shape relations between whites and people of African descent.

Slavery in America was a harsh, cruel institution. Plantation slaves were worked from sunrise to sundown (Foner 1983). Yet, despite the truculent character of slavery and the long hours of labour, slaves were not without a social life. After sundown and away from work and masters, slaves hunted, fished, gathered wild crops, sang, danced and engaged in story-telling and other forms of entertainment (Foner 1983). In fact, black participation in sport in America has its origin in plantation activities.

American Southerners participated in a number of recreational activities, such as horse racing, cock fighting, gambling, wrestling and boxing (Sammons 1988). Slaves were involved in most of these activities primarily for the entertainment, but sometimes for the profit, of planters. Perhaps the most profitable of plantation sports, for planters and a few slaves, was boxing.

Boxing is a sport that was popular in England in the eighteenth century. It was imported to America by the sons of wealthy southern planters who went to England, before the Revolutionary War, in pursuit of academic training and 'culture' (Rust and Rust 1985). Later, southern planters sponsored intra- and interplantation matches between black boxers.

Boxing matches provided entertainment for whites and a diversion from the hard life of a slave. A slave who showed exceptional boxing ability was rewarded, because his talent could render a fortune for a master who bet heavily on him and won (Rust and Rust 1985). Therefore, extraordinary boxing slaves were given special privileges to inspire them to victory. And, in a few cases, slaves were manumitted as a result of their boxing ability. Even more rare was the black man who was able to earn a living at boxing. One of these rare boxers was Tom Molineaux.

Molineaux was a slave on a Richmond, Virginia plantation. Like his father and others in his family, he was a remarkable boxer. In one fight, against another slave, his master wagered $100,000 and offered to manumit him if he won. His master profited handsomely and Molineaux travelled to England, where prizefighting was received more enthusiastically, in search of his idol, Bill Richmond (Rust and Rust 1985; Chalk, 1975).

Richmond was, according to Rust and Rust (1985) and Chalk (1975), the first African American to box for a living. He was born, free, in New York and it was there, during the Revolutionary War, that he captured the attention of British sailors with his boxing skills. After the war he left for England under the patronage of a British officer. There he was educated and engaged in prizefighting against famous (white) fighters. He fought until the age of fifty-six, and was considered a hero to many British (Rust and Rust 1985) and to others like Tom Molineaux.

Under Richmond's guidance, Molineaux positioned himself for a fight against the British (and then world) heavyweight bare-knuckle champion, Tom Cribb. Twenty-thousand people, including members of British nobility, turned out for the much awaited title bout (Chalk 1975; Orr 1969). They fought for more than twenty rounds before Molineaux knocked Cribb unconscious. While Molineaux's corner began rejoicing in their victory, an unseemly event occurred; Cribb's corner complained that

Molineaux had lead weights in his glove. The referee apparently suspended the count allowing Cribb to regain consciousness. The bout was continued and Molineaux lost in the fortieth round.

The next year, in a return engagement, Molineaux was knocked out in the eleventh round. The losses were obviously hard on him; his boxing career and health declined and he died, a few years later, broke and dispirited (Chalk 1975).

Molineaux is a startling example of the 'rags to riches to rags' cycle which still plagues black athletes over 180 years after his boxing career ended. His boxing ability took him from plantation slave to free man to a match against an esteemed white pugilist. He was involved in the first interracial title bout. Molineaux was a contender for the most coveted athletic prize during his lifetime – the heavyweight championship of the world. He most certainly knew fame and fortune, but in the end the acclaim and possessions escaped him. While it may be an overstatement to suggest he was the prototype of the African American athlete, it would not be hyperbolical to state that many black sportsmen have followed suit in their quest for, grasp of, and loss of prestige and prosperity.

Peter Jackson and the colour line

For nearly 100 years after Molineaux's fight against Cribb, no African American was allowed an opportunity to compete for the heavyweight title. However, this was not due to a lack of talent or interest among black boxers. George Godfrey and Charles Hadley are but two of the black boxers who sought a match with the popular champion John L. Sullivan; their offers, like others, were refused (Rust and Rust 1985). Sullivan fought blacks on his way to fame and the title, but when he reached prominence as a fighter, he drew the colour line. Once be became world heavyweight champion Sullivan never again faced a black boxer.

Peter Jackson came close, perhaps closer than any other African American in the nineteenth century, to fighting for the heavyweight title. He was born in the Virgin islands and emigrated to Australia when he was very young. After becoming the Australian heavyweight champion in 1886, Jackson emigrated to San Francisco in search of prestige and financial gain.

Jackson attempted to arrange for his first fight in America against a white boxer, Joe McAuliffe. However, McAuliffe, like many other white boxers, drew the colour line (Wiggins 1985). Jackson, instead, met and defeated George Godfrey for the coloured heavyweight championship of the world. As coloured champion, Jackson found white boxers were more eager to fight him, because a defeat over the best black boxer could garner for whites an important, perhaps title, fight. Jackson hoped that his defeats of white opponents (for example, McAuliffe, Patsy Cardiff, Frank Slavin and Jem Smith) would do the same for him – set him up for a title bout.

Jackson was not alone in seeking a fight between himself and Sullivan. In 1890 several athletic clubs made impressive offers to host a fight between the two boxers. Sullivan turned down all offers; he would not meet a black fighter in the ring and certainly not one as talented as Jackson (Wiggins 1985). Discouraged, Jackson continued to fight. In 1891 he fought James Corbett to a 61-round draw. While the Jackson–Corbett fight failed to enhance Jackson's position with Sullivan, it propelled Corbett to a title fight with Sullivan which Corbett won. This turn of events caused Jackson to cut short his stay in England to seek a rematch with Corbett.

Jackson and Corbett agreed to a fight, but they disagreed on the location of the bout. Corbett wanted to fight in Jacksonville, Florida, but Jackson refused. Interracial contests were not a welcome spectacle in America and an interracial heavyweight championship fight in the South (i.e. the southern states of the United States) could be particularly dangerous to a black man who emerged victorious over a white fighter. Jackson thought it wise to avoid fighting Corbett in the Deep south. Thus, he surrendered his chance to compete for the title. It is possible that Corbett's tactics were designed to avoid risking his title against Jackson (Wiggins 1985). Jackson turned to heavy drinking. He died at the age of forty from tuberculosis or perhaps, as Wiggins (1985) says, from a broken heart. His misfortune was being black in a society that valued the ability and accomplishments of whites only.

While Jackson and others sought heavyweight title bouts against white challengers, African Americans in the lower-weight classes were making their mark on boxing. Because they were smaller in size, their fights did not carry the same implications for racial and national superiority that accompanied heavyweight fights.

On 27 June 1890 George 'Little Chocolate' Dixon defeated Nunc Wallace, the British featherweight champion, with an eighteenth-round knockout, to become the first African American to hold a title in any sport (Ashe 1988).[2] The next year he won the American bantamweight title with a knockout of Cal McCarthy in Boston.

A decade later – in 1901 – a second African American became a boxing title-holder when Joe Walcott won the welterweight title from Rube Ferns. And the following year another African American, Joe Gans, won the lightweight title with a first-round knockout of Frank Erne. In 1904, two top black boxers fought for the welterweight title – Walcott and Aaron 'Dixie Kid' Brown, which Brown won on a foul in the twentieth round.

Like their heavyweight counterparts most of the above-mentioned boxers retained little of their fortune during their latter years. Dixon, who won an enormous amount of money, succumbed to alcohol and died broke at the age of thirty-seven. Walcott lived to be sixty-three but he, too, died broke (the victim of a hit-and-run accident). The Dixie Kid died penniless after attempting suicide at the age of fifty-two. Of the early black boxing champions, only Joe Gans was financially secure when he died.

Pioneer cyclists and jockeys

The decade of the 1890s has been referred to as the 'darkest period in race relations in US history' (Ritchie 1988). In addition to the record number of lynchings (1,217), this decade was the setting for a most pernicious ruling by the Supreme Court. In the Plessy vs. Ferguson case in 1896, the Court established the 'separate but equal' doctrine – separate facilities for the races were lawful as long as they were equal (Farley 1995). Ironically, this decade also witnessed the crowning of the second African American champion in any sport (after Dixon in boxing) when Major Taylor became the world and American sprint cycling champion in 1899.[3] Like African American non-athletes, he fought against a segregated system which viewed blacks as both inferior and threatening to whites.

Major Taylor was a champion cyclist during the period preceding the advent of the automobile and auto-racing, when cycling was one of the most popular spectator sports in America. Taylor won his first races as a teenager. By the time he was seventeen, he left Indianapolis for Worcester, Massachusetts, where he was able to compete in integrated contests. Taylor was not so fortunate in the South. The League of American Wheelmen (LAW), at the insistence of its southern delegations, barred blacks from membership in the organization. This cost Taylor dearly as it meant lost opportunities to increase his earnings and exclusion from races that counted in the tabulation of rankings.

In 1898 Taylor held seven world records in his speciality – the sprints. In 1899 he won the one-mile world championship in Montreal, followed by the American championship in 1899 and 1900 (on total points from qualifying events).

In 1901 Taylor left the United States for the first of several tours of Europe where cycling was the most popular sport at the time. He was heartily welcomed by the French and he dominated the sport, but his refusal to race on Sundays – for religious reasons – did not allow him to compete for the world championships in Europe in 1902 or 1903. Still, he was able to add to his victories, earnings and popularity in Europe without enduring the prejudice he faced in America.

When Taylor retired from the sport of cycling he was 32 years old, an international star and very wealthy. However, bad business investments cost him his savings, his house and other valuables. When he died of heart and kidney problems, his body lay unclaimed in Chicago for more than a week. He was buried in a common 'pauper's grave' in a Jim Crow (segregated) section of a cemetery where he remained until he was reburied 16 years later by a Chicago bicycle association. In 1982, Indianapolis, his home town and the city that banned him from one of its racetracks in 1896, named its velodrome after him.

Major Taylor was, indeed, an extraordinary athlete and individual, but he was not the first African American to ride to victory. That distinction goes to black jockeys.

Before Africans in America engaged in boxing and cycling they were involved in another sport – horse-racing. This was especially true of African Americans who worked on southern plantations. In the South most jockeys were slaves, while in the North the jockeys were, usually, English or local whites (Ashe 1988). In the early 1800s, before the advent of thorough-bred racing meets in America, black jockeys won a number of prestigious races, including the celebrated Match Races[4] (Ashe 1988).

At the first Kentucky Derby (1875) the winner – Oliver Lewis – was black as were thirteen of the other fourteen jockeys. Another black rider, Jimmy Winkfield, in four starts recorded two victories (1901 and 1902), a second and third place, to give him the best winning average in Kentucky Derby history (Rust and Rust 1985). He later went to Europe and continued racing and winning. Isaac Murphy won the Kentucky Derby in 1884, 1890 and 1891 – the first to win the Derby three times. Murphy won a number of other important races as well. Willie Simms won the Kentucky Derby twice (1896 and 1898), won at Sheepshead Bay (NY) five times and went to England were he attained international fame (Rust and Rust 1985).

Like Major Taylor, black jockeys faced resentment from white riders. It was not unusual for white riders to work in concert in order to force blacks to the rails. Eventually, they were forced from the sport of horse-racing. One event which attributed to their disappearance was when the Jockey Club – a licensing agency for jockeys – was formed in 1894; it barred blacks from membership.

Perhaps also contributing to the demise of the black jockey was Jack Johnson's defeat of Burns (1908) and later Jim Jeffries, 'the Great White hope' (1910). Johnson's victory so outraged white America that African Americans felt the repercussions in and outside the world of sport. Americans were neither yet prepared to celebrate the accomplishments of African American athletes nor to accept them as champions in presti-gious sporting events – boxing or otherwise. Shortly after Johnson's defeat of Jeffries, black jockeys vanished from the Kentucky Derby and other horse-racing events (Rust and Rust 1985).

America's games: America's way

More than seventy years before Jackie Robinson took the field in Jersey City, New Jersey in 1946 as a second baseman for the Montreal Royals, John W. 'Bud' Fowler – in 1872 – joined a minor league team in New Castle, Pennsylvania to become the first black professional baseball player (Peterson 1970).

By the next decade as many as thirty African Americans participated on white professional teams.[5] This number included Moses 'Fleetwood' Walker who, as a catcher for the Toledo Blue Stockings in 1884, became the first African American major league baseball player; he was followed by his brother Welday Walker and other standouts, such as Frank Grant and George Stovey. However, many white players resented the presence of black team-mates and opponents. Convinced that white players would quit rather than compete with or against black players, the International League, in 1887, declined to sign African Americans to contracts. Shortly afterwards there was a 'blackout' in professional baseball.

. College sports were similar to professional baseball in their Jim Crow (segregated) policies; however, a few African Americans were allowed to participate in baseball, football, basketball and track and field, usually at northern colleges (Harris 1993).[6] Still, few African Americans found programmes that would welcome their talents; those who did found discriminatory practices awaiting them. Some schools, particularly those in the South, refused to play against teams with black players. In many cases the integrated teams left black players at home or on the bench. Other southern teams forfeited games rather than face black opponents. These exclusionary practices mirrored larger societal customs during this period, African Americans being excluded from most forms of social inter-action with whites. White Americans were not ready to tolerate the presence of African Americans in their games. But ready or not, Jack Johnson, an outstanding black boxer, was seeking the most prominent position in sport: the world heavyweight championship.

Jack Johnson: the intrepid champion

The beginning of the twentieth century in America, much like the end of the nineteenth century, was a period of white supremacy. Segregated laws and practices governed nearly every aspect of life, including which wards of hospitals serviced whites and African Americans, the doors through which they entered restaurants, theatres and other public institutions, and even the water fountains that they were allowed to drink from (especially in the South). For example, not only were whites and African Americans born into separate sections of hospitals in the South, but they were also buried in different sections of the same cemetery. These customs ensured white dominance 'from the cradle to the grave'.

The institution of sport also operated in ways that maintained white supremacy; many of the contests were for whites only. African Americans contended for the 'Coloured Heavyweight' title, but whites refused to meet African Americans for heavyweight title fights. It was a common practice for white fighters to meet black boxers on their way to promi-nence, but to draw the colour line – avoid black boxers – once they distinguished themselves as pugilists. A white fighter's loss to an African American was presumed to bring shame to himself and his race.[7] For this reason heavyweight champions such as John L. Sullivan, 'Gentleman' Jim Corbett and Jim Jeffries never met black fighters in the ring while they held the title, although the latter two had fought black fighters 'on the way up' (Roberts 1983; Wiggins 1985).

Jack Johnson, who had been the 'Coloured Heavyweight Champion', wanted to fight for the 'world' heavyweight title, but he, like other African Americans, was initially ignored. However, Johnson was relentless in his pursuit of the title; he followed Tommy Burns from New York to England, France and Australia in search of the bout. Burns's decision to meet Johnson in a match for the title upset many whites, such as former champion John L. Sullivan, who declared, 'Shame on the man who upsets good American precedents because there are dollars' (Gilmore 1975: 27). Burns had parted company with Sullivan's and other white athletes' custom of drawing the colour line.

In Australia in December 1908, Jack Johnson taunted, laughed at and played with Tommy Burns, winning every round until the police stopped the fight in the fourteenth round. Johnson had defeated Burns to become the first black heavyweight title holder, but he found his accomplishment trivialized by the American press. They claimed that he was not in the same category as Sullivan, Corbett and Jeffries, former white champions (Roberts 1983). Reporter Jack London summoned Jim Jeffries, the former heavyweight champion, from his alfalfa farm to remove the ever-present 'golden' smile from Jack Johnson's face.[8] It was time, London and Jeffries felt, for white America to reclaim its athletic superiority. Jeffries, *a real champion*, would take care of Johnson, and in the process, restore white superiority to boxing.

The 'Great White Hope'

Johnson's fight with Burns had drawn little interest, considering the magnitude of the event – he was the first black man to fight for the heavyweight title in nearly 100 years. His bout against Jeffries in Reno, Nevada was decidedly different; it was a colossal affair. More than 20,000 fans – including over 100 correspondents and writers from the United States, Europe and Australia – came to witness what many viewed as the fight for racial superiority. Jeffries was white America's 'great white hope'.

Most expected Jeffries to win because he was white, but also because he was believed to possess physical ability, discipline, courage, restraint, and intellectual ability which Johnson was said to lack. Johnson was described as undisciplined, impulsive, carefree, childlike, cowardly (or 'yellow'), and a dullard in comparison to Jeffries – traits widely associated with people of colour.

Before the fight Jeffries announced,

> When the gloves are knotted on my hands and I stand ready to defend what is really my title, it will be at the request of the public which forced me out of retirement. I realize full well just what depends on

me, and I am not going to disappoint the public. That portion of the white race that has been looking to me to defend its athletic superiority may feel assured that I am fit to do my very best.

(Farr 1964: 107)

Jeffries probably came to regret that proclamation as Johnson became the first fighter to ever knock Jeffries down (which he did several times) and out. The win over Jeffries also signalled an end to unchallenged notions of white supremacy in the ring. As London wrote, 'Once again has Johnson sent down to defeat the chosen representative of the white race, and this time the greatest of them all' (Bankes 1992: 180).

Backlash

African Americans rejoiced after Johnson's victory. Many felt that he had 'uplifted' a downtrodden race. Others likened Jeffries' defeat to a second Emancipation Proclamation (Gilmore 1975). African Americans had, once again, thrown off white shackles, freeing themselves, this time, from another kind of slavery – ideological racism.

Not surprisingly, whites were angered by Johnson's triumph. Some whites sought to suppress black jubilation by preventing parades and other festivities honouring Johnson's accomplishment. As the fight results spread around the country, rioting broke out in nearly every city and town in America (Gilmore 1975). Whites and African Americans clashed from the South to the North, leaving at least eight people dead and scores injured in the wake of the Johnson–Jeffries fight (Farr 1964). Major cities forbade the showing of the film, claiming that the sight of a black man thrashing a white man heightened racial tension (although the sight of whites whipping blacks was not considered to be similarly disquieting).

Johnson's defeat of Jeffries was enough to anger most white Americans, but his lifestyle, and especially his penchant for ignoring important social taboos, was an affront to many Americans. Johnson was extravagant: he drove expensive cars; he was an impeccable dresser who often changed clothes three or four times daily; he adorned himself with expensive diamonds; and he carried a roll of thousand dollar bills (Wiggins 1971; Gilmore 1975) which he loved to spend on having a good time. For example, with the $5,000 he received for a fight against Jack O'Brien, Johnson purchased a $3,000 automobile and an $1,800 diamond ring (Roberts 1983). Johnson's public display of his wealth offended many whites, who chafed at the fact that a black man, in the early 1900s, was more affluent than they were.

In addition, Johnson showed disdain for, rather than deference to, whites. For example, when he met Tommy Burns at the signing for the championship bout Burns, waving a pistol, called out, 'Hello nigger', and Johnson, in a clear violation of racial protocol, replied, 'Hello ya yellow Canuck bastard' (Bankes 1992: 142). But what most incensed whites was

Johnson's liaisons with white women. Johnson's public affairs with white women so enraged whites that Congressman Rodenberry introduced a bill in the United States' House of Representatives that would prohibit inter-racial marriages in the United States. Miscegenation was already unlawful in several states, but it was not a federal offence. Rodenberry stated that

> Intermarriage between whites and blacks is repulsive and averse to every sentiment of pure American spirit. It is abhorrent and repugnant to the very principles of a pure Saxon government. It is subversive of social peace. It is destructive of moral supremacy, and ultimately this slavery of white women to black beasts will bring this nation to a conflict as fatal and as bloody as ever reddened the soil of Virginia or crimsoned the mountain paths of Pennsylvania. . . . Let us uproot and exterminate now this debasing, ultra-demoralizing, un-American and inhuman leprosy.
>
> (Gilmore 1973: 32)

Despite instigation from Rodenberry and other politicians who pleaded with the government to help them 'protect' white women from Johnson and other African Americans,[9] no bills to forbid interracial marriages were passed (Roberts 1983). But Johnson's troubles did not end there. He would soon be in trouble with the Mann Act.

The Mann Act, or 'White Slave Traffic Act', enacted in 1910, forbade the interstate transportation of women for immoral purposes (Gilmore 1975). It was intended to prohibit commercial vice – cases where foreign women were smuggled into the United States to engage in prostitution. Johnson was charged with violating the Mann Act for sending money to Belle Schreiber, a prostitute and Johnson's former mistress, enabling her to travel from Pittsburgh, Pennsylvania to Chicago, Illinois (Roberts 1983). Johnson admitted knowing Schreiber and having sent her money, but he did not take the charges seriously. He believed that he could pay a fine and be on his way. After an all-white jury found Johnson guilty of violating the Mann Act, the judge, George Carpenter, citing Johnson's stature in the black community, let it be known that a fine was not penalty enough: Johnson was fined $1,000 *and* sentenced to one year in prison. Deciding he had had enough, Johnson fled the United States for Europe.

Life on the run was trying for Johnson. Although he was still the heavy-weight champion, he had difficulty finding fights and making a living in Europe. He turned to wrestling, bull-fighting and vaudeville performances for income (Roberts 1983; Gilmore 1975). In 1915, two years after his escape from America, Johnson put his title on the line in a fight against the gargantuan – 6' 6", 260 lb – Jess Willard. By knocking Johnson out in the twenty-sixth round, Willard became the 'great white hope' that Jeffries had sought to be. Whites rejoiced. Boxers and promoters vowed to keep the title from black interlopers. For twenty-two years, no other

African American would be allowed to fight for the heavyweight title. Prospective black contenders would have to first prove that they were not a threat to the established order.

Johnson returned to Europe for another five years before coming back to the United States, in 1920, to serve his one year prison sentence. While he was not idolized by whites like previous heavyweight champions, Johnson was held in high esteem by many African Americans. He had destroyed one of the barriers they faced: white beliefs about African American inferiority. Johnson forced whites to see what African Americans could do in fair competition with whites: there would be some defeats, but there would also be victories. White did not necessarily mean superior.

The black middle class disavowed and denounced Johnson, believing that he had brought hardship to African Americans (for example, some African Americans found their jobs terminated in the wake of Johnson's defeat of white fighters), and he had embarrassed the black community through his liaisons with white women (Gilmore 1975; Gilmore 1973). Still, Johnson was among the first in a long line of African Americans to demonstrate blacks' abilities to participate in one-time white sports. He challenged and may have been the one to change white thinking about race and physical ability. Even his fall from grace could not change that. He paved the way for African American athletes to follow. However, they would have to follow a different path to gain social acceptance.

Black appeasement, white approbation

Jack Johnson was the torch bearer for the first generation of twentieth century African American athletes. The next generation witnessed the formation of the Negro Leagues in professional baseball (Tygiel 1983); barn-storming teams such as the all-black Renaissance Big Five in basketball (Peterson 1990); and the inclusion of a few African Americans on white professional football teams before the colour line was drawn in 1933 (Carroll 1992). In college a few black athletes, usually 'superspades', which include Fritz Pollard and Paul Robeson, played on northern and western teams. In 1916 Fritz Pollard, All-American from Brown University, became the first of many African Americans to compete in the Rose Bowl (Harris 1995). In the 1920s he also became the first African American to coach and play quarterback in the NFL. Paul Robeson, All-America at Rutgers, was a team-mate of Pollard on the Akron Pros. Robeson, a Phi Beta Kappa, attended law school at Columbia University and later became a renowned actor, singer and activist. Most black college athletes, however, were in track and field programmes. By the time of the 1936 Olympics there were 100–200 African American athletes scattered throughout programmes in the United States (Behee 1972). Black athletes were more prominent than before, but they were still not revered as heroes by white America. Jesse Owens and Joe Louis would change that.

Jesse Owens and Joe Louis were among the youngest children born, in Alabama, to large families that sharecropped. Their families left the South seeking better jobs and opportunities in the urban North cities of Cleveland and Detroit, respectively.

Duelling the master race

Jesse Owens attended college at Ohio State University where he became one of the most outstanding athletes in history. Thus, at the Big Ten Championship meet at the University of Michigan, 25 May 1935, an injured Jesse Owens tied the world record for the 100 yard dash (9.4 seconds) and broke the world mark for the 220 yard low hurdles (22.6 seconds), the 220 yard sprint (20.3 seconds) and the long jump (26 feet 8¼ inches). In one hour he broke three long-held world records and tied another. The next month Owens scored 40 of Ohio University's 40⅕ points in a meet which his team lost against the University of Southern California. Yet, Owens is best known for his performance at the 1936 Berlin 'Nazi' Olympics.

The XIth Olympic Games were important to Germany, as they indicated the Europeans nations' willingness to collaborate with Germany (Herz and Altmann 1996). But given Hitler's views on the inferiority of non-Aryans and the fact that Germany was becoming a totalitarian police state, there was bound to be controversy. American Jews, appalled by Hitler's open discrimination against Jews, called for a boycott of the 'Nazi Games' by the United States. Meanwhile, the German government called for black athletes to be barred from the games. claiming it was degrading and disgraceful to have to compete with 'Negroes' for trophies (Herz and Altmann 1996).

The American black press, although divided, also had strong opinions about the German Olympics. Some newspapers advocated boycotting the Games, as participation might be taken as a sign of approval of Nazi beliefs and practices. Others felt that the Olympic Games would be the perfect setting to challenge Hitler's notions about the inferiority of non-Aryans (Wiggins 1983). Every defeat of a German would be a blow to Aryan Supremacy.

It was the decision of the American Athletic Union to participate in the Olympics. Although the Germans won the unofficial medal count, Jesse Owens' performance was magnificent. Owens tied the world record of 10.3 seconds in the 100 metre dash; set an Olympic record of 26' 5¼" in the long jump; set an Olympic record of 20.7 seconds in the 200 metre sprint; and ran the opening leg of the finals of the record setting 400 metre relay (which was run in 39.8 seconds). Owens alone scored 40 points; the German male track team scored 60 points (Baker 1986).

Owens, the brightest of the Olympic stars, had become a hero to black and white Americans (although whites referred to him, condescendingly, as 'a credit to his race'). In winning four gold medals, he had led a team of Americans which included 18 other African Americans, and demolished notions of Aryan pre-eminence in physical contests. Louis would later pick up where Owens had left off.

Before the opening of the Olympic Games, Joe Louis met German boxer, Max Schmeling in a bout that was expected to position the winner for a match against James Braddock, the heavyweight title holder. While there were a few references to a fight between a representative of the 'master race' and a son of Africa (Sammons 1988), there was little animosity toward Schmeling. In fact, many Americans viewed this as a fight between a black man and a white man, not a German and an American. Therefore, because he was white, Schmeling had many fans in America.

Surprisingly Schmeling, a 10–1 underdog, scored a twelfth-round knockout over Louis. Upon his return to Germany he was praised by Hitler, with whom he lunched, for a 'German victory'. A despondent Louis worked to get himself back into contention for the title. He felt he had left himself and African Americans down.

Louis, more than Owens, was viewed as an emissary for the black community. Few other African Americans were in the public eye like Louis and he was careful not to 'bring shame to the race' by antagonizing whites like Johnson had. Louis's public persona was humble, nonthreatening and modest. He was counselled to never show pleasure in beating whites and to never have his picture taken with white women (Mead 1985). In short, Louis was coached to be acceptable to whites. Because he was talented and observed the prescribed roles that whites had for African Americans, he was, indeed, accepted by whites. In 1935 he was named 'Boxer of the Year' by *Ring Magazine* and 'Athlete of the Year' by the Associated Press (Capeci and Wilkerson 1983), honours that Jack Johnson would never have received no matter how many opponents he had defeated.

In the year after losing to Max Schmeling Louis defeated seven fighters in eight months. In June, 1937 he became the first African American in twenty-two years to fight for the heavyweight championship. He defeated James Braddock with an eighth round knockout in front of 45,000 spectators – 20,000 of them black fans – to become the second black heavyweight champion. But his most important fight was yet to come.

Sweet revenge

During the two years since Louis and Schmeling had met in the ring Hitler had sought to expand his influence over Germany. This, along with Germany's persecution of Jews, disturbed many Americans. In addition, Schmeling's reception by Hitler following his first fight with Louis, and the German's use of the victory as a sign of Aryan superiority troubled Americans. This led to increased American hostility towards Germans and Schmeling as a representative of Nazism.

Whereas the first fight between Louis and Schmeling was viewed as a bout between a black and white opponent, the second was viewed by many Americans as a contest between nations, the United States versus Germany, and ideology/democracy versus fascism. America was now represented by an African American, a decided change in America's position towards non-whites. Even President Franklin D. Roosevelt became involved: he sent his private car to bring Louis to the White House where he felt Louis' muscles and proclaimed, 'Joe, we're depending on those muscles for America' (Louis *et al.* 1978: 137). Louis, like Owens, had become a key functionary for America – he was performing a crucial role for the entire system. For once, his performance had the support of all America, not just the black community. He was expected to send Germany a message about America's ability to do combat.

In one round Louis completely destroyed Schmeling and concerns about Aryan supremacy; democracy had triumphed over fascism. Later, Louis consolidated his position as a beloved (black) American when he enlisted, as a private, in the United States Army, preferring to forgo a deferment that he might have been granted. His presence and recruitment activities for the military encouraged others to participate in the World War II effort. He also fought numerous exhibitions, contributing his share of purses – a considerable amount of money – to the Navy Relief and Army Relief Funds. Yet, all the while, Louis was one of the 'Coloured Troops' in so far as the United States military was segregated by race.

Although they were American champions, Owens and Louis were not immune from the prevalent racial stereotypes of their era (for example, blacks are better athletes because they are closer to the primitive than whites), nor were they excused from loathsome racial customs, such as being confined to the 'coloured section' of restaurants, buses, theatres, etc. During the early part of Louis' career he was often depicted as a 'Sambo' by newspapers – he was presented as an ape-like figure with a small head, ape-like arms, large lips, dark skin and bulging eyes (Wiggins 1988). Owens and Louis were both national figures and black men – a contradictory status in the 1930s (Evans 1985).

Nevertheless, they became the first two black heroes to America for much the same reason: they had performed phenomenally in international events where, as representatives of America, they defeated 'foreign enemies'. They were, later, credited with improving race relations in America, in large part because of their deferential behaviour. Louis' non-threatening bearing caused many influential whites – from former heavyweight champions to politicians – to declare that interracial bouts were no longer disruptive of racial harmony (Sammons 1988), a reversal of views from Johnson's reign as heavyweight champion. Moreover, Louis and Owens are credited with opening the door for Jackie Robinson and other African Americans to play integrated professional ball. They were the first to go from race heroes to national idols.

Desegregation of American team sports

Jackie Robinson is widely credited with breaking the colour line in professional team sports in America when he signed a contract with Brooklyn Dodgers in 1945. This is a misrepresentation of his accomplishment. Professional football – the National Football League (NFL) and American Football League (AFL) – had a few, although not more than five, African Americans on team rosters in the 1920s. While it appears there was no organized blackout, some teams objected to playing against African Americans (Carroll 1992). By 1933 professional football had drawn the colour line.

Even professional 'white' baseball had black players on its rosters before Robinson's signing, but that was before the turn of the century. After World War II, baseball was still America's game and no African American had yet appeared on a white 'major league' roster during the twentieth century. They played, instead, in the Negro Leagues, a multimillion dollar business – one of the largest black-owned businesses in the United States (Rogosin 1983).

The Negro Leagues showcased black talent for black and white audiences; they were known for great play and improvisation. For example, night baseball and East–West all-star games both originated in the Negro Leagues; white baseball adopted these innovations years later. The Negro Leagues were also known for barnstorming – playing exhibitions, which comprised most of their games – against all kinds of opponents ranging from black to white teams as well as local teams to major league 'white teams' (whom they often defeated) (Rogosin 1983). Negro Leaguers also endured all kinds of conditions – playing in major league parks; playing on open fields without backdrops; sleeping in buses, dugouts and by the side of the road (owing to hotel policy of racial discrimination); sleeping two or three to a bed; and playing several games in a day. Roy Campanella, who played for a decade in both the Negro Leagues and the white majors, claimed to have played catcher in four games in one day on several occasions while with the Baltimore Elite Giants of the Negro Leagues (Rogosin 1983).

Although life was hard in the Negro Leagues, they gave black players a chance to make a living playing a sport players loved, and they were a training ground for a number of the most outstanding African Americans to play baseball, including Josh Gibson and Smokey Joe Williams, who never played white baseball, as well as many who later played in the white major leagues, such as Satchel Paige, Willie Mays, Hank Aaron, Larry Doby, and Jackie Robinson – the first player to go from the Negro Leagues to white baseball.

Robinson, it was widely felt, was not the best ball player in the Negro Leagues; that honour would arguably go to Satchel Paige, the extraordinary pitcher who was, at one time, the highest paid ball player, black or white, in America. However, Branch Rickey, general manager of the

Brooklyn Dodgers felt that Robinson had the perfect 'combination' of characteristics for the premier black player in the white majors. Having thoroughly investigated Robinson's college, military and sports background, he decided that Robinson had the skills to play for the Dodgers, but his other 'assets' were just as important: Robinson was a veteran of predominantly white teams. He had earned a varsity letter in four sports at the University of California, Los Angeles (UCLA) where he was a star in football, baseball, basketball and track (Tygiel 1983). In addition, Robinson was college-educated and had served as a second lieutenant in the Army during World War II. While in the Army Robinson had demonstrated his willingness to fight for his rights on numerous occasions, including attempting to integrate facilities at military bases. Rickey saw in Robinson a courageous and talented man who would suppress his feelings and emotions in the face of white insults, for the good of Rickey's 'experiment'.[10] Or, as Buck Leonard, one of the Negro League stars saw it, 'we had a whole lot better ball players than Jackie, but Jackie was chosen 'cause he had played with the white boys' (Rogosin 1983: 203).

While the collaboration of Rickey and Robinson was important, in truth, a host of other factors, outside of baseball, had an impact on baseball's desegregation. Many African Americans welcomed the chance to demonstrate patriotism during World War II, but there was also concern and increasing activism among black Americans. Black soldiers questioned the policies of a country that would have them fight for democracy abroad while subjecting them to virulent discrimination at home. They began to talk about a 'Double V' campaign – a war versus foreign enemies and domestic prejudice (Tygiel 1983). Following the war, black reporters such as Wendell Smith of the *Pittsburgh Courier* and Sam Lacy of the *Chicago Defender*, intensified the pressure on major league teams to integrate, arguing, as many had, that if blacks could fight and die alongside whites, they could play ball with whites too. And, in 1942, New York, home to the Brooklyn Dodgers, passed the Quinn-Ives antidiscrimination law which banned racial discrimination in hiring. In 1945, three years after the Quinn-Ives law was passed, several candidates for political offices in New York attempted to pressure owners of the city's baseball teams to sign a pledge declaring they would not discriminate in hiring. Therefore, in addition to Rickey's interest in securing black talent for his team, this was an opportune time to integrate baseball.

Robinson was encouraged to emulate the behaviour of Joe Louis – appease rather than offend whites. But Robinson was not like Louis. He was not accustomed to suffering indignities; he took pride in retaliation (Robinson 1995). Yet, he was convinced, by Rickey, that any retaliation would have tragic consequences for himself and other African Americans who hoped to play professional white baseball. For two years Robinson endured racist taunts by baseball fans and opponents, 'hate mail', segregated accommodation and restaurants, and an attempt by his prospective team-mates – and later by the St. Louis Cardinals – to boycott games if he was included in the line-up, all without retribution. He continually made sacrifices to avoid jeopardizing the chances of other African American ball players. However, when black players were firmly established in the league, Robinson was free to express himself like other ball players; he was free to respond, as he deemed appropriate, to attempts to humiliate him. Thereafter, many who had admired him for submissive and non-retaliatory public behaviour began to view him as an ungrateful insurgent. Robinson felt he had done his job – he had nullified all the white reasons for excluding African Americans from baseball. An onslaught followed.

Many Negro Leaguers initially felt that Robinson was not a complete player; but, with their assistance, he became an outstanding major leaguer. During his first year with the Brooklyn Dodgers he was named the National League Rookie of the Year. Two years later, in 1949, Robinson led the league in batting and stolen bases and was named the National League Most Valuable Player. A six-time all-star who helped his team to six league pennants (league championships), Robinson ushered in an era of black dominance in professional team sports. Shortly after Robinson signed with the Dodgers they added four other black players to the roster. Although some teams lagged behind, by 1959 every major league baseball team had at least one black player (Rogosin 1983).

Robinson's signing, and later performance, reverberated throughout team sports. Professional football re-integrated in 1946 when Robinson's former UCLA backfield mate, Kenny Washington signed with the Los Angeles Rams. Woody Strode, another former UCLA team-mate of Robinson, was signed, also by the Rams that same year, to begin professional football's desegregation (Strode 1990). Nearly four years later, Chuck Cooper and Earl Lloyd became the first black players in the National Basketball Association. An important obstacle had been conquered in sport during the 1940s and 1950s. Black athletes would soon come to dominate these same sports that had, for years, ignored their performances. They were thrilled to be included in the white leagues. However, the next decade would bring restlessness and rebellion as they witnessed white America's ambivalence towards them: they were accepted on the field only.

Increased participation and resistance

During the 1950s and 1960s a number of racial barriers fell in sport. Althea Gibson won the French tennis Open in 1956 followed by back-to-back titles both at Wimbledon and Forest Hills, NY in 1957 and 1958 (Shelden 1996). There were also black firsts in the National Hockey League (Willie O'Ree in 1957); in golf on the PGA (Charlie Sifford in 1961) and LPGA (Renee Powell in 1967) tours; in professional basketball as head coaches (John McLendon in the ABA and Bill Russell in the NBA); in baseball

(Emmett Ashford as first black umpire in 1965); and in various other areas of professional sport (Eitzen and Sage 1996).

In college sports, African Americans began to show up on more team rosters in the major sports. By 1948 black athletes appeared on one out of every ten predominantly white college teams, although they constituted only 1 per cent of all basketball players at these colleges. From this it is easy to see that few teams had more than one black player representing them. Furthermore, black athletes were not allowed to be second or third teamers; a disproportionate number of them were rookies of the year, conferred most valuable players and All-Americans (Harris 1993).

Most southern colleges did not relax their ban on integration until the latter part of the 1960s. Some northern colleges that had lifted their own 'gentlemen's agreement' found it necessary to modify their southern schedule in order that black athletes be allowed to play in games. Others simply left black players on the sidelines when they visited or hosted southern teams (Harris 1993). In a sure sign that white southern schools were not prepared to welcome black athletes, African American students (non-athletes) were met by angry white mobs when they attempted to integrate the University of Mississippi in 1962 and the University of Alabama in 1963. Furthermore, Mississippi colleges sat out NCAA college basketball tournaments in 1959 and 1961 and a bowl game in 1961 – all prestigious events – rather than compete against black athletes.

In 1966, Texas Western (now University of Texas, El Paso), utilizing an all-black starting five – a first for a basketball team at a predominantly white university – upset the all-white University of Kentucky team to win the national championship. Shortly thereafter Kentucky accepted black players on its teams. Most other white colleges desegregated, if they had not already done so.

But desegregation in American sports did not mean full acceptance of African American athletes. Black players in college and the professional ranks were roomed in undesirable hotels, while their white team-mates often reposed in luxury; many restaurants, even in hotels which would admit them, were off-limits to black players; and black players who were permitted to stay at white hotels were not allowed to be roomed with whites. Moreover, interracial interaction was frowned upon, if not banned. While Jackie Robinson's team-mates chatted and played cards during road trips, he was often excluded from social interaction with other Dodgers (Robinson 1995). Hank Aaron, while playing for the Milwaukee Braves, was once pulled over by the Kentucky police for riding in the car beside a white woman (who was sister to the driver, Aaron's friend). Once the police officer confirmed that Aaron was not 'with' the white woman, he made Aaron leave the car to avoid the appearance of a black man fraternizing with a white female.

During the 1960s a number of black athletes began to complain about their treatment by the predominantly white sports establishment.

Professional athletes began to complain about being underpaid, and debarred from occupying certain sports positions – especially leadership positions. Collegiate athletes felt that they were exploited by schools that welcomed their athletic ability, yet ignored their academic and social needs. After their academic eligibility was completed, they were treated like pariahs by their Alma Mater.

Many whites – fans, coaches, administrators, students and alumni – failed to understand what black athletes had to lament. Sport, they felt, had lifted scores of black men and women from the 'ghettoes' and improved their lot in life. According to the athletic director at the University of Texas, El Paso, 'In general, the nigger athlete is a little hungrier, and we have been blessed with having some real outstanding ones. We think they've done a lot for us, and we think we've done a lot for them' (Olsen 1968: 15). Many black athletes disagreed; they challenged white demands that they be humble and grateful. Collegiate athletes presented universities with their own demands: an end to restrictions on their social activities, including interracial dating; the discontinuation of demeaning, racist language directed at black athletes; the curtailment of segregated accommodation; and an end to stacking – the practice of assigning players to positions by race. Some college programmes responded by suspending black athletes for insubordination; others simply removed them from the team, effectively curtailing their athletic careers. But many black athletes of the 1960s were not inclined to be like Louis and Owens – obsequious and non-threatening. Instead, many chose to be like Muhammad Ali.

Ali was, as Cassius Clay, a blessing for boxing. He was brash, loquacious, attractive, talented and, for sports reporters, quotable. He danced around opponents, daring them to hit him. He spouted self-penned poetry about his upcoming matches, giving his antagonists often humorous, but not alto- gether innocuous, nicknames. He brought attention and flair to boxing and helped to rescue it from the doldrums. Cassius Clay was tolerated by many Americans and well-liked by some until he announced, two days after becoming the heavyweight champion, that he had joined the Nation of Islam, a religious group headed by Elijah Mohammad. He further incensed many Americans by declaring that he was dropping his 'slave name', Cassius Clay, to be known as Cassius X. Later he took the 'divine' name, Muhammad Ali.

Many whites, and some African Americans, were upset by Ali's affili- ation to the Nation of Islam (or 'Black Muslims' as the Nation of Islam was commonly called). The Nation of Islam, and its most prominent spokesperson, Malcolm X, were outspoken about America's history of oppression of African Americans. In the 1960s, Black Muslims declared that whites were the enemies of blacks everywhere, as they had been responsible for evil; whites were devils, they claimed. But, more impor- tantly to Ali and a host of other people of colour, the Nation of Islam preached black pride to African Americans, countering feelings of black inferiority. They reasoned that God was black, not white, therefore black was divine not tainted. While their anti-Christian message was not well-received in the black community – at least judging by the number of converts – their message of black glorification and exaltation struck a receptive chord among African Americans, especially those who felt disenfranchised. Still, some African Americans eschewed the Nation of Islam.

Former black heavyweight champions, Floyd Patterson and Joe Louis, denounced Ali for joining the Nation of Islam. Patterson declared the Black Muslims 'a menace to the United States and to the "Negro race". . . . The image of a Black Muslim as the world heavyweight champion disgraces the sport and the nation', he declared (Hauser 1991: 139). He promised to defeat Ali and return the title to (Christian) America, which he was unable to do (Harris 1995).[11] Other African Americans were similarly discouraged by Ali's religious conversion.

Two years after declaring himself a member of the Nation of Islam, Ali saw his draft status changed from 1-Y (not qualified for military service) to 1-A. He announced that he would not serve in the armed forces, requesting that he be awarded conscientious objector status on religious grounds.[12] In 1967, his request denied, Ali refused to be inducted into the service. One hour later – before being charged or convicted of a crime – New York State's Athletic Commission suspended his boxing licence. Every other jurisdiction soon followed, thus barring him from further fights (Hauser 1991).

Initially, after his association with the Nation of Islam was disclosed, many black athletes were probably ambivalent towards Ali; he was anti-Christianity, anti-vice, anti-race-mixing. All told, he was too chaste for their tastes. However, black athletes came to revere Ali as he refused to waver on his principles: he would not serve in the armed forces (or, as he said, support the domination of people of colour by a white government) even if it meant being stripped of his title. Ali was in the forefront of the black athletic revolution of the 1960s. He made it easier for black athletes who followed to challenge the system.

In 1968, at the Olympic Games in Mexico City, African Americans Tommie Smith and John Carlos finished first and third in the 200 metre dash. When Tommie Smith and John Carlos raised their black-gloved fists in a 'black power' salute on the victory stand, they engendered feelings of pride in many African Americans. Smith, Carlos and many other African American athletes had used the Olympic international stage as a forum to protest against racial inequities in America. The proposed boycott of the Olympics and the resultant protests by black athletes have been described as 'the cornerstone in the wakening of black America' by author Donald Spivey (1985).

According to tennis great Arthur Ashe, Ali's sacrifice made their gesture possible (Hauser 1991). Ali influenced generations of black athletes and ushered in the era of a new black athlete – a more assertive athlete, prepared to challenge racial injustice. As Georgetown University coach, John Thompson remembers, 'Ali pulled us away from that docility, where black people who were successful sat around acting docile ... certainly Ali was an inspiration to me. Very definitely, he contributed to the man I am today' (Hauser 1991: 449).

Black athletes of the 1960s and early 1970s demanded better treatment from a white public and establishment that often felt African American athletes were lucky to receive the rewards and adulation they bestowed on them. Novelist Ronald Fair claimed that the dominant figure in the struggle for equality in America had become the new black athlete because he or she had one of the commanding positions in black society. Whereas black athletes used to avoid confrontation with authority for fear of losing their position, Fair said the new black athletic hero is bold, speaks his or her mind, and is willing to take a stand (Olsen 1968). The humility of Louis, Owens and others was out of step with the rebelliousness of the 1960s.

Great athletes (sometimes great people) but not great officials

In October, 1972, before the second game of the World Series between Cincinnati Reds and the Pittsburgh Pirates, Jackie Robinson was honoured for his contributions to baseball. A fighter to the end, Robinson said to the thousands gathered, 'When I look down the third base line, I want to see a black man coaching. Then I'll be able to say we've made progress' (Robinson 1996: 199). Robinson never lived to see that day in baseball history. He died a week later, but not before writing:

> The sickness of baseball – and it is being more and more openly dis-cussed today – is that it exploits and uses up young, gifted black and brown talent on the playing field, then throws them away and forgets about them after they have given the best years and the best energies of their lives. Baseball moguls and their top advisers seem to earnestly believe that the bodies, the physical stamina, and the easy reflexes of black stars, make them highly desirable but that, somehow, they are lacking in the gray matter that it supposedly takes to serve as managers, officials and executives in policy-making positions. Some prominent personalities in the game have even said it out loud; that they do not believe the average black player has the skill to be in a command position on the field or from the dugout or in the up-front office.
>
> (Robinson 1995: 258–9).

Nearly fifteen years after his death Al Campanis, Robinson's white former team-mate with the Montreal Royals and one of the few white players to join Robinson's all-star barnstorming team, appeared on a television programme that paid tribute to Robinson and his legacy. Campanis, then vice-president of the Los Angeles Dodgers – the franchise that made Robinson a pioneer – claims that African Americans lack the 'necessities' – his reference to intellectual and other abilities – to manage baseball teams. He added, however, that 'They are outstanding athletes, very God-gifted, and they're wonderful people.... They're gifted with great musculature and various other things' (quoted in Harris 1991: 25). These, according to Campanis, are the assets that make African Americans great athletes but do not translate into front-office positions. With this Campanis ignited a sometimes heated debate about black ability – whether sports ability is determined by race and whether African Americans, and black people around the world, are genetically superior as athletes (and, according to some people, inferior intellectually).

More than a decade earlier Robert Kane, senior writer for *Sports Illustrated*, purported to examine 'black dominance' in American sports in an extensive, although methodologically flawed article entitled 'Black is best'. Kane condescendingly complimented African Americans for their sports accomplishments, especially since the breaking of the colour barriers in team sports, concluding that they had physiological (i.e. better suited for sports), psychological (for example, relaxation under pressure) and historical advantages (i.e. slavery) over whites which led to their out-standing sports performances. As the ideas of Kane, Campanis and others indicate, whites had, in a brief period of time, gone from claiming that African Americans lacked the ability to participate in sports with whites (which was used as a justification for segregated sports) to declaring that African Americans are better at sports through no 'fault' of their own (certainly not through hard work) but, rather, because of divine or natural intervention. Thus, it was possible to admire black athlete performances as one would other creatures' magnificence,[13] while simultaneously holding on to strongly held beliefs about racial superiority (i.e. blacks are not as intelligent, disciplined, or industrious as whites).

Searching for a new endline

The belief in black athletic superiority may at once serve to mollify white concerns about their athletic ability (i.e. 'it's not that you're inept, it's that they were born better'), and keep African Americans out of the sports positions many whites covet when their playing days are over. Still, some African Americans have managed to obtain positions directing and admin-istrating sport franchises.

In the 1980s few professional teams had black head coaches, general managers, or other front-office personnel. Excluding basketball, the number of black coaches was truly abysmal. By 1994 the NBA still led the leagues with five black coaches (19 per cent), followed by Major

League Baseball with four (14 per cent) and the NFL with two (7 per cent). In addition, a small percentage of African Americans were in top management positions (for example, president or vice-president of the organization) and a few were part-owners of franchises (Lapchick 1996). In addition, African Americans have won a number of 'coach of the year' awards, and a few championships in sport. As Lapchick points out in *Sport in Society*, sport, perhaps more than other institutions in America, has allowed African Americans to become managers and executives. But, they continue to be underrepresented relative to the number of athletes in these sports. During the 1992–1993 seasons African Americans made up 16 per cent of the professional baseball, 68 per cent of the football and 77 per cent of the basketball players; their percentages as coaches and front-office personnel pale by comparison.

In college sport, African Americans comprised only 6 per cent of the students at predominantly white colleges and universities in 1994, but 42 per cent of the football players, 37 per cent of the women basketball players, and 60 per cent of the men basketball players at the most competitive (Division I-A) level (Lapchick 1996). Yet only 4 per cent of college head coaches were African American, with a higher percentage in basketball (fewer than 20 per cent) than in football (where there are only a handful) or baseball (where there are no collegiate programme heads – managers). From the above, it is apparent that black athletes are readily accepted on college and professional teams as athletes but only in non-supervisory positions. Basketball and football especially are sports where, typically, whites control and direct black talent. It is unlikely that Jackie Robinson would see progress in this.

Stars, superstars and mega-stars

During the 1980s and 1990s there was a resurgence of discussion about black intellect and athletic ability. Newspaper reporters and television shows presented debates about the reasons for the lack of black coaches and player-leaders (for example, quarterbacks in football and catchers in baseball). The National Broadcasting Corporation (NBC) devoted several hours to a presentation and discussion of black dominance in sport, hosted by its top news anchor.

In college, new regulations heightened the public conversation about black intellect and sport. The NCAA implemented a series of guidelines, Proposition 48, Proposition 42, and Proposition 16, which raised the minimum Grade Point Average and standardized test scores that athletes would have to obtain to accept an athletic scholarship. While some argued that the standardized tests were culturally or racially biased and a way to diminish the number of African Americans at predominately white universities, others argued that new, higher standards were necessary to avoid the continued exploitation of black athletes (for example, by bringing academically unprepared student-athletes into colleges and universities where they could not make the grade). The public discussions led many to question the academic competency of black athletes. This occurred at a time when sport was simultaneously making stars, superstars and mega-stars or celebrities out of few African American athletes.

As spectator sports have become more popular in America, black athletes, who are many of the best athletes and top attractions, have been at or near the top of the escalating salaries in sport. In an article about the top five paid salaries in baseball, basketball, football and hockey (*Huge Salaries*, 1996), it was reported that African Americans comprised all the top paid players in basketball for the 1996–97 season and the top four in Major League Baseball (MLB) for the 1996 season. (They were not among the top five paid football players – only white quarterbacks were repre-sented – nor among the top hockey players.) All of the players on the above list made in excess of $5,000,000 per year in salary alone, headed by Michael Jordan's estimated $30,000,000 for one season. The top profes-sional boxers often exceed Jordan's expected salary. Several professional basketball players recently signed seven-year contracts that will pay them more than $100,000,000.

In addition, some athletes have commercial endorsements that exceed their salary (for example, Michael Jordan's commercial endorsements were estimated at $40,000,000). While the salaries of most professional athletes pale in comparison to the above, the average salary in the NBA and MLB exceeds $1,000,000 and football is nearing that mark. The minimum season wage in the NBA is now $250,000. If one adds to the above the money from business interests (for example, Magic Johnson was a part-owner of the Los Angeles Lakers and has a chain of 'Magic Theatres'), money and fame from movies, videos, etc. that athletes star or appear in, it is easy to see how some black athletes have gone from stars to celebrities. In fact, in an interesting twist on celebrity, in cities like New York, Chicago, Dallas and Los Angeles, it is unusual *not* to see movie stars, television show hosts, politicians and other celebrities star-struck by black male athletes. African American athletes are now among the brightest of the stars. They have gone from the shadow to the summit.

Notes

1 I am not suggesting that all African American athletes fit this description. Certainly some are beset by problems such as drug and alcohol abuse, but as a group they are worshipped by many.

2 Chalk (1975) reports that Dixon became the first African American title-holder in any sport when he claimed the world bantamweight title vacated by the retiring Tommy Kelly whom Dixon had earlier fought to a draw.

3 I have relied heavily on the work of Andrew Ritchie's *Major Taylor: The Extraordinary Career of a Champion Bicycle Racer* (1988) in this section.

4 According to Ashe (1988) and Orr (1969) match races brought together

sectional favourites for one prominent race which was usually accompanied by heavy wagering.

5 According to Peterson (1970), there were African Americans in a number of white leagues during the 1880s and 1890s – the Eastern Interstate League, the Middle States League, the Illinois–Indiana League, the Atlantic Association, the Connecticut League, etc. In some of the years that followed there were a few African Americans participating in one or more of these leagues; in other years there were none. In 1898 the Acme Coloured Giants – an all-black team – played in the Iron and Oil League. When they folded, African Americans were not to be seen in white baseball for nearly fifty years.

6 Perhaps because in track and field the evaluation of one's performance was less subjective and participation required very little social interaction, relative to other sports, it seemed to attract African Americans more than other collegiate sports.

7 The sense of shame whites suffered from losing to African Americans can be illustrated by 'Fireman' Jim Flynn's declaration that he would rather die – he wanted to be shot – than lose to Johnson (Roberts 1983). Johnson (1992) claims that Jeffries' father threatened to disown him after his loss to Johnson.

8 I have used London's writings, as compiled by Bankes (1992), extensively because he attended the fights and provided eyewitness accounts for an American and a Canadian newspaper.

9 Apparently, white men not only believed that black men were desirous of and would pursue white women, but they also believed white women to be helpless – unable to resist – these alleged sexual advances by black men.

10 Rickey claimed he had religious reasons for integrating baseball.

11 Ali was so upset at Patterson's statements and Patterson's insistence on calling him 'Clay' rather than 'Ali' that he brutally punished Patterson. Ali refused to knock Patterson out, while repeatedly taunting him with screams of 'what's my name?'

12 Concerning his objection to participating in any war, other than a holy war declared by Allah, Ali stated that, 'We [members of the Nation of Islam] are not, according to the Holy Qur'an, to even as much as aid in passing a cup of water to the wounded' (Hauser 1991: 155).

13 Reporters and announcers are fond of making comparisons of black athletes with animals. For example, African American athletes are often referred to as 'horses' or 'work horses', 'bulls', and sometimes simply referred to as 'animals', as in 'he's a real animal, that one'.

References

Ashe, A. R. Jr. (1988) *A Hard Road to Glory: A History of the African-American Athlete*, New York: Warner Books.

Baker, W. (1986) *Jesse Owens: An American Life*, New York: The Free Press.

Bankes, J. (ed.) (1992) *Jack London,* Dubuque, IA: Wm C. Brown Publishers.

Barrow, J. Jr. and Munder, B. (1988), *Joe Louis: 50 Years an American Hero*, New York: McGraw-Hill.

Capeci, D. Jr. and Wilkerson, M. (1983) 'Multifarious Hero: Joe Louis, American Society and Race Relations During the World Crisis, 1935–1945', *Journal of Sport History* 10(3): 5–25.

Carroll, J. (1992) *Fritz Pollard: Pioneer in Racial Advancement*, Urbana, IL: University of Illinois Press.

Chalk, O. (1975) *Pioneers of Black Sport*, New York: Dodd, Mead & Co.

Eitzen, D. and Sage, G. (1996) *Sociology of North American Sport*, sixth edition, Madison, WI: Brown and Benchmark Publishers.

Evans, A. (1985) 'Joe Louis as Key Functionary: White Reactions Toward a Black Champion', *Journal of Black Studios* 11(1): 95–111.

Farley, J. (1995) *Majority-Minority Relations*, third edition, Englewood Cliffs, NJ: Simon and Schuster.

Farr, F. (1964) *Black Champion*, New York: Charles Scribner's Sons.

Foner, P. (1983) *History of Black Americans: from the Emergence of the Cotton Kingdom to the Eve of the Compromise of 1850*, Westport, CT: Greenwood Press.

Franklin, J. and Moss, A. Jr. (1988) *From Slavery to Freedom*, sixth edition, NY: Alfred A. Knoff.

Gilmore, A. (1973) 'Jack Johnson and white women: the national impact'. *Journal of Negro History* 58(Jan): 18–38.

—— (1975) *Bad Nigger!: the National Impact of Jack Johnson*. Port Washington, NY: Kennikat Press.

Harris, O. (1991) 'The Image of the African American in Psychological Journals, 1895–1923', *Black Scholar* 2 (Jan): 25–29.

—— (1993) 'African American Predominance in Sport', in D. Brooks and R. Althouse (eds) *Racism in College Athletics: The African American Athlete's Experience*. Morgantown, WV: Fitness Information Technology, Inc., 51–74.

—— (1995) 'Fritz Pollard', in D. Porter (ed.) *African American Sports Greats: a Bibliographical Dictionary*. Westport, CT: Greenwood Press.

Hauser, T. (1991) *Muhammad Ali: His Life and Times*. New York: Simon and Shuster.

Herz, D. and Altmann, A. (1996) 'Berlin 1936: The Games of the XIth Olympiad', in J. Findling and K. Pelle (eds) *Historical Dictionary of the Modern Olympic Movement*. Westport CT: Greenwood Press, 84–94.

'Huge Salaries "Unfathomable" to Many People', *USA Today*, July 16, 1996, 1A, 2A.

Johnson, J. (1992) *Jack Johnson: In the Ring and Out*. New York: Citadel Press.

Lapchick, R. (1996) *Race in Sport*. Thousand Oaks, CA: Sage Publications Inc.

Louis, J. with Rust, E. and Rust, A., Jr. (1978) *Joe Louis: My Life*. New York: Harcourt Brace Javonovich.

Masotti, L. Hadden, J., Seminatore, K. and Corsi, J. (1970) *A Time to Burn*. Chicago, Il: Rand McNally.

Mead, C. (1985) *Champion: Joe Louis, Black Hero in White America*. New York: Penguin Books.

Olsen, J. (1968) 'The Black Athlete: A Shameful Story. Part I, The Cruel Deception', *Sports Illustrated*. July 1, 1968.

Orr, J. (1969) *The Black Athlete: His Story in American History*. NY: Lion Books.

Peterson, R. (1970) *Only The Ball Was White*. New York: McGraw-Hill.

—— (1990) *Cages to Jumpshots: Pro Basketball's Early Years*. New York: Oxford University Press.

Pinkney, A. (1969) *Black Americans*. Englewood Cliffs, NJ: Prentice-Hall.

Ritchie, A. (1988) *Major Taylor: the Extraordinary Career of a Champion Bicycle Racer*. San Francisco: Bicycle Books.

Roberts, R. (1983) *Papa Jack: Jack Johnson and the Era of White Hopes*. New York: Free Press.

Robinson, J. (1995) *I Never Had it Made: an Autobiography*. Hopewell, NJ: The Ecco Press.

Robinson, S. (1996) *Stealing Home: an Intimate Family Portrait*. New York: HarperCollins Publishers.

Rogosin, D. (1983) *Invisible Men: Life in Baseball's Negro Leagues*. New York, NY: Macmillan Publishing.

Rust, E. and Rust, A. Jr. (1985) *Art Rust's Illustrated History of the Black Athlete*. Garden City, NY: Doubleday and Co.

Sackler, H. (1968) *The Great White Hope: a Play by Howard Sackler*. New York: Dial Press.

Sammons, J. (1988) *Beyond the Ring: The Role of Boxing in American Society*. Urbana, IL: University of Illinois Press.

Shelden, M. (1996) 'Althea Gibson'. in D. Porter (ed.) *African American Sports Greats: a Bibliographical Dictionary*. Westport, CT: Greenwood Press, pp. 110–12.

Spivey, D. (1985) 'Black Consciousness and Olympic Protest Movement, 1964–1980', in D. Spivey (ed.) *Sport in America: New Historical Perspectives*. Westport, CT: Greenwood Press, 239–62.

Strode, W. (1990) *Goal Dust*. Lanham, MD: Madison Books.

Tygiel, J. (1983) *Baseball's Great Experiment: Jackie Robinson and His Legacy*. New York: Oxford University Press.

Wiggins, D. (1985) 'Peter Jackson and the Elusive Heavyweight Championship: A Black Athlete's Struggle Against the Late Nineteenth Century Color Line', *Journal of Sport History* 12(2): 143–68.

Wiggins, W. Jr. (1971) 'Jack Johnson as Bad Nigger: The Folklore of His Life', *The Black Scholar* 2(Jan): 35–46.

Wiggins, W. (1988) 'Boxing's Sambo Twins: Racial Stereotypes in Jack Johnson and Joe Louis Newspaper Cartoons, 1908–1938', *Journal of Sport History* 15(3): 242–54.

9 Disability sport

Gudrun Doll-Tepper

Introduction

During recent years the level of society's awareness of the situation and needs of persons with a disability has grown. This has led to significant changes in legal mandates. An outstanding example of the introduction of new law requirements is the 'Americans with Disabilities Act' which came into effect in the USA in 1990.

The interest and participation of individuals with disabilities in physical education and sport are continually growing. Remarkable changes are evident as far as the level of excellence in sport is concerned: Paralympic Games have become highlights in the world of sport and are already the world's second largest sports event after the Olympic Games. It is essential that persons with disabilities are given the same opportunities and rights as the so-called 'non-disabled' persons, especially in

- physical education in schools
- leisure time/recreational activities
- competitive/high performance sport.

These goals are strongly advocated and supported by professionals all over the world in the area of adapted physical activity and sport for persons with a disability.

The following sections will describe historical and current developments in the sports movement of persons with a disability and focus on selected issues, including the relationship between the Olympic and Paralympic movements and the inclusion of athletes with disabilities in the non-disabled sport movement.

History of the disability sport movement

Historically, there are many examples of individuals with disabilities participating in physical activities and sport (see DePauw and Gavron 1995). Already in 1924, the Comité International des Sports des Sourds (CISS) was founded and in that year the first World Games for the Deaf were held in Paris, France.

In 1944, Sir Ludwig Guttman created the Spinal Injuries Centre at Stoke Mandeville Hospital in Aylesbury, England. He initiated the first Stoke Mandeville Games for people with a spinal column injury in 1948. Although the emphasis in the beginning of the sports movement for persons with physical disabilities was on therapy and rehabilitation, Guttman's vision was to stage games for wheelchair athletes annually in Stoke Mandeville and every four years in the host city of the Olympic Games. His dream was to incorporate sport events for athletes with disabilities into the sports movement for able-bodied athletes and into the Olympic Games. Fifty years later it can be stated that some progress has been made with regard to the realization of this aim; however, a number of obstacles must still be overcome. An essential barrier is the diversification of the organizations into different disability groups. This trend dates back to historical developments after World War II.

Participants in the International Stoke Mandeville Games in 1952 were only those with a spinal injury. These Games were held under the auspices of the newly established International Stoke Mandeville Games Federation (ISMGF). It took another eight years before the first games were held outside England.

In 1960, the first summer Paralympic Games were held right after the Olympic Games in Rome. However, the term 'Paralympic' was not used at that time and the title of the games for athletes with a disability changed every four years. In 1988, the term 'Paralympic Games' was officially introduced and it has been used ever since. In the following text and tables, 'Paralympic Games' and 'Paralympic movement' will be presented as umbrella terms to describe international events and developments of sport for athletes with a disability.

In 1964, after the establishment of the ISMGF Guttman initiated another sport organization for athletes with physical and sensory impairments and disabilities: the ISOD, the International Sport Organization for the Disabled. The International Cerebral Palsy Society was established in 1968, and led to the foundation of the CP-ISRA, Cerebral Palsy-International Sport and Recreation Association, in 1978. Other disability groups also formed their own organizations: the IBSA (International Blind Sports Association) in 1981, and the INAS-FMH (International Sports Federation for Persons with Mental Handicap) in 1986.

In order to combine efforts in the disability sports movement an International Coordinating Committee (ICC) was created in 1982, bringing together the ISMGF, the ISOD, the IBSA, and the CP-ISRA. In 1986, the INAS-FMH became a full member of the ICC. In 1987, the ICC held a seminar in Arnhem, the Netherlands, in which the International Organizations of Sports for the Disabled (IOSD) and the member nations discussed the possibilities of a new world organization that would have a democratic structure and national and regional representation from the IOSD's athletes (see Steadward 1996).

In 1989, at the Inaugural General Assembly, the International Paralympic Committee (IPC) was established in Düsseldorf, Germany. From this inaugural meeting until 1995, all international sport organizations for the disabled were members of the IPC. However in 1995, the Comité International des Sports des Sourds withdrew its membership. Currently the following five international sports organizations for the disabled belong to the IPC: the ISMWSF (the ISMGF changed into the ISMWF – International Stoke Mandeville Wheelchair Sports Federation), the ISOD, the IBSA, the CP-ISRA and the INAS-FMH.

Independent of these developments in the 1960s another sports organization was created in the USA – the Special Olympics. The Special Olympics offers a wide variety of sports activities and competitions for persons with mental retardation. The Special Olympics International (SOI) hosts summer and winter games every four years and receives world-wide recognition for their efforts in promoting the abilities of individuals with intellectual difficulties. Differences between the Special Olympics and the INAS-FMH exist mainly with respect to their philosophical approaches and the focus they place on recreational and competitive activities (Special Olympics) versus élite sport (INAS-FMH). Figure 9.1 provides an overview of the current structure of international sports organizations for persons with a disability.

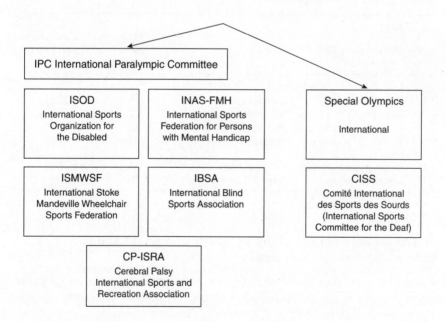

Figure 9.1 International sports organizations for individuals with disabilities.

With regard to the Paralympic Games, Tables 9.1 and 9.2 give an interesting overview of the sites (as compared to the Olympic Games), the number of participating nations and the number of participants.

Table 9.1 Past Summer Paralympics

	Sites		Paralympic participating nations	Paralympic participants
Year	Olympics	Paralympics		
1960	Rome, Italy	Rome, Italy	23	400
1964	Tokyo, Japan	Tokyo, Japan	22	390
1968	Mexico City, Mexico	Tel Aviv, Israel	29	1,100
1972	Munich, Germany	Heidelberg, Germany	44	1,400
1976	Montreal, Canada	Toronto, Canada	42	2,700
1980	Moscow, USSR	Arnhem, the Netherlands	42	2,550
1984	Los Angeles, USA	New York, USA	45	2,500
		Aylesbury, UK	41	1,430
1988	Seoul, Korea	Seoul, Korea	65	4,300
1992	Barcelona	Barcelona, Spain	94	4,000
1992*		Madrid, Spain	73	2,500
1996	Atlanta, USA	Atlanta, USA	121	3,500

* For the first time in history: Paralympic Games for Persons with Mental Handicap.

Table 9.2 Past Winter Paralympics

	Sites		Paralympic participating nations	Paralympic participants
Year	Olympics	Paralympics		
1976	Innsbruck, Austria	Örnskoldsvik, Sweden	14	250
1980	Lake Placid, USA	Geilo, Norway	18	350
1984	Sarajevo, Yugoslavia	Innsbruck, Austria	22	500
1988	Calgary, Canada	Innsbruck, Austria	22	700
1992	Tignes-Albertville, France	Tignes-Albertville, France	24	600
1994	Lillehammer, Norway	Lillehammer, Norway	31	1,000
1996	Nagano, Japan	Nagano, Japan	30	700

Relations between the disability sports movement and the able-bodied sports movement

During the past fifty years the disability sports movement has made great progress. There are three different circles of thought in current discussions concerning the role and impact of the Paralympic Games and the physical achievements of athletes with different disabilities (see Doll-Tepper and Von Selzam 1994):

- Complete inclusion of the Paralympics in the Olympic Games;
- Independence of the Paralympic Movement from the Olympic Games; and
- Co-operation.

Increased formal collaboration between the International Olympic Committee (IOC) and the International Paralympic Committee (IPC), especially with regard to the bidding process and the organization of the Olympic and Paralympic Games, could greatly enhance the value of both events. This idea is also shared by leading experts in the Olympic and Paralympic movements. Fernand Landry (1993), researcher in the field of sports and Olympism, states that the Paralympics as part of the Olympic movement would contribute further to the momentum of social change and would result in a resurfacing of the fundamental values of Olympism. Hans Lindström (1992), member of the IPC Executive Committee, also advocates the integration of sport for athletes with disabilities into the international sports movement for able-bodied athletes, while at the same time safeguarding and preserving the identity of sports for athletes with a disability.

In this context it is important to emphasize efforts made within the International Paralympic Committee to deal with the issues of integration. As early as 1989, important decisions were made with regard to a reduction in the number of classes in each competition and the introduction of an integrated functional classification system. The unanimous support for integration of disabled athletes into able-bodied competitions, such as world championships and Olympic Games, led to the approval of a presidential committee of the IPC. This committee was called the International Committee on Athletes with a Disability (ICI), but later changed its name to the Commission for Inclusion of Athletes with a Disability (CIAD).

One of the main goals of the CIAD is 'to facilitate the successful organization of selected full medal events for athletes with a disability into major international competitions and into the full ecosystem of sport society' (Steadward 1996: 36).

The sports world has witnessed a number of integrated events. For example, as early as the 1984 Olympic Summer and Winter Games, athletes with disabilities competed in a few selected events, but only with exhibition or demonstration status. The President of the IPC, Dr Robert Steadward, states: 'There is certainly no doubt that these demonstration events included in the past Olympic Games have stimulated both public and athlete interest but the ultimate experience in competitive sport is still the quest for the Olympic gold medal. It is this quest for full medal status that CIAD now pursues'. (Steadward 1996: 36–7).

The integration/inclusion issue currently splits the disability sports movement: there is strong and enthusiastic support on the one side and rejection and resistance on the other. In December 1994, the IPC President was given an opportunity to speak on this matter to the IOC Executive Board and the Association of National Olympic Committees (ANOC). The IOC President initiated this meeting, stating that:

> The goal of the Olympic Movement is to contribute to building a peaceful and better world by educating youth through sport practised without discrimination of any kind. Discrimination, therefore, was not acceptable in either spirit or in practice on the basis of disability. Discrimination on the basis of disability was no different and was as objectionable as discrimination on the basis of race, colour, sex, religion or politics.
>
> (Steadward 1994: 3)

The question of whether or not full medal events will be included in the 2000 Olympic Games in Sydney, Australia, remains open. Efforts have currently been made also on national levels to include disability sports events in championship competitions and festivals. These developments may increase the level of public awareness and acceptance of athletes with a disability and thus lead to changes in the sports world both on national and international levels.

International aspects of teaching and research

Professionals all over the world are becoming increasingly involved in creating better living conditions for persons with disabilities. This includes the introduction of new training programmes for professionals, the development of research with improved wheelchairs, prostheses, and sports equipment as well as the reduction of architectural barriers.

In 1973, the International Federation of Adapted Physical Activity (IFAPA), a cross-disciplinary organization, was founded, bringing together specialists in a range of disciplines, including adapted physical activity, disability sport, sports medicine, sports/human movement sciences, psychology, special education, pedagogy, and physical therapy. Only recently regional branches for professionals have been established in different areas of the world; for example, the European Association for Research into Adapted Physical Activity (EARAPA), the Asian Society for Adapted Physical Education and Exercise (ASAPE), and the North American Federation of Adapted Physical Activity (NAFAPA). In addition, improved co-operation has been established between the IFAPA and the International Council of Sport Science and Physical Education (ICSSPE), the International Paralympic Committee (IPC) and other international organizations dealing with sports and movement sciences. Recently, the IPC has also created its own Sport Science Committee in order to serve the needs of athletes with a disability more effectively. The mission of the International Paralympic Committee Sport Science Committee (IPCSSC) is to enhance knowledge about Paralympic Sport through collaboration and co-operation with athletes, coaches, sports administrators, sports medicine personnel and researchers. Members of the IPCSSC include administrators, sports medicine personnel and researchers. The IPCSSC is charged with the needs assessment, development, evaluation, dissemination and application of a body of knowledge about Paralympic Sport relevant to (a) the initiation and continuation of sports participation, (b) sports performance, and (c) retirement from sport. This mission is achieved through activities directed toward integration of theory and practice and the promotion of sports science education.

Important steps have been made with regard to the training of professionals, including the preparation of teachers as well as coaches and volunteers. Pre-service and in-service training programmes have been developed in many parts of the world, aiming to meet the needs of professionals who teach or coach not only in segregated environments but especially in integrated settings.

In 1991, a unique professional training programme was introduced in Europe, based on the Erasmus programme. A European Master's Degree in Adapted Physical Activity is being offered to students from different European universities in order to give them an opportunity to achieve specific expertise in the area of adapted physical activity and sport for persons with a disability. A textbook provides detailed information on the study content (see van Coppenolle *et al.* 1993).

Research in adapted physical activity and disability sport has undergone many changes. Early research in adapted physical activity had a strong focus on physical education settings and dealt mainly with the therapeutic and rehabilitative benefits of physical activity (see Doll-Tepper and DePauw 1996). In the 1970s and 1980s a sport science orientated research emerged focusing on various aspects of sport for persons with a disability. DePauw (1988: 80) summarized research topics in the following seven areas:

- effects of training and competition
- selection of training of coaches, volunteers and officials
- technological advances in sport research
- sociological/psychological aspects of sport
- differences/similarities among athletes with and without a disability
- demographics of disability sport
- legal, philosophical, and historical bases for sport.

Collaborative research projects have been proposed by the IPC Sport Science Committee. The following key research topics were identified (see Doll-Tepper *et al.* 1994):

- classification
- integration
- applicability of existing principles underlying performance
- enhancing sport performance
- barriers to sport participation
- attitudes
- empowerment through sport
- retirement from sport
- inclusion (intellectually disabled, deaf, able-bodied)
- spectatorship
- media
- equity issues (gender, ethnicity, etc.)
- measurement of performance
- process of educating and disseminating information
- sport injury (etiology, prevention, treatment)
- youth sport
- ethical issues
- initial and continuing participation (motivation, adherence).

Attitudes about the inclusion of persons with a disability in physical education and sport in various settings (schools, sports clubs, etc.) play an important role in the overall process of improving the acceptance of these persons in society. In a research study on the attitudes of college students towards the inclusion of individuals with a disability in physical education and sport conducted by DePauw and Goc Karp (1990), it was found that the subjects held negative and stereotyped attitudes. The students showed strong feelings of concern with the outcomes of mainstreaming, especially with regard to time and burden upon teachers. They felt that integration inhibits collaboration, does not improve the individual's self-concept and is not beneficial for able-bodied or disabled persons (see DePauw and Goc Karp 1990).

Two comparative studies carried out in Europe (Downs and Williams (1994) and Doll-Tepper *et al.* (1994a)) found more positive attitudes towards including individuals with physical disabilities and learning problems into physical education and sport. However, strong concern was expressed concerning the lack of preparation during professional training.

Research projects carried out by Rizzo and Vispoel (1991) have shown that perceived teacher competence (i.e. perceived ability to teach students with impairments and disabilities) is significantly related to attitudes. In addition, academic preparation and years of teaching students with disabilities had significant positive correlations with perceived competence. Despite some limitations of the above-mentioned studies, they can be considered as important steps for the further development of professional preparation and they highlight the changes necessary to achieve more acceptance and positive attitudes towards individuals with disabilities. Despite some examples of research in the different subdisciplines of sports science there is still a lack of scientific analysis and discussion on the integration issue.

In this context a remarkable trend can be identified. Most recent publications in disability sport, less research-based but rather focusing on personal experiences, emphasize the aspect of inclusion, as well as the role and importance of sporting excellence in the lives of athletes with a disability. Without a doubt, these case studies and biographies can contribute to improved insight, understanding and acceptance. One of the first to share his personal experience as an athlete with a spinal injury with the larger public was Rick Hansen from Canada who wrote a book about his 'Man in Motion' tour around the world from 1985–7 (Hansen and Taylor 1987). His enthusiasm and encouragement culminate in his famous words: 'Never give up on your dreams'.

Marianne Buggenhagen, a German sportswoman in a wheelchair basketball team, was recognized as Female Athlete of the Year in Germany in 1994. In her recently published biography she describes the various challenges she is facing in everyday life and in the sports world (Buggenhagen 1996). Her experiences can be best summarized by 'empowerment through sport' and they are in no way restricted to very few athletes with disabilities. Reinhild Möller, one of the most remarkable German amputee athletes both in summer and winter sports, has competed for almost two decades in the international disability sport arena. After graduating from high school where she always took part in regular physical education, she decided – after a short interlude in which she was trained as an optician – to register for a master's degree programme in physical education at the University of Heidelberg, Germany. In an article entitled 'What do you mean by disabled?' she reports on her experiences as a world champion and states: 'In those days: I was disabled, I was a girl, a girl from the countryside. Today I am not disabled, I am a woman, a woman of the world' (Möller 1996: 237). Her four gold medals in skiing in the Paralympic Winter Games in Lillehammer, Norway, in 1994, opened new doors to her: she was given a ten-year sponsorship contract of one million dollars. Success stories like these have contributed to a changing perception of disability sport by the media and the public. However, many obstacles must still be overcome.

Vanlandewijck and Chappel have pointed out the purposes of classification: to provide an equitable starting point for competition for every class of athletes, to stimulate the broadest possible participation of people in competitive sport, and to prevent 'dropping out' by severely disabled athletes (see Vanlandewijck and Chappel 1996).

From the perspective of wheelchair sports the classification issue is presented as follows: The goal in the classification of wheelchair athletes is to enable each competitor, even those with the most severe disability, to compete in a fair manner with other competitors who have similar degrees of disability. There is also an ongoing discussion about classification in summer and winter sports for athletes with physical disabilities and sensory impairments, especially visual impairments and blindness.

All disability groups are affected by changes in the classification system; however, it must be emphasized that specific problems occur for this with a 'minimal disability'. Steadward (1996) states: 'Some of these individuals may not be disadvantaged at all as technology improves and standards quickly escalate' (Steadward 1996: 34).

If a person wishes to participate in international sports events for athletes with a disability, he or she has to have a minimal disability as defined by the different disability sports organizations. These definitions may differ for each sport. In order to maintain credibility, sports must clearly define eligibility criteria for competition (see De Potter 1994) and these criteria are currently being developed by each sports committee within the IPC (see Vanlandewijck and Chappel 1996).

There are also concerns being expressed about the classification system in general. For example, the International Sports Federation for Persons with a Mental Handicap (INAS-FMH) states:

> The aim should be to accord all individuals the same rights and freedoms. A person with a physical, sensory or mental handicap or impairment should not be denied the same rights as someone without such an impairment. The 'able-bodied' sportsmen and women compete in open competition. There is no classification system. The Olympics are open to all but only the best in the world compete. In the case of those with an intellectual impairment, INAS-FMH believes that competitions should be equally open at Paralympic and World Games. Once an athlete has been registered with INAS-FMH there is no need for classification. In this respect, the position of the mentally handicapped/intellectually impaired differs from those athletes who have a physical or sensory impairment where classification is essential to ensure fair competition.
>
> (INAS-FMH 1994: 2).

Classification is not the only issue on which INAS-FMH has challenged other IPC disability sports groups. The integration of athletes with mental handicaps into the Paralympic Games has also been a hotly contested issue. Their integration in the Atlanta games in 1996 was an important step for their world-wide acceptance as élite athletes. However, there is ongoing controversy among representatives of the different international sport organizations for the disabled as far as the participation of athletes with mental handicaps in world championships and Paralympic Games is concerned (see Steadward 1996).

This chapter can only reflect some of the current issues and challenges. Detailed reports can be taken from publications such as Doll-Tepper *et al.* (1990), Steadward *et al.* (1994), DePauw and Gavron (1995) and Doll-Tepper and DePauw (1996).

Disability sport is also challenged by the interesting question of whether or not able-bodied athletes should be allowed to participate in sports events for athletes with disabilities. To date, this 'reverse integration' is restricted to recreational forms of sports participation. In Canada, however, able-bodied athletes have competed at league level since 1986 and at national championship level since 1992. The German Wheelchair Sports Federation has just approved a change in its constitution and bye-laws that allows able-bodied athletes to participate in wheelchair sports. Nevertheless, on the international sports scene able-bodied athletes have no access to events for athletes with disabilities. The IPC General Assembly in 1993 formally agreed that able-bodied athletes should not be given access to international competitions. These developments were not seen as integration and are therefore neither encouraged nor introduced (see Lindström 1994).

Future perspectives

The International Paralympic Committee (IPC) is developing closer co-operation with the International Olympic Committee (IOC) and the international sport federations to gain international and Olympic recognition for athletes with disabilities in sport at the highest level. However, only a very small percentage of the world-wide population with disabilities is physically active. In many parts of the world there are only very limited opportunities for persons with disabilities to participate in sport at all performance levels, and very few athletes with a disability have achieved excellence in sport. Changes can only be implemented when psychosocial and architectural barriers are removed. In summary, barriers may be overcome by:

- improving opportunities for access in schools, in the community and in sport clubs and organizations;
- encouraging positive attitudes toward persons with disabilities in all areas of society, and specifically in physical education and sport;
- increasing awareness of the needs, interest and competence of individuals with disabilities; and
- eliminating prejudices within the community against individuals with disabilities.

With regard to élite sport for athletes with a disability, there are also many barriers that have to be overcome before the gap between able-bodied and disability sport, or Olympic and Paralympic sport, can be bridged. The formation of the IPC represents an important step in this direction, because it has a sports-specific, rather than a disability-specific, orientation. Furthermore, it aims to establish a policy for integrating athletes with disabilities into the generic sports movement. At the same time, all efforts are being made to preserve the identity of the sports movement for athletes with a disability. Different visions for the future of the Paralympic movement exist, some aiming at closer co-operation with the IOC and the able-bodied sports movement and others advocating the autonomy of the disability sports movement. Challenges exist with regard to a rapprochement of these movements, but also to identification of common goals of the different disability sports organizations within the Paralympic movement. In addition, similarities and differences (for example between INAS-FMH and Special Olympics) must be identified and discussed. Moreover, philosophical positions concerning the sports movement of the deaf and their role within the world of sport also need further clarification.

We are challenged as professionals in the field of adapted physical education/activity by facing up to the following needs:

- to provide physical education for all children with disabilities in all types of schools and especially in so-called mainstreamed classes and schools;
- to modify the curricula in schools, in teachers' colleges and universities where a teacher's preparation and training takes place; and
- to improve in-service training in order to qualify physical education teachers and other professionals to deal appropriately with the needs of persons with disabilities.

Initiatives are already underway in many universities world-wide which need to be further implemented and extended to integrate specific areas of adapted physical education/activity and sport for persons with disabilities into practical and theoretical courses, for example integrating wheelchair basketball into basketball courses for university students in sports science/movement sciences.

In some sports science courses aspects of adapted physical activity are being added to the curricula. A few of these examples include:

- the historical development of sport for the disabled/the Paralympic movement (in sports history classes);
- therapeutic approaches for individuals with psychological problems and motivational factors in athletes with a disability (in sports psychology classes);
- the pros and cons of integrating children with disabilities into regular schools and physical education classes (in sports pedagogy classes);
- sociological aspects of élite sport for athletes with a disability (in sports sociology classes); and
- analysis of motor behaviour of individuals with impairments and disabilities (in sports medicine/exercise physiology classes).

It may also be necessary to introduce new qualifications on a post-graduate basis, such as the previously described European Master's Degree in Adapted Physical Activity. However, we not only need specialists in adapted physical education/activity, we also need to ensure that all teachers and coaches have basic knowledge and experience in 'physical activity and disability'. In addition, coaches for top-level sports and recreation specialists also need to be trained in adapted physical activities and sport for individuals with disabilities.

In connection with modifications to professional training, intensified efforts in interdisciplinary research on a national and an international level must be undertaken. Important steps in this direction can be expected from professionals who increasingly co-operate in international projects and organizations. The biennial symposia of IFAPA, focusing on current trends in adapted physical activity and the recently introduced Paralympic Congresses, can serve as important forums for the exchange of expertise.

If we successfully improve the training of professionals, encourage inter-disciplinary and multidisciplinary scientific collaboration and offer more attractive and advanced programmes for individuals with disabilities – especially in integrated settings – out efforts will contribute to an important societal goal as the third millennium approaches: better quality of life for all individuals in all facets of society, including physical education and sport.

References

Buggenhagen, M. (1996) *Ich bin von Kopf bis Fuß auf Leben eingestellt*, Berlin.

De Potter, J.-C. (1994) 'Adapted physical activity at the dawn of the 21st century' in Yabe, K., Kusano, K. and Nakata, H. (eds) *Adapted Physical Activity: Health and Fitness*, Tokyo: Springer, 257–63.

DePauw, K. (1998) 'Sport for Individuals with Disabilities: Research opportunities', in *Adapted Physical Activity Quarterly* 5(1): 80–9.

DePauw, K. and Gavron, S., (1995) *Disability and Sport*, Champaign, IL: Human Kinetics.

DePauw, K. and Goc Karp, G. (1990) 'Attitudes of selected college students toward including disabled individuals in integrated settings', in Doll-Tepper, G. *et al.* (eds), *Adapted Physical Activity – An Interdisciplinary Approach*, Berlin/Heidelberg/New York.

Doll-Tepper, G. and DePauw, K. (1996) 'Theory and practice of adapted physical activity: research perspectives', in *Sport Science Review, Adapted Physical Activity* 5(1): 1–11.

Doll-Tepper, G. and Von Selzam, H. (1994) 'Towards 2000 – the Paralympics', in Steadward, R., Nelson, E., and Wheeler, G. (eds) *The Outlook – Vista '93*, Edmonton: Rick Hansen Centre, 478–87.

Doll-Tepper, G., Dahms, C, Doll, B. and Von Selzam, H. (eds) (1990) *Adapted Physical Activity – An Interdisciplinary Approach*, Berlin/Heidelberg/New York.

Doll-Tepper, G., Schmidt-Gotz, E., Lienert, C., Döen, U. and Hecker, R. (1994a)

Einstellungen von Sportlehrkräften zur Integration von Menschen mit Behinderungen in Schule und Verein, Cologne.

Doll-Tepper, G. *et al.* (1994b) *The Future of Sport Science in the Paralympic Movement*, Berlin.

Downs, P. and Williams, T. (1994) 'Student attitudes toward integration of people with disabilities in activity settings: a European comparison', in *APAQ* 11(1): 32–43.

Hansen, R. and Taylor, J. (1987) *Rick Hansen – Man in Motion,* Vancouver/ Toronto.

INAS-FMH (1994), *International Sports Federation for Persons with Mental Handicap, Eligibility and Classification*, Härnösand, INAS-FMH Publ., 1–4.

Landry, F. (1993) 'Paralympism, Olympism and the sport for handicapped people', in Once, F. (ed.), *I Paralympic Congress Barcelona 1992*, Barcelona, 28–59.

Lindström, H. (1992) 'Integration of sport for athletes with disabilities into sport programs for able-bodied athletes', in *Palaestra* (spring) 28–32: 58–9.

—— (1994) 'Integration of sport for athletes with disabilities on international level – perspectives for the future', in *Proceedings of the Second Paralympic Congress*, Lillehammer and Oslo: Royal Norwegian Ministry of Cultural Affairs, 273–84.

Möller, R. (1996) 'Was heißt hier behindert? Erfahrungen einer Weltmeisterin, in Pfister, G. (ed.) *Fit und gesund mit Sport, Frauen in Bewegung*, Berlin, 237–41.

Rizzo, T. and Vispoel, W. (1991) 'Physical Educators' Attributes and Attitudes Toward Teaching Students with Handicaps', *APAQ* 8: 4–11.

Steadward, R. (1994) 'Athletes with Disabilities and their Quest for Olympic Inclusion', paper presented at the Joint Assembly of the IOC Executive Board and the Association of National Olympic Committees, Atlanta.

Steadward, R. (1996) 'Integration and sport in the Paralympic movement', *Sport Science Review, Adapted Physical Activity*, 5(1): 26–41.

Steadward, R., Nelson, E. and Wheeler, G. (1994) *The Outlook – Vista '93*, Edmonton: Rick Hansen Centre.

Van Coppenolle *et al.* (eds) (1993) *European Master's Degree in Adapted Physical Activity – Textbook*, Leuven and Amersfoort.

Vanlandewijck, Y. and Chappel, R., (1996) 'Integration and Classification Issues in Competitive Sports for Athletes with Disabilities', in *Sport Science Review, Adapted Physical Activity*, 5(1): 65–88.

10 The homosexual and homoerotic in sport

Arnd Krüger

Sexuality is one of the variables of human experience, sex one of its constants. Sexual desire has stimulated humans at all places and in all times, but the object of that desire varies from culture to culture and from era to era. Most people are right handed, but some are not. Most people are heterosexual, some are not. The question of sport and sexuality has long been a taboo theme; this was the case for heterosexuality and even more so for homosexuality. But the phenomenon has been around for a long time, so it has its rightful place in this book.

It is important first of all to differentiate between homosexual feelings, acts, behaviour, moral positions and the reactions of society towards them (Ruse 1988). In our postmodern era there are many more possible views of this phenomenon than a hetero- and a homosexual, a male or a female one. We should therefore be careful in labelling people one way or another, as much as this might provide voyeuristic pleasure (Gutterman 1994; Urry 1990).

In today's world there is a good chance that between 5 and 10 per cent of any western cultural is homosexual by most people's definition. As gender relations are culturally constructed, I am not concerned here with them in different cultural traditions. According to the Kinsey Reports (Kinsey *et al.* 1948; 1953), as many as 10 per cent of the population is homosexual to some extent, but the figures depend upon the definition of 'gay'. With other definitions other figures are discussed locally (with the possible bias of self-reporting) with 2.3 per cent and 1.1 per cent (Muir 1993), while a more recent representative figure for Britain is given as 4 per cent (David 1997).

Athletes are average people in many of their outlooks, but as they are more concerned with their body, the chances are that the rate of homo-eroticism among them is even somewhat higher. So, take twenty-two soccer players, one referee and two of his or her assistants on the field, statistically at least one if not two are gay. If you have 10,000 spectators, more than 500 can safely be assumed to be homosexuals. What does that mean for the sport, what for the visual or practical experience of homosexuals and the rest?

The male athlete, particularly the weightlifter and body-builder (Klein 1993) can be considered a foremost gay icon. Dancers, too, are often considered homosexuals as they find their way in a mostly female world. The tomboy female physical education teacher and athlete is often considered a lesbian *per se*. Homosexuality in sport has long been considered a taboo topic that was whispered but not written about. Gay men in sports might even be underrepresented as they subvert the objective that 'sport makes a boy into a man', while lesbians might be overrepresented in sports as competitive sport turns girls into conflicted women (Lenskyj 1994). Self-realization and the celebration of the beauty of the body are often themes of homoerotic literature. They are also at the core of what much of sport is about. It is therefore surprising how little of sports-related literature deals with our topic.

Just as much as gender is culturally constructed, so are gender relations. The role of sexuality in society is changing perpetually, so is the role of sport, as has been demonstrated in other chapters in this book. Over time, sport has become one of the major agents in the social production of masculinity (Whitson 1990) – and most women define themselves with the help of their body, though not always their athletic body. We should, however, be aware that the cultural construction of gender in western cultures relies upon the production of sexuality as a stable and oppositional heterosexuality. Gender then only exists in the service of the conventional dichotomy of heterosexism (Butler 1993).

The one-dimensional Kinsey scale of zero (heterosexual) to six (homosexual) has its advantages of describing many phenomena which cannot simply be classified as homo- or heterosexual. Yet these scales leave out the multidimensional qualitative side which cannot be quantified by such data as how many orgasms one has had with one sex or another (McWhirter *et al.* 1990) over a given period of time. Particularly in such activities as competitive sport which are often sexually segregated, the question arises of what kind of homosexuality one is actually talking about (Altman *et al.* 1988). In the Kinsey survey, 37 per cent reported one or more same-sex orgasms after adolescence (4, 5 and 6 on the scale). Yet, there are many more *soft* facts of homoeroticism and male or female bonding that need to be considered. Looking at it through the eyes of a scientist and leaving out interviews, subjective realizations, and the artists' descriptions and depictions will not really do justice to the phenomenon. 'Art is more than mere science: where science sees life through dead systems, art sees it in its unity and makes of it an experience – the only form in which we can really grasp, really feel life' (Hewitt 1996: 131). In this chapter we will look at some of the reasons why homosexuality and homosexual behaviour have so seldom been dealt with in the context of sport and the human body although it is such a prevalent theme (Pronger 1990).

Sport is part of culture, culture is concerned with 'shared meanings' (Hall 1997). Meaning comes with naming a phenomenon. The term 'homosexual' is relatively recent. It was coined by Karl Maria Kertbeny in the context of a reform of the Prussian legal code (1869) and spread rapidly in all European languages. We should, however, not assume that homosexuality was invented as a fixed category with the usage of the term. There are many facts that indicate a gay culture has existed since antiquity in our civilization. In the context of sports history we should look at gay history just as much as at homophobia and other forms of heterosexual prejudice. Much of the knowledge of the continuity of gay history has been suppressed and censored, and little if any has been dealt with in the context of sport prior to the 1960s. But to understand the function of sport in the construction of gender roles, we also have to look at gay culture to acquire a better understanding (Norton 1997).

Can an event in sport such as wrestling have the same meaning for a homo- or a heterosexual wrestler? The 'culture industry' which makes use of the originality and creativity of the sports world to generate the image of standardization and pseudo-individuality (Negus 1997) has a hard time coping with such phenomena as homosexuality in sport. For a long time the phenomenon has been marginalized, negated or refuted. The tradition of the heterosexual male as main provider for an independent sport system was invented in the late nineteenth century (Hobsbawm and Ranger 1983). Yet it can be postulated that there have always been gays and lesbians in sport. Like any minority, they might have had a different perspective of sport which in turn emphasizes the relativity of any subjective viewpoint. The question of homosexuality is therefore useful to understand better the relativity of any view of sport (Krüger 1995a).

The supposed unity of the sport system, the seemingly internal homogeneity, which is often treated as being natural, is but a cultural construction which needs to exclude – sometimes only tacitly – some, the silenced and unspoken other, in order to function. Laclau (1990) argues in following Derrida that the construction of a social identity is an act of power which establishes a hierarchy often violently and enforces hegemonic thought. According to Foucault (*Quel Corps?* 1975) we should be aware that a body technique such as sport is an instrument of power and that the control of sexuality is yet another powerful tool to achieve homogeneity (Foucault 1988/90). In following Hall (1980), I therefore propose that we should read the question of homosexual behaviour in sport from an oppositional position and ask why society needs such acts of discrimination, power and liminality to assure heterosexual totalitarianism. A dominant hegemonic position which marginalizes sexual orientation based on mutual consent between adults invites a suspicion that something else is being attempted. Higgins (1996) referring to Britain calls this the 'heterosexual dictatorship'. Butler (1989) therefore proposes to make 'gender trouble' to undermine the old binary restrictions (male/female, active/passive, etc.) 'Queer studies' are the result, as they are concerned not just with gay history and culture, but also with the present struggle against discrimination and for the civil rights of persons with a different sexual orientation. The multiplicity of possible sexuality which occurs in non-heterosexual contexts cannot by itself overturn the hegemonic heterosexual/reproductive discourse, but may be capable of disrupting and weakening it. The butch lesbian, the drag queen, the *femme* lesbian, the macho gay all offer forms of sexuality which radically problematize the hegemony of a unidimensional heterosexuality.

Interest in the role of the body in social thought is a relatively recent phenomenon (Shilling 1993), yet the phenomena have always been around and will be looked at in our context from antiquity onward. An attempt to put the history of body language into cultural terms without looking at homosexuality in sport (Blake 1996) is bound to be inconclusive. To understand the particularities of modern gender relations and orientations we have to look at the development of modern thought and culture, especially as they relate to the body and body techniques such as sport (Featherstone and Turner 1995).

We should also be cautious not to take our twentieth-century notion of homosexuality and transfer it into the past. Distinguishing homosexual from heterosexual men or women is a concept that has existed at least since antiquity, but we have to be aware that writing the history of homosexuality and sport as a history of power relations is not identical with writing the history of homosexuality as physical desire. Just as we can identify the erotic nature of the body in action and in sport over time (Guttmann 1993), just as certain traits in athletic behaviour like the search for memorable and recordable performances has always been present (Carter and Krüger 1990), so we can discuss the homosexual as part of athletic behaviour.

Antiquity

The term *lesbian* is derived from the fact that in Greek antiquity female homosexual behaviour was frequent on the Greek island of Lesbos. Sappho, one of the more famous lesbians of antiquity, and many other lesbians came from that island. Male as well as female homosexual behaviour was neither unusual, nor discriminated against in classical Greece, provided that it occurred by mutual consent (Dover 1978). Many of the finest love songs of antiquity have long been falsely interpreted as being heterosexually oriented, while they were gay in reality (Snyder 1991). Aristotle believed that some people were naturally inclined to homosexual behaviour (*Nichomachean Ethics*) and speculated why some adult men prefer to be penetrated anally. Is this the origin of homosexuality as a distinct *culture*?

The centre of male daily activity was the gymnasium, where physical as well as intellectual training of the future elite took place – homosexual relations there were often seen in conjunction with physical activity.

Pederasty, sexual relations of an adult man with a young boy, was considered the highest form of love by Plato, who was not only one of the best-known philosophers of his time, but also an Olympic champion. The Greek who enjoyed physical beauty as an important asset considered the well-formed body of the young male athlete, combined with vigour and a skill in the arts, one of society's highest values. Pindar's (518–438 BC) *Olympian Odes* that celebrate the victors of the ancient Olympic Games – and which have inspired generations of modern schoolboys and athletes, including Pierre De Coubertin – also show that homoeroticism, male physical attractiveness and athleticism were one and the same for the Greeks (Pronger 1995). At the Olympic Games and many other athletic competitions, no female spectators were admitted as the performances of the beautiful nude males were reserved for male spectatorship as undisturbed homoerotic pleasure.

Swimming and bathing have a long tradition of being related to athleticism (Krüger 1984) and movement therapy (Krüger 1995b) Yet Sprawson (1992) offers many examples of the erotic pleasures of men swimming naked with other men and boys through the ages. The gay saunas of the twentieth century seem quite commonplace compared to the myriad pleasures of classical antiquity. Tiberius enjoyed swimming between rose petals while specially trained naked boys swam up his legs and nibbled.

Theocritus (*c.* 308–240 BC), whose homoerotic idylls focus largely on the pains of lost or frustrated love, describes in his *Hylas* (Idyll 13) – one of the most famous homosexual lyrics of the ancient world – the relationship of Hercules to 'golden haired Hylas'. Even the strong demi-god, hero of generations of strongmen and body-builders, could not resist the beautiful boy. Does the idyll thus subvert the heroic virtue of the ancient Greek, or does it show that we cannot apply our present-day value system to what we know of antiquity (Mastronarde 1968)? Hylas drowned when he was trying to fetch water for his lover as the nymphs of the river fell in love with him and wanted to keep him. 'The struggles and frustrations of (homosexual) love stand in for the mortal peril of heroic combat', concludes Halperin (1983), as Hercules – unable to save his lover – went mad from grief. Theocritus thus shows that homosexual love is stronger than the physical might of Hercules, a demi-god and the greatest hero of his time. Theocritus' idylls are the basis of the pastoral tradition of homoerotic plays which have been with us since then (Frontain 1995b).

There are hundreds of works of all genres in Ancient Greek dealing with the sexual relations of men with boys (Licht 1993). The most important theoretical work is probably Plato's *Symposion* (Banquet) in which the men present discuss the power of Eros, the god of love. This is a unique piece which celebrates the different forms of love and sexual relations: Aristophanes defines love as the search for the other half of the once unified human – separated in two parts by the gods. And that other half may be of the same sex or of the other. Socrates defines love as the search for immortality, which puts the seeds for children in the womb of women and fills similarly the soul of boys and youths with wisdom and virtue. The really good teacher must also be a good paedophile and love the boys he is teaching. A lover of men must be more manly than a lover of women. For Socrates the love of boys was a step in the right direction, but the love of beauty in general was more important. Marriage, according to Lucian's *Erotes*, was considered a life-pressing necessity, while the love of boys was the privilege of the wise. With the reception of Hellenism in the public schools and universities of the late nineteenth century (the basis for the invention of modern international competitive sport, including the Olympic Games), what of this Greek homosexual behaviour was also received? (Dowling 1994)

In practical terms we know much about Greek homosexuality (and some Roman) from the work of Plutarch who gives rich detail as to who had homosexual relations with whom and in which way. He praises the Athenians and Spartans, as here homosexuality took place among equals, while in Elis, Thebes and Crete homosexual acts were performed with slaves as well. In his *Lycurgus* he also praises the lesbianism of the Spartan ladies. As the Spartans were considered the best warriors, male and female homosexuality was expressly linked with success in war. Male bonding as the basis for military success has been with us ever since.

Roman and Greek cultures differed drastically with regard to the acceptance of homosexual behaviour. In Ancient Greece educational mentorship – pedagogy – went along automatically with pederasty and was supposed to prepare the free-born youth for active duties as citizens. Consequently, homosexual relationships with male slaves were considered inappropriate and unacceptable. The Roman paradigm was the direct opposite. A nation of conquerors, the Romans approved of sexual relations with purchased or captured slaves of either sex. Cato complained, about 200 BC that a beautiful slave boy cost as much as a farm. Homosexual relations with a free-born youth compromised the boy's manhood and civic status, as one should never take a passive role in male relations. In a macho society, the argument that having been a *catamite* will always show and instil in that person the subordinate spirit of a woman, was made against Cataline, Pompey, Caesar, Marcus Antonius etc. On the other hand, the Romans admired Greek culture and eventually took over many forms of Greek sensuality. It can safely be assumed that on the whole the Romans were inclined towards bisexuality. Ovid's *Metamorphoses* are full of sexual stories which freely change from homo- to heteroerotics. The emphasis was not on the gender of a man's sexual companion, but on his role in that sexual relationship. As long as a man took the active part, his status and masculinity were favoured. We therefore also find some of the most misogynist works of all in Roman literature (Crompton 1995).

The Judeo-Christian tradition was quite ambivalent in the beginning. The Old Testament as basis of the Jewish faith is also the history of the

Jewish people attempting to attain its identity among surrounding peoples. The Old Testament therefore condemns *excessive* homosexual behaviour (male or female) as this was the trait of some of the neighbours of the Jewish people who used temple prostitutes of both sexes. This can particularly be seen in the context of the destruction of Sodom (Gen. 19: 1–11) whose citizens were known for their male homosexual behaviour in conjunction with their religious ceremonies. On the other hand, there are rich descriptions of love between men 'surpassing the love of women' (2 Sam. 1: 19–26) as in the case of David. This made Michelangelo's statue of David 'the Western world's most pervasive symbol of male beauty and one of the staples of gay popular culture' (Frontain 1995a) – used as an insider's marker for the gay movement. There is little in the Old Testament that has been interpreted in a lesbian way one way or the other although Ruth 1: 16 is open to positive lesbian interpretation.

In the New Testament neither Jesus nor any of the apostles spoke up against homosexual behaviour, but St. Paul in letters to the Corinthians and the Romans (Boswell, 1980) interprets Paul's advice as being directed against excessive homosexual behaviour and not against *any* homosexual activity. There is little in the New Testament that has been interpreted in a lesbian way. Again, the question of finding one's own identity among religious communities of the time seemed to have been in the forefront of the interest of Paul and later church fathers. When the Judeo-Christian tradition developed eventually into a strong force against homosexuality, reinterpreting the Bible in a way that seemed to condemn the vice of sodomy, we have to look for the reasons.

Middle Ages

As homosexual behaviour was associated with paganism, there was more and more opposition against it from Church fathers. Augustinus speaks in his *Confessiones* against any sexual activity outside of marriage and rejects explicitly homosexual behaviour, which he considers to be against nature. The Rules of Clemens of Alexandria of the third century become the codex according to which many human activities were interpreted. For him sexuality for other purposes than procreation is against the laws of nature (Sommer 1990). With the close connection between the Church and the Roman Empire from the fourth century onwards, acts of homosexuality were legally penalized. Emperor Constantine – who also finally prohibited the ancient Olympic Games as pagan rites – condemned it, but was vague about the punishment. The *Codex Theodosianus* of 438 decreed that homosexual men should be burned in public. The death penalty in various forms remained the norm for the following centuries, particularly as the occurrence of homosexual behaviour was seen in conjunction with the plague, poor harvests and hunger – God was ravaging the land in the same way as he had destroyed Sodom. This Biblical text remained the main argument for centuries. It was frequently discussed in church laws, by the major theologians and included into the law of the land. Burning was part of Roman Law and as such became Carolinian Law of Charles the Bald and by this the basis for all Western law. As all natural order was part of God's creation (Thomas Aquinas), unnatural acts of devils and witches, such as homosexuality, were punished by excommunication and burning at the stake. Homosexual behaviour was often equated with heresy and persecuted as such (Spreitzer 1988). Although the rules were not always enforced, it laid the basis for homosexuality being a *vice* that is used as a form of strategic denunciation right up to our time.

Renaissance

The emergence of the modern spirit in the Renaissance went side by side with reception of antiquity and rejection of the rigour of the Middle Ages, condemning many practices without bothering to understand them. Individualization also meant that the differences in such private matters as homosexuality were more widely discussed and not just taken as acts of Satan (Gerard and Hekma 1989). With the reception of antiquity, 'Socratic love' became an accepted formula for what had been around Italy for a long time: the master/servant relationship often had sexual connotations. It was an accepted practice that the apprentice in a shop, the boy helping an artist, or the page of a nobleman was also having a sexual relationship with his master. As long as the master also supported the youth and did not employ force to rape the boy, nobody was concerned.

Homosexuality was discussed in major Renaissance texts. Castiglione, the author of the famous book on education, including physical education, *Il Cortegiano* (1528), questioned the concept of Socratic love, the non-physical love of beauty and wisdom. If Socrates was searching for wisdom, why did he prefer to have young boys in his bed and not old men, although the latter would certainly have been wiser? If he was searching for beauty, why were they in bed at night although in the daytime Socrates would certainly have a better chance to recognize beauty and wisdom? Questioning Socrates' and Plato's sexual behaviour and alleging their homosexuality made the 'vice' much more respectable.

Venice had a homosexual subculture that was, on the one hand, involved in prostitution, smuggling and robbery, and, on the other, in male bonding in such traditional male preserves as the army, the navy, the monasteries, the schools (Ruggiero 1985). In Florence sodomy was a widespread phenomenon that warranted quite a differentiated penal system: youths under the age of 15 received no penalty, up to the age of 25 only a mild sentence, while above it was much higher. It also was staggered according to social rank. 'Sodomy' is a wide term. In contemporary usage it refers to anal intercourse, whether homo- or heterosexually conducted. In historical usage 'sodomy' denotes a class of mostly same-sex non-reproductive sex acts, for which there were no other terms at the time. It included sex acts conducted with animals. Religious, medical, literary and legal traditions have often referred to it as *non nominandum*, the 'love that does not speak its name' (Lord Douglas), 'of which least mention is best' (Craft 1994). When in 1515 the winner of the annual *palio* (horse race) was a citizen of Siena nicknamed Sodoma and his supporters ran through the city shouting and singing his name, the police stepped in to restore the peace – as the unmentionable word had been yelled in what was considered an act of blasphemy. What sort of sodomy was he conducting with his mare? Handelman (1984) has shown that the religious symbolism of the *palio* with the prayers for the help of the Virgin Mary symbolically transforms the mare into the Mother of Jesus.

When the laws against sodomy were, however, really enforced, an exodus of prominent taxpayers after 1550 soon ended the enforcement in the city state, as it would have gone bankrupt without their taxes. The relaxation of their vigilance against homosexuality, however, did not indicate that society was less against the 'vice', it just made sure that it was not performed any more in public. Famous artists like Leonardo da Vinci, Botticelli, Michelangelo, Cellini etc. all had been arrested at one time or another for public sexual relations with boys, but a city that enjoyed its artists did not fine them too harshly in order to avoid driving them away. Dancing and fencing schools were also seen as the centre of sodomy as young single active men were looking at each others' movements – and that often ended in gay relations (Rocke 1996).

The recent discourse about the historical construction of homosexuality is concerned with the question of when homosexuals began to identify themselves as a different category, when they were being seen as a distinct minority. Was it through the medical discourse of the middle and end of the nineteenth century when the term homosexuality was coined? Throughout the Middle Ages only single-act sinners were identified. In the Renaissance, with the possibility of freer expression, homosexuality was widely discussed (although mostly referring to historical examples of Greek antiquity), but the homosexual drive was not recognized, as recognition is the first step towards legitimization – even if recognition is only made for the sake of condemnation.

In that respect Foucault was right when stating that the condemnation of homosexuality by the medical discourse of the nineteenth century was the basis for its legitimized existence. But the Renaissance shows that the social discourse made homosexuals distinctly different at least 350 years before the medical discourse revealed it. The cinquecento understood not only the connections between homosexuality and homoeroticism, but also linked homoeroticism with Platonic and Socratic love and sodomy. That should have made sodomy central to Platonism, which was, however, a yet unthinkable taboo. Platonic love therefore had to be for the time being within non-sexual heterosexuality – and never homosexuality (Dall'Orto 1989).

The situation in England was slightly different in that the discussion about sodomy took place a century later and from a different perspective. The English empiricists simply had to realize that there were homosexuals, that they were not sodomites dancing with Satan to overthrow heaven, but that they were friends and neighbours who happened to have a different taste and not a different creed. Neither was there more public discussion about homosexuality, nor many court cases – the English had their sexual relations more at home than in public and therefore could ignore it much longer. When it was put on stage or in poetry it could be taken lightly, but the artistic discourse, for example, in Shakespeare, prepared the ground for some considerable changes (Smith 1991). The appearance in England of a separate homosexual culture and a distinctive homosexual identity was part of a wider picture of society that had been transformed into modern thinking (Bray 1982). With John Locke the individuality of the separate case was no longer what was searched for, but the abstract idea of things beyond the particular case.

The shift towards the rational explanation of phenomena formerly inexplicable can also be seen in the area of physical activity and treatment of the body. While for Nicholas Wynman (1538) swimming was a wonder, unnatural of man (swimming was therefore used as a test of whether witchcraft was at play), Everard Digby (1587) wrote a demysticized biomechanical study of swimming which was concerned with gravity, drag and the most effective way to define and teach the *art*. The phenomenon was explained in natural terms and no longer were the separate occurrences described as separate unexplainable acts (Krüger 1984).

Enlightenment

In the following centuries much depended upon the country and the rules as to whether the climate was positive or negative with regard to homosexual behaviour. Sodomy and debauchery were always considered sins, but how did one deal with them? While the Prussian court of Frederick the Great was tolerant in this respect – Frederick and his brother were thought to have homosexual interests themselves – Cromwell's rule was intolerant against all vices (Fone 1995). Voltaire, French philosopher at the Prussian court, had a short homosexual encounter and did not enjoy it. He treats homosexuals as a separate species and includes them in his *Dictionnaire philosophique* (1764) under *L'Amour nommé Socratique*. Here he also included a long international list of famous pederasts, thus establishing the identity as a group – and not just listing certain acts.

In this Voltaire also made a grammatical error which became a standing joke for almost the next 100 years: Gesner (1753), one of the better known professors of the classics at the prestigious Göttingen Academy in the Kingdom of Hanover, had given a lecture at the Göttingen Academy (in Latin) on *Socrates Sanctus Paederasta*. Gesner defended Socrates and Plato against the interpretation that they were physically making love to boys and – following the argument of Erasmus of Rotterdam – concluded that the 'Holy Socrates' was just loving them spiritually. Voltaire, who had spent much time at the sexually permissive court of Potsdam and had obviously not read the lecture, just knew the title and translated it with a grammatical error into *Socrates, the Holy Pederast*. Thus, *le Saint Bourge* became the joke of eighteenth century academia when talking about male homosexuality (Derks 1990).

The French court was considered effeminate, but the French Revolution erased all laws against public homosexual behaviour – yet Napoleon re-introduced and enforced such laws (Copley 1989). In sporting terms, as Renaissance athleticism declined, upper-class sports such as riding and fencing (Krüger 1987) were performed in a perfectly drilled fashion. Only towards the end of the eighteenth century Rousseau revived a more natural attitude in falling back on the 'good wild creature' as civilization had corrupted the *mœurs*. According to his opinion, a 'wild' young man, growing up with natural physical exercises, would find no need to mastur-bate. In Germany, GutsMuths and Jahn revived physical activity for the school system and the physical education of the young to have strong guerrilla warfare against Napoleonic rule. Although male bonding played an important role for Jahn, he was not particularly concerned with sexu-ality. Dr Tissot, whose *Gymnastique médicale et chirurgicale* (1780) was translated into all major European languages, became the medical basis for much of GutsMuths. In his work Tissot was much concerned that masturbation was the vice of the day – and a lot of his recommendations for gymnastics and sport have to be seen as a remedy for this. Although the discussion originated in England (Stengers and Van Neck 1984), most of the research seemed to have been done in France and Germany – from where the introduction of school physical education for all children took its course through Europe. Masturbation was considered a basic problem in traditional medicine which was much concerned with the maintenance and loss of all bodily fluids (Krüger 1995b).

The question of political correctness and the notion of the avoidance of homosexuality in the military comes to mind when discussing the career of Ernst von Pfuel. He had been in his younger years the gay friend of the famous German poet Heinrich von Kleist – and it is through his letters that we learn about their gayness. But then he started a military career, serving in many different armies – up to the rank of general (and later liberal MP in the Prussian Parliament). He is best known as the inventor of the von Pfuel method of teaching swimming in the army, a method that enabled the Prussians, but later also Belgians and others, to cross rivers and thus be more mobile. Did he love the homoerotic pleasure in seeing his soldiers stripped or was he really concerned with improving the mobility of his infantry? (Steakley 1989; Diem 1971).

Sir Francis Bacon (1561–1626) revolutionized the world of learning. A Renaissance man and lawyer-politician who became Lord Chancellor of James I, much of his writing is the basis of the future development of science and human learning. When considering the influence of his rationalism in the world of learning, it should not be overlooked that he was also defending homosexuality among men, as according to him they were better men for it (Cady 1975). Descartes, Shaftesbury, Haller, Montaigne, Winckelmann, Linné, Diderot, Kant, Lessing, Rousseau, Lichtenberg, to name but a few, all influenced our thinking in that they no longer carried the burden of the Dark Ages, but brought light into the world. They are thus the basis for the democracies arising out of the American and French Revolutions. After the re-evaluation of nature, then of society, came re-evaluation of human nature. This was not left to the medical profession, but authors like the Marquis De Sade (1740–1814) contributed to our understanding.

There was relatively little lesbian literature at the time, although women started to write and were also becoming more and more a market as readers. But when Amalie Freiin von Imhoff published a lesbian poem 'The Sisters of Lesbos' – advised by the most famous of all German poets Goethe – in an anthology edited by the equally famous Schiller, the reactions were quite mixed. The main problem seemed to have been that the anthology was geared towards a male market enjoying the pornographic double thrill of two females engaged in sexual acts (Derks 1990).

The more the consensus of dealing with homosexuality disappeared, the more it became a political matter to be discussed. Foucault placed his argument about the regimentation of human sexuality into the general context of forcing the population into modernity with a high degree of uniformity and making them ready for modern modes of production and government by standardizing how sexuality had to be performed (Dumm 1996). Yet there remained homosexual subcultures in many larger cities of Europe which refused to be brought into line (Norton 1992).

For the Enlightenment, the role of censorship should not be underestimated. Shakespeare's Sonnets were available only in a falsified version for 140 years. *Sodom, or, The Quintessence of Debauchery*, attributed to John Wilmot, Earl of Rochester, was the first literary work to be censored in England (1684) on grounds of obscenity and pornography. There then started a long line of censorship of homosexual texts, which motivated many authors to publish in Latin to circumvent censorship. Often censorship permitted the publication only after extensive changes: in Michelangelo's poems 'he' was turned into 'she' throughout; Plato's *Army of Lovers* was turned into an army of knights and ladies. In addition there was a lot of self-censorship as open homosexual expression often would have resulted in inability to publish at all (Cady 1975). In this respect, homosexuality, besides being censored, became a taboo topic. Although there was much homosexual behaviour and description thereof, there was little systematic discussion.

It can be argued (Mayer 1975) that the Enlightenment failed in Europe as it could not accept social outsiders such as homosexuals. Bodily concerns became eventually stronger than the theoretical notion of enlightenment. With the onset of the Industrial Revolution, social tensions became more virulent, and with the use of the steam engine a lot of male dominance based on physical superiority vanished. Along with it arose a strong 'tabooization' of sexual themes, generally known as Victorianism. At the same time, the rise of organized sport occurred, often considered a cure for all social evils – particularly homosexuality and masturbation. Tired from sport, a cold shower was supposed to suppress the remainder of all sexual desires. At the same time, it was supposed to further manly virtues, a chivalric Spartan fighting spirit and an *esprit de corps*.

The rise of sport in England

While in the previous pages we have been more concerned with understanding the human body and human behaviour, we should now look closer at the rise of sport in the nineteenth century. Of course, sport existed prior to this time. It has been argued that for the rules, the search for physical perfection and human behaviour, we should not forget early modern sport (Carter and Krüger 1990), but most features of modern sports arose in the second half of the nineteenth century. Tony Mangan (1981) has traced many of the origins of modern sports to the English public school and college system around 1850.

Before the middle of the nineteenth century, rebellions within the schools were not uncommon. Bored, brutalized youth turned against their teachers. With the introduction of sport and male bonding in smaller units, the House System in the schools, the Tutorials at universities, major revolutions could be prevented. The last rebellion at Marlborough (1850) brought about a major educational revolution: back to Greek athleticism and the combining of sport with a strict rules code (fair play), compulsory team games, the creation of extensive (and expensive) playing fields. 'The transformation of upper middle class masculinity began – from well-bred hooligans to well-bred heroes' (Mangan 1995).

The notion of 'manliness' was central to the evolution of the Victorian image of the ideal male. In the first half of the century such key terms as physical courage, chivalric ideals, virtuous fortitude were coupled with military and patriotic virtue, and with Christian virtues. In the second half of the century the virility had become neo-Spartan. The norms of the public school system prevailed and eventually spread to the United States and the Empire. Although much athleticism was included in the term 'muscular Christianity' there was less and less Christianity in the actual form and more and more of the games ethic.

Modern discussion about the games ethic leaves out many aspects of homosexuality that should not be overlooked. With the use of Greek

Studies, a legitimate form of discussion of homosexuality arose (Dowling 1994). In Ancient Greece the conjunction of manliness, homosexuality, and hero worship had been obvious. The Empire that was to be built and maintained had to have a firm basis in the friendship of men who knew how others were thinking. For these purposes the team sports system was very practical – and so sport was put at the basis of colonial expansion and administration of a vast Empire. But many former athletes also maintained long-lasting close friendships that allude the homosexual ties (Lane 1995).

Boarding schools and the armed forces have long been identified as breeding grounds for same-sex love. They play an important role in the rise of sport. I am not insisting that sport arose out of a desire to channel homosexuality in a socially acceptable manner but, with the help of such sports as rugby, physical contact was desirable, the image of the tough man was perpetuated who would not give up under physical strain, and same-sex contact was no longer reduced to the dormitory. Scrummaging is the most striking characteristic of rugby. The scrummage is an organized hug. It provides direct, hard-pressing physical contact by team members. Was this why organized rugby became so popular in the colonies where there was traditionally a shortage of women on the one hand, and a strong taboo of homosexuality on the other? Colonial men were unable to receive that affection and physical contact in other situations. So the drinking and singing after the match – another possibility for close physical contact (Nauright and Chandler 1996) – was another important aspect not only of rugby but also of other team games. On the other hand, it can be seen that – just as in Roman literature – it is the effeminate role in homosexuality that is seen as a danger to the rise of the Empire – and not the love for other men *per se*. For Coubertin sport served a double function; on the one hand, it worked out the young man hard enough to reduce any sexual drive and, on the other, athletic success in itself provided a certain amount of satisfaction so that sexual exploits or masturbation should prove to be superfluous. Coubertin followed Tissie, who considered athletic training a school for chastity, as successful athletes were searching for their auto-satisfaction without sexual exploits (Baillette 1986).

With Charles Darwin an old notion of homosexuality was reinforced: the stress was on survival of the fittest and the struggle for female mates. Heterosexuality was once again considered natural while homosexuality was unnatural. This was no longer based upon the divine order of the world, but was scientifically proven. The scientific argument of the nineteenth century is, however, no more conclusive than that of previous ones: cannibalism is natural in the animal world, and although it is by that fact certainly natural for humans, it is not desirable.

In the 1890s the medical profession started to occupy itself extensively with homosexuality, inverted sexual instincts and male sexual morbidity. Although this brought some sort of relief to the gay community in that it was recognized as such, it meant at the same time that its members were now no longer considered sinners, but simply sick. Havelock Ellis and John Symonds maintained that the sexual development of the homosexual had been retarded, as it had not fully developed in early childhood. They therefore maintained that it was not an illness but an abnormality. Some physicians of the early twentieth century would not even go that far and insisted that it was the lability of the nervous system that was inborn and that in some cases this would lead to homosexuality – but could be treated by hypnosis (Geuter 1994). The educated homosexuals at Oxford tried to show, on the other side, that in Greek culture many of the finest intellects had been homosexuals and that homosexuality should be considered an opportunity to halt the cultural decline of Britain (Dowling 1994). A lot of literature condemned masturbation either as it was supposed to lead to insanity or death, but also as it was a waste for the reproduction of a strong people, and it was weakening the nervous system (Ernst 1991). The notion of abstention from intercourse and masturbation by athletes was based on these same 'scientific' ideas.

We are used to the idea of the prudish, sexually repressed Victorian who is guarding him- or herself against all temptations. In the theoretical discussions about the differences of the sexes a strong dichotomy was constructed – it was no longer the *other* sex but the *opposite*, men were considered superior beings by far – and that demanded that men should maintain manly virtues. The Aesthetic Movement questioned that position in arts and letters, but with the conviction of Oscar Wilde (two years for homosexual acts), public sentiment clearly favoured those who upheld public morals and suppressed all that were acting against them. Homosexuality in the context of active and not effeminate men was, however, widely accepted: Sir Arthur Conan Doyle (inventor of the Sherlock Holmes stories, and chairman of the Finance Committee of the English Olympic Committee) could include, in his story of lifelong male bonding between Holmes and Dr Watson, some of the finest prose of homosexual and homosocial congeniality (Richards 1987).

A number of clergymen and directors of public schools had been convicted over the years for homosexual acts with their pupils and students, but on the whole the homoerotic system was alive. The image of a strong masculinity involving male bonding does, however, always have homosexual connotations.

Along with latent homosexuality very often goes a misogynist attitude. Coubertin's rejection of the participation of women in the Olympic Games has been explained as part of his traditional view of Ancient Greek Olympic Games. He even went as far as to offer his resignation from the IOC if women received the same rights (Krüger 1997). But a love for Ancient Greece and Hellenism has been identified as a marker for homosexual interest (Dowling 1994). With his construction of organizations involving strong male bonding and his desire to show off masculinity and manliness, he is typical of the 'homosociability' of his time.

Early twentieth-century sport

In the late nineteenth century an additional tradition of athletic behaviour started to manifest itself: a *physical culture* by which men and eventually women started to work on their body and present it to a wider audience. It is from this time that body-builders became icons of homosexuality, although there were many who were exhibitionists and not necessarily gay. This was an international movement concerned with a strong body, often following the classical Greek example (Andrieu 1988) and with male beauty (Andrieu 1992). Texts by such authors as the Dane I. P. Müller sold over one million copies and heavily advocated homoerotic performances by male and female persons to work on the perfection of their body (Bonde 1991). Even Lenin *müllered* in prison.

The situation with dancers and gymnasts seems to have been somewhat different. Here the percentage of gay men in a world that has traditionally seen women as many of the best performers has been relatively high (Hanna 1988).

In terms of moral attitudes the watershed of the twentieth century may well be the 1968/9 cultural revolution. In the time before, homosexuality in sport was still more speculated than talked about. One of the best homosexual athletes was Dr Otto Peltzer, world record holder in the 800 metre, half mile, and 1000 metre runs. Only as long as he was world class could he make the German team; as soon as this was no longer the case, he was no longer nominated. Because of his homosexuality and free-speaking, he spent some time in a Nazi concentration camp. Only his superb physique assured his survival. But after the war, when he was one of the few West German athletes who actively pursued an anti-fascist policy, his homosexuality was turned against him. Ritter von Halt, Hitler's last *Reichssportführer,* a stout Nazi and named as war criminal by the Nuremberg Court, was elected President of the German Olympic Committee and Honorary President of the Athletics Federation in 1949. Peltzer's arguments for a new start after the war, without a Nazi in such a prominent position, were counteracted by continuing to call him by the Nazi derogatory *Otto der Seltsame* (Otto the Strange), thus assuming that the argument of a gay is valueless in the straight world of sport (Krüger 1975).

Peltzer grew up within the German youth movement that was known for its free morals, including camp (homo)sexuality. Ever since Walt Whitman lived his homosexuality in his wood camps, and with the attachment of Baden-Powell to 'camp', the idea of 'camp' gained special meaning for homosexuals (Bergman 1993). When the Nazis persecuted former members of the youth movement, it was more for their non-conformism than their homosexuality, which just served as a vehicle to ensure public support for the persecution. The same can be said about the persecution of Catholic priests – particularly those who had been active in the Catholic youth and sports movement. It was not that they were any more or less homosexual, but they could hardly be brought to court for telling the truth – so they were indicted for homosexuality (Jellonnek 1990).

The Nazis had an opportunistic relationship in regard to homosexuality. On the one hand – just like any other close-knit group of strong male bonding – there was a relatively large percentage of homosexuals among them. Yet, homosexuality was used as a powerful tool to cleanse Nazi ranks of members who were undesirable for other *political* reasons. In the world of physical culture, Hans Surèn was one of the most prolific writers and coaches. His body was always shining, oiled and sun tanned. Exercises he created were mainly for men exercising in the nude. Hitler was personally an ardent Surèn fan and always had a signed photograph of him hanging in his office. Eventually, Surèn was fired from a leadership position by the Nazis for causing a public scandal: he was seen masturbating on his balcony (Krüger 1991).

The reasoning behind the strong actions of the Nazis against open homosexuality in its ranks reminds one of Victorian England. For the war effort anything that hindered the birth of children was persecuted – but what made matters worse was (as in the Middle Ages), if you dared to break the law on such a matter as homosexuality, in which other fields of male bonding would you become active? Any assembly of people and any organization was subject to surveillance to assure totalitarian dictatorship. If you were secretly meeting your gay friend, what else could you plan in secrecy? It was supported by the gymnastic and sports movement in spite of the fact that this had traditionally been a strong male reserve with a strong male homoerotic and homosocial tendency in many sports. Already in the 1920s there were estimates that as many as 1.2 million male homosexuals lived in Germany, so that obviously in any all-male organization there was bound to be a relatively large number. The Nazis therefore waged a selective war against them which led to the concentration camp for many (Plant 1991).

What has been said here of Germany was more or less the case in most other countries. In the United States the fear of effeminacy was so strong that President Teddy Roosevelt stepped in to assure that the football rules would not be softened. There have been severe rules against homosexuality in the armed forces of all countries, but under the rules of full war they were handled in a sensible way, i.e. 'a simple rule was observed by both heterosexuals and homosexuals – no sexual activity within the confines of the barracks or elsewhere on duty' (David 1997). The sports movement tried, however, to pretend that it was clear of all homosexual activities. Homophobia was used to pressure athletes into the mainstream sexuality of the day.

Gay and lesbian liberation

Most historians of homosexuality do not distinguish between homosexuality and homophobia; they prefer to study laws against gay behaviour, rather than gay experience, thus shifting attention from gays to gaybashers. I am fully aware that I have been falling into the same fallacy – as there is little available in primary or secondary literature before the cultural revolution of the late 1960s which has not been impeded to some extent by (self-)censorship. There is no adequate sociological theory dealing with the phenomenon (Lautmann 1977), and Foucault's social constructionism, as useful as it is to identify some homosexual phenomena, does not fit all the historical facts. Social constructionists maintain that significant changes took place in the nineteenth century – because that is when their Marxist theory required them to take place. That way they redefine the 'homosexual' (who is now called as such by Ellis, Freud and others) as the 'modern homosexual' who has class awareness and is moving towards class consciousness which enables him or her to radically question such concepts as gender and be more concerned with the class struggle. But as I have shown, there were plenty of gays with a separate identity long before the advent of capitalism – and homosexuality was equally persecuted in the emerging communist societies as a 'barbaric hangover of bourgeois societies' (Weeks 1997).

The situation is even more complicated in the case of lesbians. A lot of the lesbian heritage may be distorted by the male prerogative to be properly educated and to publish. Some lesbian literature and particularly pictures and videos are written and produced to please a heterosexual male market that readily absorbed the double thrill of seeing or hearing two nude women enjoying their bodies. Lesbian feminism in the early 1970s consciously intended to sever lesbians from their cultural roots (Case 1996). The forced disinheritance of lesbians of the 1940s and 1950s by lesbian feminists is a case in mind. The experience of black and working-class lesbians was erased from politically correct lesbian history. Only relatively recently have gay and lesbian activists joined forces in their political battle for equal rights (Nestle and Preston 1995).

Given the long association between athleticism and manliness, women athletes had a hard time right from the beginning. A look at the table of medals at the Olympic Games shows that such problems were bigger in some countries than in others. Germany, Scandinavia and Eastern Europe provided a larger amount of liberalism and did not automatically equate any women who dared to go in for sport as being lesbian, as in the USA or UK. For decades critics of women's sport have linked athletic drive in women and mannishness to a lesbian orientation. When women had achieved greater rights in sports through Title IX in the United States, widespread homophobia was used to push women out of coaching jobs for women which they had held before.

The homophobic argument is used against women coaches recruiting. 'If she likes your daughter so much, beware of her getting into a lesbian affair with the coach ... better send her to a healthy climate', assuming that a lesbian coach creates a lesbian atmosphere in a team (Griffin 1992;

1993). The old theory of homosexuality as sexual inversion, which was used in the 1880s, was still being used in conjunction with sport. Athletic drive was associated with manliness – so if you have that drive as a girl, you are manly and bound to end up in lesbianism. A strict heterosexual upbringing created many difficulties for sporting teenage girls, who could not see why it was accepted to play soccer with boys at age twelve, but not at age fourteen, and they often found themselves drawn into female sports and developed gay preferences (Palzkill 1990). Olympic Champion Babe Didrikson, later to become a professional golfer, seemed to be a good example. In some cultures it was assumed more than in others that you had to be lesbian to be any good in sport. Martina Navratilova, number one in women's world tennis for years, stood up for her lesbian rights (Cahn 1994).

The cultural revolution of 1968/9 brought different changes to different countries. In Germany and France heterosexual orgies were the order of the day, as monogamy was considered the main *oppression* for the majority. Gay liberation started in the United States. The jock strap, icon of gay Americans and Britons, only came into usage in Germany and France through the spread of cultural influences from Hollywood, while previously a normal slip that covered the buttocks was worn.

Black American athletes protested against exploitation and racism in American sport (Edwards 1969), German athletes revolted against their management and boycotted the European Athletics Championships in Athens 1969 (Krüger 1975), American gays and lesbians had their Stonewall Revolt in New York in June 1969 (Lisker 1969) when they violently defended their right to assemble in private. Homosexuality in the United States became a human rights issue from that time onward (Fone 1995), while in other countries the questions raised were more in the cultural sphere. The right of physical self-determination of one's body was soon linked in the USA with the question of legalized abortion, while in other countries those questions were kept apart (Brugger 1993). On the whole, the sports movement was, however, conservative and avoided the homosexual challenge. Sport, as a male socializing agent, has been described as one of the bulwarks of a patriarchal society; feminism was seen as a challenge, but also the influx of women into sport was discouraged in the United States (Sabo and Runfola 1980). The result of the cultural revolution was, however, on the whole a 'coming out' (Altman *et al.* 1988). It is therefore not surprising that eventually homosexual athletes would start their own Gay Games (1982) – to do their sport with pride in the open.

The gay movement was hit hard by the spreading of the HIV virus and AIDS. Here you could see the mediaeval mechanisms, assuming that God was destroying Sodom a second time by sending the deadly virus, particularly to *perverts*. There were, however, a large number of heterosexually transmitted cases, besides where the transmission had occurred by sharing the same injection needle and also through unclean blood banks. When Magic Johnson tested positive for HIV, a discussion about AIDS in sport went through the media. Fortunately, for the self-esteem of the sports system, Johnson had caught the disease by a heterosexual contact – or at least that is what he said (Wachs and Dworkin 1997).

Doping also has a sexual side. With more and more anabolic steroids being used in sports by both sexes, the testosterone level of athletes of both sexes has been elevated. While this had the effect of raising the level of aggression in male sports with its brutalizing effects in such sports as American football, soccer, ice hockey, and a disproportionate rise in sexual assault among athletes on steroids (Crosset *et al.* 1995), the results for female athletes have been less clear. Do virilizing physical effects such as a deeper voice, stronger muscles, more body hair, enlarged clitoris also have an effect on the sexual orientation of female athletes? Is it a question of when steroids are used in the development of the athlete and her sexuality? Much more research is needed, but difficult to conduct because of the double taboo of drugs and homosexuality.

Part of the coming out of gay athletes has become the Gay Games which were first organized by Dr Tom Waddell, a San Francisco gay activist. The first week-long festival in his hometown in 1982 brought together 1,350 athletes from 12 countries, participating in 14 events, assisted by 600 gay volunteers and judges. The Gay Games were modelled from the beginning on the modern Olympics. At first they were even called the Gay Olympic Games, but the USOC as sole owner of the name rights to Olympic objected and so all the following were just the Gay Games. Gay Games II, 8 days in August 1986, again in San Francisco, had 3,500 participants (40 per cent women) from 19 countries participating in 19 events. This time the city of San Francisco even subsidised the Games. Gay Games III, 7,500 athletes from 39 countries, participating in 23 athletic events, brought the sport in August 1990 to Vancouver, Canada. Dr Waddell died of AIDS and the games have been henceforth a memorial to this sporting visionary. Gay Games IV had already more than 10,000 gay athletes from 40 countries, 7,000 gay volunteers, for a week in June 1994 in New York City. Gay Games V were held in the first week of August 1998 in Amsterdam. From all five continents, 12,500 participants in the sport and 2,500 more in the cultural events were expected. Gay Games VI have been awarded to Sydney for the year 2002. Will Olympic cities host the Gay Games in the future using their athletic facilities? The Federation of Gay Games had three more bids for the Games (Montreal, Dallas, Long Beach), but decided on Sydney to spread the word around the world (Uncle Donald's 1998).

Gay sports have had a considerable influence in Europe. From the very beginning, European gays participated in the USA, came home and often started their own gay sports clubs, although in many cases sports were just one activity of a general gay club. The situation in Europe was quite different. In most cases there has been, however, no unity between male and female homosexual activities. In this they were very similar to the basic organization of sport. Gay Sports Zürich is one of the few gay sports clubs that plays volleyball in the regular league – and was welcomed into the federation by a standing ovation. On the other hand, the Comité Gay Paris – Ile De France had a particularly hard time: the French sporting press does not even report the Gay Games and French homosexual intellectuals ignore sports as they have a different attitude towards their body (Buttgeleit and Groneberg 1996).

The Gay Eurogames were started in The Hague in 1992 as a result of the Gay Games. Eurogames II were also held in the Netherlands, while Eurogames III took place in Frankfurt in 1995, IV in Berlin in 1996, and V in Paris in 1997. The European Gay and Lesbian Sports Federation under the chairmanship of its Dutch President Ben Baks is discussing a typical problem for sports of a European magnitude: should there be a limit to the number of permitted participants? Is the limit reached with the 3,500 present in the last games? Are the Eurogames an élite sport event for which one has to qualify nationally or is it a major sports-for-all event in the spirit of the large city marathon races? In Berlin the male cheerleading competition showed the closeness to travesty shows that attract many spectators – but was not necessarily what many of the athletes wanted.

Although these international events seem to be a big step forward in demonstrating gay and lesbian pride, there are not only steps forward in the public discussion of such matters of gender construction. The old question remains of whether homosexuality is inborn or acquired. In the name of that research question the Nazis killed many people, but now twin (Whitman *et al.* 1993) and genome (Hamer *et al.* 1993) studies are being conducted to show that homosexuality is somehow genetically predetermined. So far the results are inconclusive. What would it mean if a genetic or other biological base for homosexuality were to be found? Judging from the past history of human homosexuality, it would probably mean devising a cure, legalizing abortion of homosexual fetuses, sterilizing homosexuals, or burning them at the stake as in the past but now with seemingly better biological justification.

The sports system is split on the coming out of gay members. The German Football Federation (DFB) officially prohibited members of the women's national team from participating in the 1995 Gay Eurogames in Frankfurt and threatened those who did take part never to play 'for Germany' again in the national side. Sports that have traditionally had a strong women's representation, like track and field, seem to have had a problem in sanctioning female participation in such sports as marathon running or hammer throwing. It took a long time for women's boxing to be accepted, as it seemed to be a bigger challenge for the definition of manliness.

With the wider public acceptance of homosexuality in the 1990s as more and more gays came out and were published on, the sport system is now less worried about the coming out of its gay members. Although homophobia is still widespread, gay and lesbian movie stars, musicians and athletes have come a long way as role models for the younger generation. Postmodernism with its rejection of meta-narrative structures of society has also helped us accept a wider range of individuality in the 'global village'. With the help of modern electronic media gay culture is moving closer to social acceptability and, within it, the sports movement is playing a prominent part together with other everyday activities as they help to advertise the physical fitness of gays and lesbians (Ridinger 1996).

References

Altman, D. (1980) *Coming Out in the Seventies.* Melbourne: Penguin Books.

Altman, D., Vance, C. *et al.* (1988) *Homosexuality, which Homosexuality? International Conference on Gay and Lesbian Studies.* Amsterdam: Schorer.

Andrieu, G. (1988) *L'homme et la force. Des marchands de la force au culte de la forme (xixe et xxe siècle).* Joinville-le-Pont: Actio.

—— (1992) *Force et beauté. Histoire de l'esthétique en éducation physique aux xixe et xxe siècles.* Bordeaux: Presses Universitaires de Bordeaux.

Baillette, F. (1986) 'Pratique sportives et hygiène sexuelle' in *Quel Corps?* (Dec. 1986), 32/33, 87–112.

Bergman, D. (ed.) (1993) *Camp Grounds. Style and Homosexuality.* Amherst: The University of Massachusetts Press.

Blake, A. (1996) *Body Language. The Meaning of Modern Sport.* London: Lawrence and Wishart.

Bonde, H. (1991) *Mandighed og sport.* Odense: Universitetsforlag.

Boswell, J. (1980) *Christianity, Social Tolerance and Homosexuality. Gay People in Western Europe from the Beginning of the Christian Era to the Fourteenth Century.* Chicago: University of Chicago Press.

Bray, A. (1982) *Homosexuality in Renaissance England.* London: Gay Men's Press.

Brugger, W. (1993) *Persönlichkeitsentfaltung als Grundwert der amerikanischen Verfassung. Dargestellt am Beispiel des Streits um den Schutz von Abtreibung und Homosexualität.* Heidelberg: C. F. Müller.

Butler, J. (1989) *Gender Trouble. Feminism and the Subversion of Identity.* London: Routledge.

—— (1993) *Bodies that Matter. The Discursive Limits of Sex.* London: Routledge.

Buttgereit, S. and Groneberg, M. (eds) (1996) *Eurogames IV. Eine Dokumentation.* Berlin: Querverlag.

Cady, J. (1975) 'Bacon, Sir Francis' in C. J. Summers (ed.) *The Gay and Lesbian Literary Heritage.* New York: Henry Holt, 70–1.

Cahn, S. K. (1994) *Coming on Strong. Gender and Sexuality in Twentieth-Century Women's Sport.* New York: Free Press.

Carter, J. M. and Krüger, A. (eds) (1990) *Ritual and Record. Sport in Pre-Industrial Societies.* Westport, CT: Greenwood.

Case, S. E. (1996) *Slit Britches. Lesbian Practice – Feminist Performance.* London: Routledge.

Castiglione, B. (1528) *Il libro del cortigiano.* Florence: P. di Giunto.

Copley, A. (1989) *Sexual Moralities in France, 1780–1980. New Ideas on the Family, Divorce, and Homosexuality.* London: Routledge.

Craft, C. (1994) *Another Kind of Love. Male Homosexual Desire in English Discourse. 1850–1920.* Berkeley: University of California Press.

Crompton, L. (1995) 'Roman Literature' in C. J. Summers (ed.), *The Gay and Lesbian Literary Heritage.* New York: Henry Holt. 594–600

Crosset, T. W., Benedict, J. R. *et al.* (1995) 'Male Student-Athletes Reported for Sexual Assault', in *J. Sport & Soc. Issues* 19(2), 126–40.

Dall'Orto, G. (1989) 'Socratic love' as a disguise for same-sex love in the Italian Renaissance', in Gerard, K. and G. Hekma (eds) *Male Homosexuality in Renaissance and Enlightenment Europe.* New York: Harrington Park Press, 33–65.

David, H. (1997) *On Queer Street. A Social History of British Homosexuality.* London: Harper Collins.

Derks, P. (1990) *Die Schande der heiligen Päderastie. Homosexualität und Öffentlichkeit in der deutschen Literatur, 1750–1850.* Berlin: Rosa Winkel.

Diem, C. (1971) *Weltgeschichte des Sports.* Stuttgart: Cotta.

Dover, K. J. (1978) *Greek Homosexuality.* Cambridge, MA: Harvard University Press.

Dowling, L. (1994) *Hellenism and Homosexuality in Victorian Oxford.* Ithaca, NY: Cornell University Press.

Dumm, T. L. (1996) *Michel Foucault and the Politics of Freedom.* London: Sage.

Edwards, H. (1969) *The Revolt of the Black Athlete.* New York: Free Press.

Ernst, R. (1991) *Weakness is a Crime. The Life of Bernarr Macfadden.* Syracuse, NY: Syracuse University Press.

Featherstone, M. and Turner, B. S. (1995) 'Body & Society. An Introduction' in *Body & Society* 1(1), 1–12.

Fone, B. R. S. (1995) *A Road to Stonewall. Male Homosexuality and Homophobia in English and American Literature. 1750–1969.* New York: Twayne.

Foucault, M. (1988/90) *The History of Sexuality.* 3 vols, New York: Vintage. (French original of 1976).

Frontain, R.-J. (1995a) 'The Bible' in C. J. Summers (ed.) *The Gay and Lesbian Literary Heritage.* New York: Henry Holt, 99–100.

—— (1995b) 'Theocritus' in C. J. Summers (ed.) *The Gay and Lesbian Literary Heritage.* New York: Henry Holt, 699–700.

Gerard, K. and Hekma, G. (eds) (1989) *Male Homosexuality in Renaissance and Enlightenment Europe.* New York: Harrington Park Press.

Gesner, J. M. (1753) 'Socrates Sanctus Paederasta. Prael a.d. V. Febr. MDCCLII' in *Commentarii Societatis Regiae Scientiarum Gottingensis.* Vol. II, Göttingen, 1–31.

Geuter, U. (1994) *Homosexualität in der deutschen Jugendbewegung. Jungenfreundschaft und Sexualität im Diskurs von Jugendbewegung. Psychoanalyse und Jugendpsychologie am Beginn des 20. Jahrhunderts.* Frankfurt: Suhrkamp.

Griffin, P. (1992) 'Changing the game. Homophobia, sexism and lesbians in sport', *Quest* 44(2), 251–65.

—— (1993) 'Homophobia in women's sports. The fear that divides us', in Cohen, G. L. (ed.) *Women in Sport. Issues and Controversies.* London: Sage, 193–203.

Gutterman, D. S. (1994) 'Postmodernism and the interrogation of masculinity', in Brod, H. and Kaufman, M. (eds) *Theorizing Masculinities.* London: Sage, 219–38.

Guttmann, A. (1993) *The Erotic in Sport.* New York: Columbia University Press.

Hall, S. (1980) 'Encoding/decoding', in Hall, S., Hobson, D. *et al.* (eds) *Culture, Media, Language.* London: Hutchinson, 128–38.

Hall, S. (ed.) (1997) *Representation. Cultural Representations and Signifying Practices.* London: Sage.

Halperin, D. M. (1983) *Before Pastoral: Theocritus and the Ancient Tradition of Bucolic Poetry.* Newhaven, CT: Yale University Press.

Hamer, D. H., Hu, S. *et al.* (1993) 'A linkage between DNA marker on the X chromosome and male sexual orientation', in *Science* 261(5119), 321–7.

Handelman, D. (1984) 'Die Madonna und die Stute, Zur symbolischen Bedeutung des palios von Siena', in A. Krüger and J. McClelland (eds) *Die Anfänge des modernen Sports in der Renaissance.* London: Arena, 58–84.

Hanna, J. L. (1988) *Dance, Sex and Gender. Signs of Identity, Dominance, Defiance, and Desire.* Chicago: University of Chicago Press.

Hewitt, A. (1996) *Political Inversions. Homosexuality, Fascism, and the Modernist Imaginary.* Stanford, CA: Stanford University Press.

Higgins, P. (1996) *Heterosexual Dictatorship. Male Homosexuality in Postwar Britain.* London: Fourth Estate.

Hobsbawm, E. and Ranger, T. (1983) *The Invention of Tradition.* Cambridge: Cambridge University Press.

Honey, J. R. de S. (1977) *Tom Brown's Universe.* London: Heinemann.

Jellonnek, B. (1990) *Homosexuelle unter dem Hakenkreuz. Die Verfolgung von Homosexuellen im Dritten Reich.* Paderborn: Schöningh.

Kiefer, O. (1993) *Sexual Life in Ancient Rome.* New York: Dorset.

Kinsey, A. C., Pomeroy, W. B. *et al.* (1948) *Sexual Behaviour in the Human Male.* Philadelphia: Saunders.

—— (1953) *Sexual Behaviour in the Human Female.* Philadelphia: Saunders.

Klein, A. M. (1993) *Little Big Man. Bodybuilding Subculture and Gender Construction.* Albany, NY: State University of NY Press.

Krüger, A. (1975) *Sport and Politik. Vom Turnvater Jahn zum Staatsamateur.* Hannover: Fackelträger.

—— (1984) 'Schwimmen. Der Wandel in der Einstellung zu einer Form der Leibesübungen', in A. Krüger and J. McClelland (eds) *Die Anfänge des modernen Sports in der Renaissance.* London: Arena, 19–42.

—— (1987) 'Die Professoren für Reitlehre. Die Anfänge der organisierten Wissenschaft vom Sport', *Stadion* 12/13 (1986/7), 241–52.

—— (1991) 'There goes this art of manliness. Naturism and social hygiene in Germany', *Journal of Sport History* 18(1), 135–58.

—— (1995a) 'Sport sciences as part of cultural studies. The responsibility of the sciences for the future', in J. Raczek (ed.) *Nauki o Kulkturze Fizycznej wobec Wyzwan Wspolczesnej Cywilizacji.* Katowice: AWF, 175–86.

—— (1995b) 'Geschichte der Bewegungstherapie', in M. Bühring and F. M. Kemper (eds) *Naturheilverfahren und unkonventionelle medizinische Richtungen.* Lose Blatt Sammlung. 8. Nachlieferung. Heidelberg: Springer, 1–20.

—— (1997) 'Forgotten decisions. The IOC on the eve of World War I', *Olympika* 6(1), 85–98.

Laclau, E. (1990) *New Reflections on the Revolutions of Our Time.* London: Verso.

Lane, C. (1995) *The Ruling Passion. British Colonial Allegory and the Paradox of Homosexual Desire.* Durham, NC: Duke University Press.

Lautmann, R. (1977) (ed.) *Seminar: Gesellschaft und Homosexualität.* Frankfurt: Suhrkamp.

Lenskyj, H. (1994) 'Sexuality and femininity in sport contexts: issues and alternatives', *J. Sport & Soc. Issues* 18(4), 356–76.

—— (1995) 'Sports literature: lesbian', in C. J. Summers (ed.) *The Gay and Lesbian Literary Heritage.* New York: Henry Holt, 678–81.

Licht, H. (1993) *Sexual Life in Ancient Greece.* New York: Dorset.

Lisker, J. (1969) 'Homo nest raided. Queen bees are stinging mad', in *New York Daily News*, July 6, 1969.

Mangan, J. A. (1981) *Athleticism in the Victorian and Edwardian Public School.* Cambridge: Cambridge University Press.

—— (1995) 'Coubertin and Cotton. European Realism and Idealism in the Making of Modern European Masculinity', in A. Krüger and A. Teja (eds), *La Commune Eredità dello Sport in Europa.* Rome: CONI, 238–41.

Mastronarde, D. J. (1968) 'Theocritus' Idyll 13: Love and the Hero', in *Transactions of the Am. Phil. Society* 99, 273–90.

Mayer, H. (1975) *Aussenseiter.* Frankfurt: Suhrkamp.

McWhirter, D. P., Sanders, S. A. *et al* (1990) *Homosexuality/Heterosexuality. Concepts of Sexual Orientation.* Oxford: Oxford University Press.

Messner, M. A. and Sabo, D. F. (1990) *Sport, Men and the Gender Order. Critical Feminist Perspectives.* Champaign, IL: Human Kinetics.

—— (1994) *Sex, Violence and Power in Sports. Rethinking Masculinity.* Freedom, CA: Crossing Press.

Muir J. G. (1993) 'Homosexuals and the ten percent fallacy', in *Wall Street Journal*, March 31.

Nauright, J. and Chandler, T. J. L. (eds) (1996) *Making men. Rugby and masculine identity.* London: Frank Cass.

Negus, K. (1997) 'The Production of Culture', in P. du Gay (ed.) *Production of Culture – Cultures of Production.* London: Sage, 67–118.

Nestle, J. and Preston, J. (eds) (1995) *Sister and Brother. Lesbians and Gay Men Write about their Lives Together.* London: Cassell.

Norton, R. (1992) *Mother Clap's Molly House. The Gay Subculture in England, 1700–1830.* London: Gay Men's Press.

—— (1997) *The Myth of the Modern Homosexual. Queer History and the Search for Cultural Unity.* London: Cassell.

Oosterhuis, H. and Kennedy, H. (eds) (1991) *Homosexuality and Male Bonding in Pre-Nazi Germany.* New York: Haworth.

Palzkill, B. (1990) *Zwischen Turnschuh und Stöckelschuh. Die Entwicklung lesbischer Identität im Sport.* Bielefeld: AJZ.

Plant, R. (1991) *Der Rosa Winkel. Der Krieg der Nazis gegen die Homosexuellen.* Frankfurt: Campus.

Pronger, B. (1990) *The Arena of Masculinity. Sports Homosexuality and the Meaning of Sex.* New York: St. Martin's Press.

—— (1995) 'Sports literature: gay male', in C. J. Summers (ed.), *The Gay and Lesbian Literary Heritage.* New York: Henry Holt, 675–78.

Quel Corps? (1975) 'Pouvoir et Corps. Interview de Michel Foucault', *Quel Corps?* (Sept/Oct)(2), 2–5.

Richards, J. (1987) '"Passing the love of women." Manly love and Victorian Society'. in J. A. Mangan and J. Walvin (eds) *Manliness and Morality. Middle*

Class Masculinity in Britain and America, 1880–1940. Manchester: Manchester University Press, 92–122.

Ridinger, R. B. M. (1996) *The Gay and Lesbian Movement. References and Resources.* New York: G. K. Hall.

Rocke, M. (1996) *Forbidden Friendships. Homosexuality and Male Culture in Renaissance Florence.* Oxford: Oxford University Press.

Ruggiero, G. (1985) *The Boundaries of Eros: Sex Crime and Sexuality in Renaissance Venice.* Oxford: Oxford University Press.

Ruse, M. (1988) *Homosexuality. A Philosophical Inquiry.* Blackwell, Oxford.

Sabo, D. F. and Runfola, R. (1980) *Jocks. Sport and Male Identity.* Englewood Cliffs, NJ: Prentice-Hall.

Segal, L. (1997) 'Sexualities', in Woodward, K. (ed.) *Identity and Difference.* London: Sage, 182–228.

Shilling, C. (1993) *The Body in Social Thought.* London: Sage.

Smith, B. R. (1991) *Homosexual Desire in Shakespeare's England.* Chicago: University of Chicago Press.

Snyder, J. M. (1991) 'Public occasion and private passion in the lyrics of Sappho of Lesbos', in S. B. Pomeroy (ed.) *Women's History and Ancient History.* Chapel Hill, NC: The University of North Carolina Press, 73–110.

Sommer, V. (1990) *Wider die Natur? Homosexualität und Evolution.* Munich: Beck.

Sprawson, C. (1992) *Haunts of the Black Masseur: the Swimmer as Hero.* London: Vintage.

Spreitzer, B. (1988) *Die Stumme Sünde. Homosexualität im Mittelalter.* Göppingen: Kümmerle.

Steakley, J. D. (1989) 'Sodomy in enlightenment Prussia. From execution to suicide', in Gerard, K. and Hekma, G. (eds) *Male Homosexuality,* 163–75.

Stengers, J. and Van Neck, A. (1984) *Histoire d'une grande peure: la masturbation.* Brussels: Editions de l'Université.

Tissot, C. J. (1780) *Gymnastique médicale et chirurgicale, ou, Essai sur l'utilité du mouvement ou des différens exercices du corps, et du repos dans la cure des maladies.* Paris: Bastien.

Uncle Donald's Castro Street (1998) 'A brief history of the Gay Games', *www.backdoor.com/castro/gaygames.html.*

Urry, J. (1990) *The Tourist Gaze. Leisure and Travel in Contemporary Societies.* London: Sage.

Wachs, F. D. and Dworkin, S. L. (1997) '"There is no such thing as a gay hero." Sexual identity and media framing of HIV-positive athletes', *J. Sport & Soc. Issues* 21(4), 327–47.

Weeks, J. (1997) *Coming out. Homosexual Politics in Britain from the Nineteenth Century to the Present.* London: Quartet.

—— (1981) *Sex, Politics, and Society. The Regulation of Sexuality Since 1800.* London: Langman.

Whitman, F. L., Diamand, M. *et al.* (1993) 'Homosexual orientation in twins: a report on 61 pairs and three triplet sets', *Arch. Sex. Behaviour* 22(2), 187–206.

Whitson, D. (1990) 'Sport in the social construction of masculinity' in M. A. Messnet and D. F. Sabo (eds) *Sport, Men, and the Gender Order.* Champaign, IL: Human Kinetics, 19–29.

11 Sport and terrorism

Bernd Wedemeyer

Introduction

The most obvious manifestation of terrorism in sport is the tragic action during the Munich Olympic Games of 1972. Early in the morning of 5 September, eight Palestinians burst into the Israeli compound of the Olympic village; they killed a coach and took ten Israeli athletes hostage. Their stated intention was to use the hostages to free arrested Palestinian terrorists in an Israeli gaol. In the end, the Palestinians and eleven Israeli athletes were killed in the ensuing shoot-out with the police.

This was an assault on Olympic peace, on the ancient truce held during the period of the games. Olympic athletes had become victims of a terrorist act (Höfer 1994: 200).

In the history of sport and terrorism, however, one finds many examples of athletes being less the victims of political terror, rather political terrorists themselves. The dark side of the political outlook of some sports organizations and athletes is that in many cases this outlook accompanies an extremely nationalistic view of one's own country. Sport, physical culture and fitness bodies have all been used in the twentieth century as weapons against the 'enemy' both inside and outside their country.

Athletes representing this standpoint normally exhibit a very conservative and often undemocratic view of the ideal form of government (Mangan 1995). The history of this tradition in this century is the focus of this chapter, particularly the collaboration between terrorism and sport in Ireland and Germany.

The political boundary between legal military sport, on the one hand, and sport practised in illegal paramilitary organizations, on the other, is often unclear. Sometimes the sole difference is the democratic or undemocratic political views of the organization itself. In short, if a group is losing, they are branded as terrorists; if it is winning, they are called respectable freedom fighters. But both sides instrumentalize sport as a political weapon (Krüger and Riordan 1996; Barrett 1977).

Specialist literature on the relationship between sport and terrorism is rare. It is much easier to obtain information on the history of paramilitary sport and the connection between nationalism and sport. Such sources, however, hardly mention terrorism at all; nor is the information on illegal sports activities adequate. What does exist is the published regulations of terrorist groups, the memoirs and autobiographies of terrorists and politicians. Many talk of their attitude to sport and the ways they kept fit. It is sources such as these that have been largely drawn on.

International aspects of sport and terrorism

Most definitions state that terrorism is a politically motivated form of criminal violence; it includes violence against states or societies by threats or acts to undermine governments. To reach a revolutionary situation, the state has to be shown to be unable to stabilize law and order. The methods employed to attain this situation are sabotage, blackmail, assault, kidnapping and assassination of individuals or groups representing the state.

Especially after World War I, when many democratic governments were established, the main motives for terrorism were nationalistic, religious, anti-democratic or anti-capitalist. Some terrorist groups fought against dictatorship. But in many cases terrorists try to overthrow governments in states where legal opposition is possible (*Brockhaus Encyclopädie* 1993, 22, 21–4).

Terrorism therefore includes anti-democratic right-wing organizations like military sports groups, as well as nationalist groups like the Irish Republican Army (IRA) and the Provisional Irish Republican Army (PIRA), the Palestine Liberation Organization (PLO) and the Basque Fatherland and Liberty group (ETA). There are also 'anti-imperialist' left-wing organizations, like the German Red Army Faction (RAF), the French Action Directe and the Italian Red Brigade. Their views are sometimes independent of traditional right- or left-wing orientations. The Kurdish Workers Party (PKK), for instance, fights for national identity, but it is politically more of a left-wing party. Groups like the PIRA or the PLO have political or national, as well as religious aims (Wilkinson 1993).

Although terrorist groups operate in different countries and from different motivations, their common goal is to overthrow the government. So various groups work closely together, especially in preparing terrorist acts or acquiring weapons (Wilkinson 1993). Another common basis for collaboration is the international use of the *Mini-Manual of the Urban Guerrilla*, written by the Brazilian guerrilla Carlos Marighella (1911–69). It has been translated into many languages, and it gives instructions for training, planning and executing terrorist acts (Marighella 1970). The third common feature is that terrorists have to be physically fit; so they all use sport, particularly military sport, to keep in training. Many of them – left- as well as right-wing groups – have trained over the last two decades in Palestinian camps in Lebanon or the Yemen (Geldard and Craig 1988). It is this instrumentalization that may be considered the dark side of 'international sport'.

Contemporary examples of terrorism and sport

The intensive use of sport in extreme right-wing paramilitary and terrorist organizations in Germany in the 1970s and 1980s represents a contemporary example of the close relationship between terrorism and sport. In 1973, the paramilitary organization Wehrsportgruppe Hoffmann (Hoffmann Military Sports Group) was founded in southern Germany. Its 600 members were followers of Hitler and the Nazis; its aim was to fight against democratic Germany in order to re-establish a Nazi dictatorship. They stockpiled weapons, attacked students and members of socialist groups, and they robbed banks. They also planned to free the Nazi leader Rudolf Hess (1894–1987), who had been second in command to Adolf Hitler and was held after the war in a Berlin prison. In 1981, members of the group were strongly suspected of murdering a Jewish publisher; in 1979, they allegedly had a hand in the Munich bomb blast during the traditional *Oktoberfest*, when several people were killed.

To get and stay fit, the members trained in shooting and unarmed combat, practised combat sports, body-building and military sports in the forests. In 1980, the German Federal government outlawed the Wehrsportgruppe Hoffmann, following which several members went abroad to continue military sports and their anti-democratic struggle (Meyer and Rabe 1979: 79). For special training, some members travelled to paramilitary camps in the Lebanon where they were instructed by Palestinians (Backes and Jesse 1993: 305).

Another such example is the Wiking Jugend (Viking Youth). This organization propagates the ideology of a Great German Nation under a dictatorship and works for a National Socialist Germanization of Europe. This involves all North European nations with 'Germanic roots' joining together to build a 'national front' against southern and eastern countries. The Viking Youth therefore has members and followers not only in Germany, but in France, Britain, Holland, Belgium, Denmark and Sweden. Because of their philosophy of a healthy mind in a healthy body (*mens sana in corpore sano*), they strongly condemn alcohol and cigarettes. To develop a 'Teutonic' body, they practise paramilitary sports, like shooting, club-throwing and armed and unarmed combat in their training camps (Meyer and Rabe 1979: 51).

At the opposite end of the political spectrum, there is the 'anti-imperialist' Red Army Faction (RAF) which had its roots in the student movement of 1968. From the beginning, RAF directed the struggle against the 'imperialist' influence of the United States, and West Germany as the main acolyte of the USA. It has never attracted more than a few hundred individuals; it supports non-capitalist and Marxist movements with the goal of overthrowing German democracy by persuading people to take part in revolution.

The attack and murder list of RAF is long and international – it has collaborated with the French Action Directe, the Irish IRA and the Italian

Red Brigade. To keep fit, RAF members have trained in Palestinian camps, learning how to shoot and engage in armed combat. In Germany, they have kept fit in special 'Ju-Jitsu/Karate' groups (Peters 1991: 84, 103). Once caught, some RAF members continued to do gymnastics and aerobics in prison.

Sport is used therefore not only as a weapon against democracy, but also as a way to discipline members of organizations and to drill them to be obedient to their leadership. For the past few decades, military sports have proved to be important to most of the illegal or semi-legal right-wing and 'anti-imperialist' groups which aim to overthrow government or commit political crimes and assaults.

The example of Ireland

An instructive relationship between sport and politics in regard to terrorism may be traced in the historical development of Ireland. Since the founding of the forerunner of the IRA, the Irish Republican or, later, Revolutionary Brotherhood – the IRB in 1858, and the setting up of the Gaelic Athletic Association (GAA) in 1884, sport, nationalism and terrorism have worked together in Ireland (Coogan 1985: 242).

The GAA has always been a nationalist association which has done its best to prevent any British sport from influencing Irish sport. From the start, the GAA formed a militant opposition to British sports. It supported traditional Irish sports like Gaelic football, hurling and handball, it banned its members from playing sports like soccer, rugby, cricket and track and field, and it outlawed any game that it did not sanction. Soccer, in particular, was discussed at considerable length (Holt 1995: 49; Morehouse 1995: 58–64). Such prohibition prevented any British individual from becoming a GAA member. Only in 1971 were these rules abandoned (Smulders 1977: 566).

After the division of Ireland into two states in 1921, the GAA tried to keep a monopoly of sport control in both states by organizing competitions for all thirty-two counties, including the six northern counties under British Protestant rule. In order to control track and field athletics, for example, the GAA founded the NACA (National Athletic and Cycling Association); the British did all they could to put a stop to this development.

In 1934, the IAAF (International Amateur Athletic Federation), of which the GAA had been a member, added a new paragraph to its rules 'which confines member associations to the political boundaries of the country or nation they represent' (Smulders 1977: 561). This led to a controversial debate within the GAA which wanted to represent the whole of Ireland: either the organization accepted the rule or it would have to leave the IAAF. In the end, the GAA refused to give up representation of the six northern counties, quit the IAAF and gave up international sport. The Irish Free State by this act became the only country to boycott the 1936 Nazi Olympics (Krüger 1972). In 1967, however the GAA rejoined the IAAF as representative of only the twenty-six counties of Southern Ireland; in so doing, it surrendered its representation of both Irish states.

During this period of sports politics, the IRB and, later, the (P)IRA supported nationalist Irish sport in pursuance of their own aims.

In the late nineteenth century, the IRB was continually facing the problem of having a poor stock of weaponry, and so 'armed insurrection was not an option' (Griffin 1990: 9). This led the IRB to the idea of becoming involved in the Irish sports movement: that way its members would be trained and organized in another nationalist and important Irish group at the same time. It also instilled a guerrilla spirit in its members, mindful of the fact that this had been the driving force behind the German Turners in the early nineteenth century, as well as the Czech and Polish Sokol movement in the late nineteenth and early twentieth centuries.

In 1884, the IRB member Michael Cusack, who was also a member of the Irish Champion Athletic Club (ICAC) and the Dublin Athletic Club (DAC), wrote an article in the Republican newspaper the *Irishman*, in which he said that the 'best athletes in Ireland are Nationalists' (Griffin 1990: 10). Given the similarities in political views, the IRB and the GAA approached one another, as a result of which Cusack became a key figure in establishing the IRB–GAA connection. Three years later, in 1887, several prominent IRB members gained top positions in the GAA (Griffin 1990: 23). Using the infiltration tactic, IRB members insinuated themselves into positions of influence in the nationwide GAA and the Gaelic League (Coogan 1985: 17).

Since 1916, the IRA gradually became the most important anti-British militant group and began to replace the old IRB. By 1920, the IRA had a virtual nationalist monopoly on violence; various sources estimate membership at between 15,000 and 100,000, including approximately 5,000 active fighters. But the problem of the relatively poor arms supply had never been resolved. Lack of weapons caused the IRA to start guerrilla training, including marching and cycling, in order to keep and stay fit. In this they were supported by the various cycling clubs of Ireland (Multhaupt 1988: 100).

From that point on, the relationship between the GAA and the IRA became close. Both sides worked hand in hand, and the GAA began to enlarge its political work. Just before the Treaty of 1921, the GAA supported Sinn Fein and arranged benefit matches for political prisoners. After the Treaty came into effect, General Eoin O'Duffy, an old IRB leader, played a big part in the policy of the GAA in banning British sports (Smulders 1977: 558). The British were aware of the relationship between the GAA, Sinn Fein and the IRB. In 1920, fourteen alleged British intelligence officers were shot in Dublin. During the afternoon soccer match in Croke Park between Dublin and Tipperary, British policemen, who thought that the players were involved in the shooting, opened fire and killed a Tipperary player and some spectators. By this action, the British only brought the GAA and the IRA closer together (Griffin 1990: 30–1).

During World War II, many IRA men were arrested and put in internment camps. The British had discovered that the IRA was receiving help from Nazi Germany (Geldard and Craig 1988: 7). The GAA Secretary, Padraig O'Caoimh, who was an IRA man, tried to support the prisoners by sending them a set of footballs and 'Medals that were keenly played for' (Coogan 1985: 197). After the War, IRA drilling began again and members infiltrated GAA clubs just as before.

In 1949, the cyclist Joe Christle founded the Gate Cycling Club; together with his club members he joined the IRA and remained a member until 1956. In the Armagh raid, 'six of the twenty raiders were club members' (Coogan 1985: 293). In 1952, Christle joined the John Mitchell Club of Sinn Fein and became one of its speakers. In the following years he organized annual eight-day cycling events and became an official of the National Cycling Association (NCA). However, he stayed in touch with revolutionary groups. He was arrested by the British in 1959, but was later released (Griffin 1990: 232; Coogan 1985: 297).

The example of Casement Park in Belfast is of a more symbolic character. The sports park was named after the Irish diplomat Roger Casement who, to support the IRB, had bought weapons in the independence struggle of 1916; later he was executed by the British Army. To name the park after an old IRA man was a political act against the British; it again characterized the relationship between the IRB, the IRA and the Irish sports movement. In 1969, the British turned the park into a tank base for their troops (Smulders 1977: 563).

Efforts were also made to use sport in the peace process – the 'Belfast Experiment' of the 1970s and 1980s. The local council tried to take jobless young people off the streets because they were a major element in the riots. Although sport in Ireland has been employed as a political weapon between the different national and political groups, the Belfast council decided to open fourteen 'Sport and Leisure Clubs'. The problem was where to build them. Initially it was planned to have Catholics and Protestants in the same leisure centres, so the clubs were constructed on the boundary between the two communities. This project failed because the clubs were 'regarded as Catholic centres by the Protestants, and as Protestant centres by the Catholics' (Sugden and Bairner 1993: 117).

The Belfast Leisure Services Department initiated a series of competitions between the centres. This 'ping-pong diplomacy', which endeavoured to improve relations through sporting activities, also failed. The result finally was a riot, and participation rates in the Belfast leisure centres are still very low (Sugden and Bairner 1993: 121).

The Irish example of the relationship between sport, politics and terrorism may be unusual, but it clearly shows how such a relationship can become a reality if circumstances allow. The extraordinary situation in Ireland is not unique: there are other examples of a close connection between sport and terrorism.

German Turners and terrorism

It can be argued that German gymnastics (*Turnen*) are founded on terrorism. Jahn, the Turner father, organized German students into the first guerrilla freedom-fighters against French Napoleonic occupation of Germany. Jahn's *Deutsche Turnkunst* (1817) can therefore be considered as the first guerrilla manual. But later on the Turners moved more into the mainstream of society and gave up their revolutionary inclinations. The Turner idea of physical fitness as part of the fight for freedom, however, remained alive in the Sokol organizations of Czechoslovakia and Poland – yet, here, ironically, the fight was against German occupation (Krüger 1975).

At the end of World War I, a revolution in Germany toppled the monarchy and established the first German democratic state based on freedom and equality. But the November 1918 Revolution was incomplete, the democratic forces were still in a minority. Because of their authoritarian monarchical structure, the old bureaucracy, the military and the judiciary remained powerful anti-democratic forces undermining the new republic (Diehl 1977: 17). Most of the social groups in Germany – political parties, social and political organizations of the aristocracy – were still anti-democratic and nationalistic (some were anti-Semitic as well). They aspired to re-establish the monarchy, or at least they preferred dictatorship. The other great anti-democratic force arraigned against the new democracy was the Communist Party, which endeavoured to introduce a communist state based on the Soviet Republic.

Because most Germans, and the anti-democratic and nationalist forces in particular, did not accept either the Treaty of Versailles or the new democratic Germany, many right-wing groups – and left-wing groups as well – opposed the conditions and tried to change society by violence and terror. Thus, they broke the law twice: by rejecting the conditions laid down by the Allies and violating the laws of the new democratic Germany.

From the start of the November 1918 Revolution up to the first democratic elections in January 1919, it was not clear which form of political government would prevail. Some political groups preferred a state based on Western democratic standards, some a state like the Soviet Republic. Yet others favoured a right-wing government with weak democratic institutions and some wanted a moderate version of a monarchy or a dictatorship. So the first attempts to introduce local democratic governments in the regions or in cities were attacked by anti-democratic forces from left and right. Riots were often led by former monarchist soldiers and officers who banded together in the illegal Free Corps (Freikorps). They had kept their weapons from the Great War or rearmed themselves although, according to the Allied conditions, all arms were forbidden. Armed local and part-time groups of Free Corps, named Auxiliary Volunteer Units (Zeitfreiwilligenverbände) and Civil Guards (Einwohnerwehren) were set up to support the small legal German army (the Reichswehr); this had also never adequately been integrated into the new state because of its long monarchist traditions.

Many of the anti-democratic and right-wing paramilitary people became members of all these groups at the same time; in some cases, individuals were also members of the legal Reichswehr. Because of the double and triple memberships, the ideological and political differences between the organizations (and also the Reichswehr) seemed small. So the anti-democratic or anti-Versailles forces in the German government and the Reichswehr supported the existence of the paramilitary groups, even though they were outlawed by the Allies.

Owing to their strong nationalist and monarchist tradition, some German Turners belonged to or sympathized with these anti-democratic groups (Bernett 1992). One of the aims of the nationalist Turners was to back the founding of a German national state; this dream had become a reality in 1871, when Chancellor Bismarck had proclaimed the German Reich under Wilhelm I, King of Prussia, and now also the first emperor of the German Reich, which included more than thirty German counties.

The Turners belonging to the Deutsche Turnerschaft, which was their principal association founded in 1861–68, supported the German emperor and his ideological and political aims – which were the national expansion of the Reich, leading to imperialism and the predominance of Germany in Europe. The monarchist Turners saw themselves as the military and national vanguard; they practised physical culture to make Germans fit, and military sports to prepare themselves for the next war. In this period, the Deutsche Turnerschaft fought against every anti-monarchist, anti-nationalist or democratic notion, particularly the new Social Democratic Party. Some democratic Turners, however, left the Turnerschaft and founded the socialist Arbeiterturnbund (Association of Worker Turners); and when it was set up in 1893, it already had 10,655 members, about 10 per cent of all German Turners (Krüger and Riordan: 1996).

In World War I, nearly a million Turners were in the army. But the lost war debilitated Germany which had to forfeit its colonies. The Allies took Germany under their control and the former German territory in the east was given to Poland or Czechoslovakia. The new democracy broke the German monarchy and the emperor. So the Turners could not identify themselves with the new state; they supported the old monarchist, imperialist and anti-democratic forces (John 1980). On the other hand, many left-wing Turners, who were also against democratic relations, backed the paramilitary and the sometimes outlawed Communist organization –

the Rote Frontkämpferbund (Red Front Fighting Association). Many of these 'fighters' were also members of the socialist Arbeiterturnbund at the same time (Bach 1981: 287).

From the late nineteenth century, English sports and Swedish gymnastics had become more and more popular in Germany. The Turners fought against these imports, even though track and field events were practised by both German Turners and British athletes. But at the start the Turners condemned English sport as a striving for records, efficiency, individualism, specialization and professionalism, in contrast to their own aims of collectivist, traditional, comprehensive and amateur *Turnen*. Later on, the Turners characterized English sport as 'foreign' according to their own xenophobic attitudes. But the Turners could not halt the encroachment of foreign sport. Because they feared losing their influence, the Turners permitted double membership of sporting and Turner federations. This is one reason for the founding of the Turn- und Sportvereine in the late nineteenth century (John 1980).

During the Weimar Republic, many Turners subscribed to traditional monarchist ideas; others supported communist principles. So individual Turners, organizations and military sports clubs were deeply involved in paramilitary groups, left- and right-wing skirmishes, uprisings and putsches. The relationship between sport and terrorism in the 1920s was so common that even contemporary literature (as in the novels of Joseph Roth – 1894–1939) and in satirical art (as in the work of George Grosz – 1893–1959) highlight these pervasive phenomena (Roth 1967: 49; Jones 1987: 121; Bernett 1992).

Because of the ideological concord and the personal relationship between the Völkisch Turner and right-wing terrorists, many terrorists and Civil Guards founded a Turner association as a cover, or they concealed themselves in right-wing Turn- und Sportvereine (Gymnastic and Sports Associations) (Könnemann 1971: 320). Some examples of these are given below.

Between 1918 and 1919, the Bavarian revolution brought a Soviet Republic to Bavaria and Munich for a few months. Many right-wing and paramilitary groups, like the Free Corps and the Civil Guards, fought against the Republic, as did a right-wing and Völkisch Secret Order called the Thule Society (Thulegesellschaft). The order was led by an extreme anti-Semite named Rudolf von Sebottendorff (1875–1945) who tried to overthrow the legal Bavarian government by assaults on communists and whipping up racial hatred against Jewish politicians (Sebottendorff 1934; Olenhusen 1990).

Some of the 200–300 members of the Thule Order were to become members of Hitler's National Socialist Party, and so the Thule Society is often described as a pioneer organization of the Nazis (Goodrick-Clarke 1992: 144–52). Some right-wing authors like Detlef Rose deny that connection (Rose 1994: 156–60). The Thule Society none the less hid weapons, planned an attack on Kurt Eisner (the elected leader of the Bavarian

Soviet Republic – who was eventually murdered in 1919 by a fellow-traveller of Thule) and worked hand in glove with the anti-Semitic right-wing Free Corps. To mask the purposes of his organization and to spread his anti-Semitic propaganda, Sebottendorff held meetings in the large rooms of a sports club, pretending that Thule was really a sports organization. He also bought a Munich anti-Semitic sports newspaper, the *Münchner Beobachter und Sportblatt*. Some Thule members worked as sports journalists themselves in order to camouflage their real aims (Sebottendorff 1934: 43–5, 207).

One of the most dangerous paramilitary Free Corps in Berlin was led by the Free Corps chief Reinhard. To disguise his banned anti-democratic organization, Reinhard called it Sportclub Olympia, sometimes Bund Olympia (Diehl 1977: 218) or Deutscher Verein für Leibesübungen Olympia (Kruppa 1988: 178). The sports club was involved in putsch plans of the Free Corps leader Captain Hermann Erhardt (1881–1971) who had taken part in the unsuccessful right-wing and anti-democratic Kapp-Putsch in Berlin in 1920, which had forced the elected government to flee from Berlin (Gumbel 1984: 68). The Olympia Sports Club held its meetings in school gyms and tried to attract young people as members because they could be more easily convinced of right-wing ideas.

At the end, the Olympia Sports Club possessed more than 2,000 members involved in military sports (Kruppa 1988: 178–80, 282). The club was banned in 1926 by the Berlin local council because of its anti-democratic activities. After that most of its members joined the Stahlhelm (Steel Helmet) which was one of the biggest organizers of military sports activities in the Weimar Republic (Mauch 1982: 69).

The same fate befell the illegal paramilitary association Bund Oberland, which operated 'under the auspices of a cover organization called the Deutscher Schützen- und Wanderbund (German Shooting and Hiking Society)' (Diehl 1977: 158). It had close relations with the former Free Corps leader Rossbach.

Major General Rossbach (1893–1967) participated in the anti-democratic Kapp-Putsch in Berlin and the Hitler Putsch of 1923 in Munich, when Hitler made a first, but still futile, attempt to overthrow the democratic state (Rossbach 1967: 78–83). After condemnation for his right-wing political activities, Rossbach decided to emigrate to Austria, where he founded terrorist organizations and camouflaged them as youth, gymnastics and dance clubs (Kruppa 1988: 282–3; Mauch 1982: 51). After his amnesty in 1925, Rossbach returned to Germany to continue his anti-democratic work and paramilitary sport (Diehl 1977: 371). From 1925, many German right-wing Turner associations helped Rossbach to provide a cover for his groups: Schill-Jugend, Völkische Turnerschaften or Spielschar Ekkehard (Bernett 1992: 429).

In the early years of the Weimar Republic, many Völkisch Turner associations helped terrorists of Hitler's SA and SS; they hid members of the terrorist Consul Organisation and the anti-democratic Kapp-Putsch, or they helped the Free Corps leader Rossbach to evade arrest. The Turners acted as a cover for these groups or trained them for their next attack on the democratic state (Könnemann 1971: 247; Bernett 1992: 428–9).

Very often members of the terror organizations went to Turner associations to make propaganda for their illegal groups or to put advertisements in popular sports journals. In 1919, the Civil Guards applied to Turner and sports associations and some rowing clubs to find strong people for their organization (Könnemann 1971: 205). In 1924, the Social Democrat lawyer Emil Julius Gumbel (1891–1966) reported on Free Corps leaders who gave lectures in sports clubs in order to attract volunteers (Gumbel 1984: 16, 26). Several Völkisch associations published their propaganda material in 1920 in the Turner newspaper *Deutsche Turnzeitung* to announce the foundation of right-wing and anti-Semitic Turner associations (1920: 267–8). The year before, the same paper printed a propaganda text of the Free Corps, *Schwarze Jäger*, which invited Turners to join them (Peiffer 1976: 34). In 1923, the same paper thanked the terrorist Bund Oberland, which had illegally fought against the Poles in Silesia, for defending the former German districts – an act which was against the Treaty of Versailles (1923: 327).

Many Turners were members of the semi-legal Civil Guards and sympathized with the Kapp-Putsch (*Deutsche Turnzeitung* 1920: 318). German Turners who lived in areas like Silesia and south-western Germany – occupied by or under the control of the Allies – were arrested because of their military sport, their (forbidden) participation in the first German Turner festival (*Deutsches Turnfest*) in 1923 and their connections with a dangerous Civil Guard named Orgesch (*Deutsche Turnzeitung* 1921: 24; 1922: 121). Turners and skating clubs fought together with the Free Corps against the Poles in Silesia; many local Silesian sports groups, like the Kosener SC, formed their own Free Corps sections in memory of Jahn and his 1813 Free Corps (*Monatsschrift für Turnen, Spiel und Sport* 1921: 137; Salomon 1951: 155).

In the new state of Czechoslovakia, set up in 1918, the local German minority tried to return the country to the Reich by supporting nationalistic, terrorist and anti-democratic actions against Czechs and Slovaks. The leader of this German minority was Konrad Henlein (1898–1945) who at the same time was leader of the German Turners in Czechoslovakia (Salomon 1951: 172–4). In 1938, when Hitler occupied the 'German' part of Czechoslovakia, the Nazi Henlein became governor of this region. He was executed by the Allies as a war criminal in 1945.

Thanks to the strong connections between Turners and terrorism, and to the conviction that physical exercise could be good for military discipline, for the total defence potential and for fighting against enemies inside and outside Germany, the tradition of military sport never completely disappeared. Many German terrorist organizations engaged in physical training as an integral part of their military training.

The left-wing Red Front Fighter Association also engaged in military sports to present itself as a well-organized and disciplined political agitation group, to defend its members in street fights against right-wing groups and to resist arrest during demonstrations. After 1929, when the organization was outlawed, the main aim was to overthrow the democratic government by trying to create a revolutionary situation. The organization trained together with worker sports clubs, preferring track and field events, shooting and combat sports; it also arranged military sport contests which were banned, but secretly carried out (Bach 1981: 287–8); Finker 1981: 52–64).

The situation at the time of the founding of Hitler's Storm Troopers, the SA, in 1921 was typical (Longerich 1989: 23). Before the organization was named Storm Troop (Sturm Abteilung), the Nazis tried to conceal the terrorist aim of the SA by calling it the Turner and Sport Division (Turn- und Sportabteilung). Some local groups of the SA founded special Turner clubs, like the Turnerschaft Ulrich von Hutten in Berlin (Werner 1964: 307). In fact, Hitler combined the terrorist training of the SA with physical training. Military sports were elements in all SA groups (Werner 1964: 367–70; Krüger and Riordan 1996; Bach 1981: 282–6; Bernett 1981). They practised boxing, ju-jitsu, gymnastics, track and field, the decathlon, combat sports and self-defence. The sports section of the SA had to be very careful because spies of the Allies and the government were always suspicious of military and paramilitary sport (Killinger 1934: 44, 57; Röhm 1934: 152).

The largest right-wing group which organized and practised paramilitary sport extensively was the Stahlhelm, the organization of and for former front soldiers. Founded in December 1918 and led by the ex-officer Franz Seldte (1882–1947) and right-wing politician Theodor Duesterberg (1875–1950), the Stahlhelm rose to half a million members. Although it was temporarily outlawed by the government, it was a huge reservoir for people discontent with the conditions of the Treaty of Versailles and who had fought against democracy and the German revolution of 1918. After 1933, the Stahlhelm joined the SA. Their anti-democratic ideas and paramilitary politics led to intensive contacts with diverse Free Corps, SA and SS and the Consul Organisation, which were the other members of 'Hitler's Heralds' (Jones 1987: 188–91). The Stahlhelm was semi-legal and not directly involved in terrorist acts. So this may be a borderline case of definition. But the organization may be called terrorist according to the accepted definition quoted earlier, and the specific historical situation in the Weimar Republic, when anti-democratic forces called for the overthrow of the democratically elected government. The Stahlhelm certainly did so.

The military sport of the Stahlhelm was well organized. Young members were forced to join sports clubs, but military sport was carried out by the Stahlhelm itself. Divided into districts and regions, they went in for scouting, open-country marches and cross-country races, running, shooting and full-pack marches (Bach 1981: 278). Most of the sports were performed in teams; it was more important to achieve good results as a team than as an individual (Krüger and Riordan 1996). The military sport and regular sports contests were organized following official rules published in the annual registers of the Stahlhelm (Hildebrandt and Kettner 1931: 213–19).

Sometimes the physical training of the above-mentioned organizations was led by members of the notorious terrorist group Organisation Consul (OC), where *Turnen* gymnastics and track and field events were very important for staying fit. In his novel *Das Spinnennetz (The Spider's Web)*, first published in 1924, Joseph Roth describes the physical training and military sports of a fictitious terrorist organization – the literary analogy of the OC (Roth 1967: 49). In fact, nearly all known prominent OC members practised *Turnen*, gymnastics and ju-jitsu (Bernett 1992: 427; Freska 1924: 307).

The OC was responsible for assaults on and murders of German politicians and intellectuals. In 1921, they shot the Finance Minister Matthias Erzberger, and in 1922 they murdered the Foreign Affairs Minister Walther Rathenau. In the same year they tried to assassinate Phillip Scheidemann, Lord Mayor of Kassel, and the famous writer and intellectual Maximilian Harden. Both assaults failed (Sabrow 1995). It is known that in all cases the OC assassins were involved in right-wing Turner, physical culture or nudism movements.

Rathenau's assassins had been *Völkisch* Turners from a young age and members of the 'Deutsch-völkischer Turnverein Jahn' (Bernett 1992: 426). They used their physical fitness to attack their victims and escape from the police (Sabrow 1995: 196). The OC member Albert Grenz, who was involved in the attack on Harden, was a member of the racist and anti-democratic Nudism Gymnastic Order of Richard Ungewitter (Lohalm 1970: 235). During the first decades of the twentieth century, nudism was part of the most right-wing and anti-democratic gymnastic movement in Germany (Krüger 1991; Gumbel 1984: 216).

Many members of the OC were convicted and sent to prison for several years. Most wrote memoirs about their experiences in gaol, which provide contemporary sports historians with substantial detail. All of them mention fitness training walks in prison. The Rathenau assassin Erich von Salomon (1902–1972), who was trained in the army in 1918, performed press ups nearly every day (Salomon 1928: 27; 1933: 50). The OC chief, 'Consul' Hermann Ehrhardt did pull-ups in his prison cell (Freska 1924: 255). Hartmut Plaas (1900–44), who was first adjutant to Ehrhardt and who also took part in the attack on Rathenau, practised callisthenics in prison. For him physical fitness was an invaluable weapon against the democratic state (Plaas 1928: 50). Manfred von Killinger (1886–1945) was one of the OC leaders and later became a functionary of the Nazis; he committed suicide in 1945 after the Nazi defeat. Like Ernst Röhm, leader of the SA, who had always been a Turner (Röhm 1934: 19, 152), Killinger had also practised track and field events, swimming and *Turnen* from an early age; he even won first prize in a boxing contest during his Free Corps period (Killinger 1928a: 156). In 1924, when he was in gaol, Killinger performed gymnastics and nudist gymnastics (Killinger 1928b: 111). He used the famous gymnastic systems of J. P. Müller and Bess Mensendieck, who wrote gymnastic books around the turn of the century; they were translated into several languages (Bonde 1991; Müller 1909; Mensendieck 1954).

Conclusions

Physical fitness exercises, sport and *Turnen* gymnastics may be practised for a variety of reasons – health, record-breaking, recreation or just fun. The uses and ideology of sport are multiple, and so are its abuses (Krockow 1972: 84).

Military sport belongs to a difficult sports category, as it may be instrumentalized in both positive and negative ways. In some situations, it may well be used to stabilize democratic governments. However, function, practice and use can easily be transformed into non-democratic and even terrorist forms without changing the main principles of engaging in sport. It all depends on the circumstances. A good example of this instrumentalization is the situation in Palestinian camps where completely different political terrorist groups have been trained in the same 'utilitarian' sports. Here the political foe of the terrorist groups is radically different even though each group fights with the same weapon – sport.

We have seen how individual athletes or Turner and sports groups can use physical training as a political or even terrorist weapon, or how they themselves may be instrumentalized by terrorism. Here sport is instrumentalized only to pursue direct political aims. On the other hand, in looking at completely different political groups (for example, the IRA and German right-wing terrorists), we see how the liberal and educational notion of sport can be transformed into anti-democratic, nationalist or even anti-Semitic terrorist weapons.

Certainly the twentieth century is littered with examples of sport linked to terrorism.

References

Bach, H. (1981) 'Volks- und Wehrsport in der Weimarer Repulik', *Sportwissenschaft* (11)3, 273–94.

Backes, U. and Jesse, E. (eds) (1993) *Politischer Extremismus in der Bundesrepublik Deutschland*, Bonn.

Barrett, M. B. (1977) *Soldiers, Sportsmen and Politicians – Military Sport in Germany 1924–1935*, Dissertation, University of Massachusetts.

Bernett, H. (1981) 'Wehrsport – ein Pseudosport', *Sportwissenschaft* (11)3, 295–308.

Bernett, H. (1992) 'Völkisch Turner als politische Terroristen', *Sportwissenschaft* (22)4, 418–39.

Bird, K. W. (1977) *Weimar, the German Naval Officer Corps and the Rise of National Socialism*, Amsterdam: B. R. Grüner.

Bonde, H. (1991) 'I. P. Müller. Danish Apostle of Health', *The International Journal of the History of Sport* (10)3, 347–69.

Coogan, T. P. (1985) *The I.R.A.*, London: HarperCollins.

Diehl, J. M. (1977) *Paramilitary Politics in Weimar Germany*, Bloomington and London: Indiana University Press.

Eyck, E. (1956) *Geschichte der Weimarer Republik*, Erlenbach-Zürich and Stuttgart: Eugen Rentsch Verlag.

Finker, K. (1981) *Geschichte des Roten Frontkämpferbundes*, Frankfurt: Verlag Marxistische Blätter.

Freska, F. (1924) *Kaptän Ehrhardt. Abenteuer und Schicksale*, Berlin: August Scherl.

Geldard, I. and Craig, K. (1988) *IRA. INLA: Foreign Support and International Connections*, London: Institute for the Study of Terrorism.

Goodrick-Clarke, N. (1992) *The Occult Roots of Nazism. Secret Aryan Cults and their Influence on Nazi Ideology*, New York: New York University Press.

Gordon, H. (1972) *The Beerhall Putsch*, Princeton, NJ.

Griffin, P. (1990) *The Politics of Irish Athletics 1850–1900,* Ballinamore, Co. Leitrim: Marathon Publications.

Gumbel, E. J. (1984) *Verschwörer. Zur Geschichte der deutschen nationalistischen Geheimbünde 1918–1924* (1st ed. 1924), Frankfurt: Verlag Das Wunderhorn.

Hildebrandt, H. and Kettner, W. (1931) *Stahlhelm-Handbuch,* Berlin: Stahlhelm-Verlag.

Höfer, A. (1994) *Der Olympische Friede. Anspruch und Wirklichkeit einer Idee*, St. Augustin: Academia.

Holt, R. (1995) 'Contrasting nationalism: sport, militarism and the unitary state in Britain and France before 1914', in *Tribal Identities. Nationalism, Europe and Sport* (ed. J.A. Mangan), London: Frank Cass, 39–54.

John, H. G. (1980) 'Die Turnbewegung im deutschen Kaiserreich von 1871 bis 1918', in *Geschichte der Leibesübungen* 1/3 (ed. H. Überhorst), Berlin: Bartels and Wernitz, 278–324.

Jones, N. H. (1987) *Hitler's Heralds. The Story of the Freikorps 1918–1923*, London: John Murray.

Killinger, M. (1928a) 'Neun Monate im Untersuchungsgefängnis in Offenburg', in *Wir klagen an! Nationalisten in den Kerkern der Bourgeoisie* (ed. H. Plaas), Berlin: Vormarsch Verlag, 153–60.

—— (1928b) *Ernstes und Heiteres aus dem Putschleben,* Berlin: Vormarsch Verlag.

—— (1934) *Die SA in Wort und Bild. Männer und Mächte*, Leipzig: Kittler.

Könnemann, E. (1971) *Einwohnerwehren und Zeitfreiwilligenverbände,* Berlin: Deutscher Militärverlag.

Kolb, E. (1993) *Die Weimarer Republik*, München: Oldenbourg Verlag.

Krockow, C. G. V. (1972) *Sport und Industriegesellschaft*, München: Piper Verlag.

Krüger, A. (1972) *Die Olympischen Spiele 1936 und die Weltmeinung*, Berlin.

—— (1975) *Sport und Politik*. Hanover: Fackelträger.

—— (1991) 'There goes this art of manliness: naturism and racial hygiene in Germany', *Journal of Sport History* 18(1), 135–58.

Krüger, A. and Lojewski, F. v. (1996) 'Ausgewählte Aspekte des Wehrsports in Niedersachsen in der Weimarer Zeit', in *Sport, Spiel und Turnen in*

232　*Bernd Wedemeyer*

Niedersachsen zwischen 1918 und 1933 (eds A. Krüger and H. Langenfeld), Hoya: NISH (in print).

Krüger, A. and Riordan, J. (eds) (1996) *The Story of Worker Sport*, Champaign, IL: Human Kinetics.

Kruppa, B. (1988) *Rechtsradikalismus in Berlin 1918–1928*, Berlin and New York.

Lohalm, U. (1970) *Völkischer Radikalismus. Die Geschichte des Deutsch Völkischen Schutz- und Trutzbundes*, Hamburg: Leibniz-Verlag.

Longerich, P. (1989) *Die braunen Bataillone. Geschichte der SA*, München: C. H. Beck.

Mangan, J. A. (ed.) (1995) *Tribal Identities. Nationalism, Europe and Sport*, London: Frank Cass.

Marighella, C. (1970) *Minimanual of the Urban Guerilla*, New World Liberation Front, s.l.

Mauch, H.-J. (1982) *Nationalistische Wehrorganisationen in der Weimarer Republik. Zur Entwicklung und Ideologie des 'Paramilitarismus'*, Frankfurt am Main: Peter Lang.

Mensendieck, B. (1954) *Look better, feel better. The world-reknowned Mensendieck System of Functional Movements – for a youthful body and vibrant health*, New York: Muller.

Meyer, A. and Rabe, K.-K. (1979) *Unsere Stunde die wird kommen. Rechtsextremismus unter Jugendlichen*, Göttingen: Lamuv.

Morehouse, H. F. (1995) 'One State, several countries: soccer and nationality in a "United" Kingdom', in *Tribal Identities. Nationalism, Europe and Sport* (ed. J. A. Mangan), London: Frank Cass, 55–74.

Müller, J. P. (1909) *My Army and Navy System*, London: Ewart & Seymour.

Multhaupt, W. F. (1988) *Die Irisch-Republikanische Armee (IRA). Von der Guerilla-Freiheitsarmee zur modernen Untergrundorganisation*, Dissertation, Bonn.

Olenhusen, A. G. v. (1990) 'Bürgerrat, Einwohnerwehr und Gegenrevolution Freiburg 1918–1920. Zugleich ein Beitrag zur Biographie des Rudolf Freiherr von Sebottendorff' in *Wege und Abwege. Beiträge zur europäischen Geistesgeschichte der Neuzeit. Festschrift für Ellic Howe* (ed. A. G. v. Olenhusen), Freiburg: Hochschul-Verlag, 115–34.

Peiffer, L. (1976) *Die deutsche Turnerschaft. Thre politische Stellung in der Zeit der Weimarer Republik und des Nationalsozialismus,* Ahrensburg: Czwalina.

Peters, B. (1991) *RAF. Terrorismus in Deutschland*, Stuttgart: Deutsche Verlags-Anstalt.

Plaas, H. (1928) 'Die verruchte Stätte', in *Wir klagen an! Nationalisten in den Kerkern der Bourgeoisie* (ed. H. Plaas), Berlin: Vormarsch Verlag, 38–59.

Röhm, E. (1934) *Die Geschichte eines Hochverräters*, München: Eher-Verlag.

Rose, D. (1994) *Die Thule-Gesellschaft. Legende Mythos Wirklichkeit*, Tübingen: Grabert.

Rossbach, G. (1967) *Mein Weg durch die Zeit*, Weilheim-Lahn: Schmidt-Verlag.

Roth, J. (1967) *Das Spinnennetz*, Cologne and Berlin: Kiepenheuer & Witsch.

Sabrow, M. (1995) *Der Rathenaumord. Rekonstruktion einer Verschwörung gegen die Republik von Weimar*, München: Oldenbourg.

Salomon, E. v. (1928) Schrei aus dem Käfig, in *Wir klagen an! Nationalisten in den Kerkern der Bourgeoisie* (ed. H. Plaas), Berlin: Vormarsch Verlag, 26–37.

—— (1933) *Die Kadetten*, Berlin: Rowohlt.

—— (1951) *Der Fragebogen*, Hamburg: Rowohlt.

Sebottendorff, R. v. (1934) *Bevor Hitler kam. Urkundliches aus der Frühzeit der nationalsozialistischen Bewegung*, München: Deukula.

Schultz, G. (1982) *Deutschland seit dem Ersten Weltkrieg 1918–1945*. Göttingen: Vandenhoeck & Ruprecht.

Smulders, H. (1977) 'Irish representation in international sport events, 1922–1932. The dialectics of autonomy and internationalism in sport', in *H.I.P.S.A. VIth International Congress. International Association for the History of Physical Education and Sport,* Dartford, 555–70.

Sugden, J. and Bairner, A. (1993) *Sport, Sectarianism and Society in a Divided Ireland*, Leicester: Leicester University Press.

Waite, R. G. L. (1952) *Vanguard of Nazism: The Free Corps Movement in Post-War Germany*, Cambridge: Harvard University Press.

Werner, A. (1964) *SA und NSDAP, SA: 'Wehrverband'. 'Parteitruppe' oder 'Revolutionsarmee'? Studien zur Geschichte der SA und der NSDAP 1920–1933*, Dissertation, Nürnberg.

Wilkinson, P. (ed.) (1993) *Terrorism: British Perspectives*, Dartmouth: Galliard.

12 Sport in South Africa

Grant Jarvie and Irene Reid

When South Africa re-entered international sport six years ago the looming new democracy was excited at having an instant role model for people of diverse cultures. From President Mandela down, politicians were quick to point out that sport had provided an ideal catalyst for change, that sport, like no other area of public life, had the capacity to break down barriers and forge the links in the nation building chain.

(The *Sunday Times* (South Africa) 5 October 1997: 22)

The new constitution of the Republic of South Africa was initially adopted on 8 May 1996 and amended by the new Constitutional Assembly, under the leadership of Nelson Mandela, on 11 October 1996. While the new constitution, with its American-styled Bill of Rights, provided the framework for the development of the new republic few areas have received more presidential support than sport. Who could forget the scenes from the 1995 rugby World Cup finals with the new president wearing the green and yellow rugby shirt, sharing the public euphoria of South Africa becoming rugby world champions and proclaiming, yet again, that sport was part of the glue that held the new republic together? The state and the African National Congress (ANC) now speak the same language of reconstruction, nation-building and development. South African Minister of Sport Steve Tshwete, talking about sport at the Commonwealth Heads of Government Conference in Edinburgh during October 1997, stated that sport provided the basis for social interaction, community building, economic development and the fostering of civic and national pride.

The image of national unity captured by the Springbok success in 1995 has been repeated in relation to other South African sporting achievements. Football has long been perceived as the sport of black South Africans and has also been viewed as a symbol of nation-building. Victory in the 1996 African Nations' Cup was followed by qualification for the 1998 World Cup finals in France. The National Party spokesman for sport Nic Koornhof remarked that 'we can all be proud of Bafana, Bafana and their spectacular contribution towards the rainbow nation's quest for excellence' (*South African Press Association* 17 August 1997: 2). Clive Barker, Bafana, Bafana's coach, had hoped that South African football would be rewarded for not tolerating rebel tours during the struggle against apartheid (*Daily Telegraph* 18 August 1997: S3). Qualification for the World Cup finals occurred only five years after being re-admitted to FIFA.

On 16 August 1997 95,000 people entered a ground built for 80,000 to watch South Africa qualify for their first football World Cup finals. A further 25,000 waited outside the locked gates. The FNB stadium near Soweto is the home of South African football. For the match against Congo another world bordering on anarchy existed inside the FNB stadium. People sat in the aisles, perched on the walls and clung to the railings. The delirious exhortations to the favoured Bafana, Bafana football stars perhaps neatly reflected, more than the rugby World Cup victory, Nelson Mandela's rainbow nation. Less than a decade ago the likes of Andre Arendse, Tinkler and Masinga were each represented by separate racial governing bodies and now they were one team, representing one nation on the world stage. The same players who would have been excluded from representing South Africa in the late 1980s were now able to look forward to their share of the £150,000 for qualifying for the 1998 World Cup finals in France. The celebrations after the 1–0 victory over the Congolese may have been viewed by the state as further confirmation of not simply another imagined community but that South Africa's most popular sport was football, albeit the most popular male sport, which in terms of participants and spectators was way ahead of establishment sports such as cricket and rugby union.

Sport as an aspect of South African life has always been an area through which different groups have actively reworked their relationships and responded to changing political and historical conditions. The majority of South African sportsmen and women throughout most of the twentieth century have had to struggle with sport under conditions not of their own choosing. For much of the twentieth century, an exclusive form of white Afrikaner nationalism, with its explicit objective of capturing the state for the then white Afrikaner nation confronted a pan-South African black nationalism which sought to incorporate the majority of South Africans into the body politic. During this era of apartheid, sport was extremely important because of the way in which it was used by the state in determining and influencing opinion towards South Africa. The practice of multiracial sport was the National Party's ideological defence against those who argued that you could not have normal sport in an abnormal society.

Given the complexity of sport, political consciousness and community in twentieth-century South Africa it is impossible to provide a comprehensive coverage of a period, which if one takes the period of apartheid from 1948–92 alone, has spawned a considerable body of literature and research. None the less in this chapter we hope to provide a short historical synthesis of sport in twentieth-century South Africa. We have tried to do this by providing a continuous historical narrative into which is woven some of the most appropriate sporting illustrations that have emerged between 1900 and the present. It is important in the first instance to recognize that sport in what is now the Republic of South Africa, with its new one law, one nation constitution, does in fact have a much earlier history which pre-dates the early 1900s. For instance, well before the beginnings of the second Anglo-Boer War (1899–1902) the following sporting bodies had already formed: the South Africa Cricket Federation (SACA); the Football Association of South Africa (FASA) and the South African Rugby Board (SARB). With the exception of cricket and horse-racing all the major sports made their appearance between 1860 and 1900. By 1908 South Africa had participated in its first Olympic Games.

Sport before apartheid

If it might be inappropriate to talk of sports in pre-colonial South Africa, it is not inappropriate to mention briefly the folk origins of modern South African sport. The sport practised in South Africa in the late 1990s has itself developed out of various phases in the development of South African society. The first British occupation of the Cape from 1795 to 1802 coincided with the foundation of the first horse-racing club in 1802. Early settler games revolved around the horse which played a crucial part in Boer working life. Hunting and especially shooting were predominant recreational activities of the time. Regular horse races between British and Dutch settlers took place after 1795. From these early beginnings, if not earlier practices, Cape horse-racing quickly spread to Kimberley and Johannesburg with the South African Jockey Club being formed in 1882.

During the most active period of imperial expansion a number of sporting events involved both the British Army and British settlers. Although the first recorded cricket match took place in 1805 the first match between settlers and Africans took place in 1854. The social significance of cricket is commented upon by Archer and Bouillon (1982: 88):

> Until the end of the 19th Century, cricket had been a social game played popularly by all groups including Africans and Coloureds. The transformation into an imperial sport for the elite, conscious of its civilising integrating mission in the world ... sharply reduced the game's audience amongst blacks, the majority of whom were excluded from playing by material costs.

By the time the second Anglo-Boer War had ended in 1902 tennis, cycling, athletics, swimming and gymnastics all had national federations. Indeed with the exception of cricket and horse-racing all the major imperial sports had made their appearance by 1900. More specifically it might be suggested that: (i) all the major sports apart from rugby/football (1862), athletics, cycling, golf, boxing and tennis appeared between 1880 and 1900; (ii) the institutionalization of several sports occurred between 1875 and 1885; during this decade the first clubs were formed in rugby, football, athletics, cycling, horse-racing, golf and tennis; (iii) sports were subsequently taken up at such a rate that the first national federations appeared only ten years afterwards and were established in all the major sports before the 1920s; and (iv) the development of colonial sports and the marginalization of indigenous sports continued. Two particularly active periods are worth mentioning, namely the interwar years and the 1950s.

Afrikaner nationalism accelerated during the 1930s and the ideological fervour of the period was often mirrored in sport. The role of rugby as a symbol for the Afrikaner way of life has often been mythologized through assertions that the values of religion, a rugged frontier life-style and co-operation were often key qualities that were reflected in the game of rugby. Liberal opinion was such that sport was also seen to be used in the social control of black leaders and urban workers while at the same time bridging the gap between the two white communities of the Boer and the Briton. Writing in 1927 the British colonel P. A. Silburn commented (Archer and Bouillon, 1982: 34):

> the Boer and the Briton . . . follow the same sports with equal fervour and skill, they belong to the same clubs and play in the same teams. . . . The love of the same sport is gradually eradicating racial antagonism, and it will be upon the sports field that it will eventually expire and be decently buried. The postponement of that day is mainly due to the non-sporting, self seeking politicians of both races . . . whose stock in trade is racialism.

The institutionalization of white sport in school physical education programmes further served as a mechanism of social differentiation. By 1939 physical education had become a compulsory subject within both school and university programmes and yet the majority of the population were hardly affected since only a small minority of black schoolchildren of school age were enrolled in school programmes. The proportion of children attending classes in black schools rose from 18.1 per cent of the children of school age in 1936 to 27.1 per cent in 1946. In 1946 only 173 of the 4,587 African schools taught at secondary level. The expansion of the South African economy not only resulted in higher standards of living for whites but also increased sporting opportunities in the sense that facilities, programmes and federations all increased during the period of industrialization. In particular the white sports boom was prominent in those industrial growth areas where increased industrial production resulted in the further exploitation of cheap black labour but also financed the installation of leisure and sporting facilities for the Afrikaner.

By the time the National Party came to power in 1948 a degree of segregation and inequality of opportunity between groups and athletes had already evolved. There was little need to impose a policy of apartheid upon specific sporting relations since a high degree of social differentiation already existed. The general laws of apartheid rule rendered multiracial sport impossible in that it was just as illegal for black and white athletes to mix openly in competition as it was in society. The attempts of the 1948 nationalist government to consolidate Afrikaner solidarity through a rigid definition of coloured ethnicity went far beyond anything attempted hitherto. The Population Registration Act, the Prohibition of Mixed Marriages Act, and Immorality Amendment Act, the Group Areas Act and the Separate Registration of Voters Act all contributed to a process of redefinition. Membership of the *volk* was limited to those who were deemed to be *white* Afrikaans-speaking Calvinists, and existing racism was bolstered by legislation in the interests of ethnic consolidation. Apartheid in other words was the real hurdle to normal sport in an abnormal society.

Apartheid: the real hurdle

The period between 1948 and 1992 was marked by the development of apartheid, international isolation from major sporting events and the internal struggle between different sporting factions within South Africa. The realities of apartheid were such that during the 1970s whites had 73 per cent of all athletic tracks, 92 per cent of all golf courses, 83 per cent of hockey fields, 84 per cent of cricket pitches, 95 per cent of squash courts, 80 per cent of badminton courts, 83 per cent of swimming baths, and 82 per cent of rugby fields (Jarvie 1989: 16). It is not necessary to provide a complete analysis of the extent to which apartheid laws influenced sport in South Africa, but it is worth mentioning several cornerstones upon which apartheid was built.

1   The population Registration Act of 1950 provided for a rigid system of racial classification in terms of white, coloured, Indian or native groups.
2   The Reservation of Separate Amenities Act of 1953 permitted owners of property to evict or exclude members of certain racial groups from the premises or amenities, including sporting amenities. The Act provided for dispensation for international black sporting stars who were deemed to be 'honorary white' citizens for the duration of their stay.
3   The Native Law Amendments Act of 1957 provided for the withholding of permission for Africans to attend gatherings outside of their own native residential area. It grew out of the Native Consolidation Act of 1956 and was reinforced further with the Group Areas Act of 1966.

4   The Group Area's Act of 1966 divided South Africa into areas of occupancy and residential segregation on the basis of race. The consequence of this for the majority of black South African sportsmen and women was that it hindered the travel to and from matches and competitions which were outside of an individual's designated residential area.
5   The Liquor Amendment Act of 1975 and 1977 originally barred all mixed drinking. The 1977 Act by introducing permits allowed for dispensation for certain authorized sporting functions. It also laid the basis for the protection of International Hotels and in this way honorary white sportsmen and women and other talented black athletes were shielded from normal apartheid conventions. It allowed the authorities to convey to the outside world that a degree of multi-racial interaction was evident within South African sport.

Black participation in sport had always been mediated by the practice of apartheid. A survey conducted in the province of Natal reflected the backlog in black sports participation in one of South Africa's four provinces (Zulu and Booth 1988). The results which were collected during the 1980s indicated that 144 sports were practised in Natal and that 215,708 people were registered with government recognized sports associations. Less than 45 per cent of those participating were black. The people's game was football with over 90 per cent of those registered to play football being black. The only other sports with significant black sports participation levels were boxing and road running. In 40 per cent of the sports registered no black participation at all was recorded. In schools too black participation and opportunity reflected the politics of apartheid. Shortly before his death in prison, Steve Biko described the differences between black and white sport (Biko 1979: 19):

> You find for instance even the organisation of sport – these are things you notice as a kid – at white schools to be absolutely thorough and indicative of good training, good upbringing, you could get in a school 15 rugby teams, we could get from our school three rugby teams. Each of those 15 teams has got uniforms for each particular kid who plays; we have got to share the uniforms amongst our three teams.

The social, cultural, emotional, economic and political resources which the majority of the South African people had at their behest meant that sporting opportunity was inherently unequal. The general laws of apartheid rendered multiracial sport impossible in that it was illegal for black and white athletes to mix openly in competition, as it was for various groups to mix socially in South African society. Hardly a decade went by without sport in South Africa being the internal and external focus of resistance against apartheid rule. The 1950s witnessed the Non-Racial Table Tennis

Board being accorded recognition by the International Table Tennis Federation and the formation of the South African Sports Association (SASA). The 1960s saw the transition of the main black sporting federations to a policy of non-racialism; the formation of the South African Non-Racial Olympic Committee (SAN-ROC); the Basil D'Olivera affair of 1966 where MCC, having selected the South African born cricketer to play with the touring side, were confronted with a protest by the Nationalist Government of President Vorster (the MCC refused to de-select the player and the tour was cancelled); the exclusion of South Africa from the Olympic Games and the strategic move of SAN-ROC to a position of exile in London. The 1970s opened with the formation of two further non-racial sporting organizations namely the South African Non-Racial Sports Organisation (SASPO) and the South African Council on Sport (SACOS); Prime Minister Vorster unveiled a new multinational sports policy which the British minister of sport rejected in that it continued to reflect the apartheid system, and the Gleneagles Agreement was signed by the Commonwealth heads of government on 15 June 1977 which condemned the development of sport under apartheid and encouraged the isolation of South Africa from the international sporting arena.

By the late 1980s at least two positions on sport had firmly emerged. The official government stance on sport was that, despite being regulated through the Department of National Education, sport was free from all statutory control. Sport, in theory, was free to go its own way. Such an ideological position has been the objective of the Directorate of Sport and Recreation Advancement, a policy that was operated through the South African Olympic and National Games Association (SAONGA) and the South African Sports Federation (SASF). Yet such a position did not merely develop overnight but did in fact emerge as a result of changing social and political positions and tensions. Dr Donges, Minister of the Interior, argued in 1956 that whites and non-whites should organize their sport separately. Prime Minister Vorster made a similar statement in 1967, while between 1971 and 1976, Dr Koornhof was charged with establishing a new multinational sports policy that was compatible with the state policy of separate development for different nations within South Africa. This remained a cornerstone of President de Klerk's liberalization policies in the early 1980s. Supporters of the state's position on sport argued on a number of occasions that sport provided an essential platform in the process of integration and bridge building. Critics of this position argued that the changes were cosmetic, ideological and indeed peripheral to the lives of the majority.

While the official government stance on sport might have been loosely termed attacking down the right, or sport was free to go its own way, those oppositional forces which attacked down the left tended to argue that you could not have normal sport in an abnormal society. The aim was to create a form of sport that was free from all forms of racism, including the structural racism that was inherent within apartheid. While the anti-apartheid sporting organizations in the 1970s were mainly SASA, SACOS and the African National Congress (ANC) a new militant organization, the National Sports Congress (NSC), was formed in the 1980s. A number of sporting organizations had historically compromised their demands yet the strength of SACOS, SAN-ROC and the NSC was their refusal to separate sporting demands from the broader demands for social change. Freedom in sport, it was argued, could only materialize as a result of true liberation which in turn necessitated the dismantling of apartheid's core statutes and policies. Yet even within these aligned sporting movements differences in policy existed. The creation of the NSC divided the non-racial sports movements. The NSC questioned the use of boycotts and non-collaboration and instead urged that negotiation with the establishment was the key to the de-racializing of South African sport. However, its lack of human and financial resources mitigated against it being the Trojan Horse which would transform or even shackle the establishment world of cricket and rugby.

In the early 1990s in no sport, argued Guelke (1993), was the transformation so dramatic than in cricket. It was cricket that in part paved the way for South Africa's re-admission to international competition. In November 1991 a three one-day test match series was played against India in which India won the series by two tests to one. That South Africa's emergence from sporting isolation should take place in India is all the more remarkable considering the absence of any formal ties between India and South Africa since 1948. The path to re-entry into international cricket was cleared by the International Cricket Council in July 1991 and the lifting of the international sporting links by the National Olympic and Sports Congress followed in October. The final obstacle was cleared with the decision of the Commonwealth heads of government, meeting in Harare, to lift immediately sanctions on travel, tourism, cultural, academic, scientific and sporting exchanges. The decision to lift sporting sanctions was in line with the recommendations of the Commonwealth Foreign Ministers meeting in New Delhi in September 1991 which had recommended a phased easing of sanctions. By 1992 South Africa had participated in the Cricket World Cup in Australia and New Zealand.

Such events were in stark contrast to the circumstances which surrounded the arrival of the last rebel cricket tour to visit South Africa in January 1990 under the captaincy of the former England captain Mike Gatting. The tour men were quick to offer their justifications: financial security, keep politics out of sport, and bridge-building in the townships being the most common. However, when this particular rebel tour had come and gone the South African Cricket Union (SACU) was still faced with the realities of apartheid in transition. The opposition to the Gatting rebel tour was much greater than previously experienced by sanction breaking sports tours. Mass protest greeted the team's arrival at Jan Smuts airport. Further demonstrations were organized outside the grounds and hotels where the players played and stayed. Eight hundred people took part in a protest outside the city's cricket ground in Bloemfontein. Only 150 watched the game. The tour coincided with a watershed in the political history of South Africa (Guelke 1993: 155). On 2 February President de Klerk announced the dropping of the ban on the African National Congress (ANC), the Pan-Africanist Congress (PAC) and the South African Communist Party (SACP). On 11 February the current president, Nelson Mandela, was released from jail. On 14 February the tour organizer Ali Bacher announced that the rebel tour had been shortened. He argued that the South African Cricket Union (SACU) had decided to curtail the tour in support of the changes announced by President de Klerk on 2 February 1990. It was the beginning of a new phase in the development of South African sport.

Sport and nation-building in the rainbow nation

> In our efforts to create a better South Africa, sport could enhance the nation-building process, lessen the level of tension and contribute towards creating a healthy disciplined society. Sport affords our people opportunities to play, plan and work together. . . . We are proud that we can contribute to the healing of our land through the comradeship and exhilaration of sport.
>
> (Steve Tshwete, Minister of Sport in South Africa,
> *The Fixture* 1995: 18)

The dismantling of apartheid and the new South African politics of the 1990s were announced by then President F. W. de Klerk in February of 1990. The release of African National Congress leader Nelson Mandela was followed by the release of other political prisoners including the current minister of sport, Steve Tshwete. The reformist mood of the 1990s involved Mrs Thatcher (then British Conservative prime minister) asking the European Community to remove sanctions on South Africa and President Samaranch of the International Olympic Committee urging the IOC to welcome South Africa back into the world of sport. In April 1994 the first free elections took place with the voters returning Nelson Mandela as State President elect. The African National Congress in conjunction with the Government of National Unity set out a Reconstruction and Development Programme (RDP) based upon six key principles. Sport was viewed as being central to the process of nation-building, reconciliation, unity and development.

More specifically the role of sport within the RDP was such that: (i) all sport and recreation agencies had to reflect the needs of *all* South Africans: (ii) the restructuring of the nation through sport could not be left to individual sporting communities or individual governing bodies; and

(iii) sport and recreation were seen as activities through which under-privileged individuals and communities could be empowered (RDP 1994: Para. 3.5.2). By 1992 the nation had competed in the Olympic Games, the first time since 1964. However it was South Africa's participation as host nation to the 1995 rugby World Cup which gave the ideal platform for sport to take centre stage within the politics of nation-building in the rainbow nation. As South Africa prepared to host the rugby World Cup President Mandela spoke of the progress and winds of change that were sweeping through the country, telling the world that they would 'see the spirit of nation-building and reconciling, manifesting itself in every section of our community' (*Guardian* 21 May 1995: 13).

The need for reconciliation and nation-building is common in countries emerging from a period of conflict. This is particularly the case in those nations, such as South Africa, that have experienced not only apartheid but where national boundaries of religion, kinship and class have often been tempered by colonial rule and western-styled political ideologies. In newly transformed nations sport often becomes a vehicle for integration and a catalyst for nation-building. Those who have commented upon the relationship between sport, nationalism and culture have tended to rely upon a number of themes invariably dressed up in different disguises to suit particular contexts or events. At a general level a number of arguments might be mentioned as follows:

1   Sport helps to reinforce not only locality but also a national identity.
2   Sporting occasions provide a safety valve or outlet of emotional energy for frustrated peoples or the nation; sport is a substitute for political action.
3   Sport is an arena through which submerged nations can assert them-selves and play a role in international affairs.
4   Sport is not and never can be an island. The social ambience of rugby and every other game is shaped and moulded by that aspect of the nation or that sector of society that give it life and sustain it. A game has no class bias but people do.
5   There are better ways of celebrating a nation than football or rugby with their assumed democratic working class status. Sport often bolsters a working-class romanticism at odds with the nation's expe-rience as a country where social mobility is possible.
6   As a form of cultural politics sport helps to reinforce national consciousness.

Sport should not be exalted with an over-determined degree of political importance and yet it is necessary to recognize the nature and content of different notions of nationalism, expressions of nationhood or ideas about South Africa or indeed the complexity of sporting culture in the republic. The message of reconciliation and unity was certainly expressed by both the outgoing President de Klerk and the incoming Nelson Mandela. As the latter cast his vote in the 1994 election he reiterated that 'we have moved from an era of pessimism, division, limited opportunities, turmoil and conflict and we are starting a new era of hope, reconciliation and nation-building' (*Guardian* 28 April 1994: 14). The message on nation-building and reconciliation was firmly embedded within the narrative of the 1995 rugby World Cup. When the event opened in Cape Town on 25 May, the President had visited 'his boys' (*Guardian*, 26 May 1995: 1) in the city the day before, saying to them, 'you will help bind our country into a single unit . . . I used to wish the Springboks to lose. Not any more, oh no . . . You fellows now represent our whole country' (*Guardian*, 25 May 1995: 21). The narrative continued throughout the tournament which culminated in the final between South Africa and New Zealand on the 24 June. Prior to the match the President appeared on the pitch wearing a replica Springbok jersey complete with the number 6 of the team captain Francois Piennar. After the game the captain commented, 'When Mr. Mandela wore a duplicate of my shirt . . . that was one of the biggest thank-yous of my life. When he gave me the trophy, he said: thank you for what you have done for South Africa . . . but I told him that nobody has done as much for our country as him' (*Guardian*, 25 June 1995: 1). The South African journalist Donald Woods added that the actions of Mandela and Piennar had made the new Springboks acceptable to most blacks and the national concept real to most whites (*Guardian*, 2 July 1995: 10).

Concluding remarks

The minister of sport remains fairly clear about the task facing South African sport. At one level 33 million people have to be provided for in terms of facilities, opportunities and development. Yet sport in South Africa does not exist outwith the legal framework of the given constitution of the Republic of South Africa. Sport is not free to go its own way and in some cases establishment sports may have to pay for past injustices and what Steve Tshwete calls the 'Mortal wounds of Apartheid'. The power of capital in South Africa is such that the supporters of cricket and rugby may work within a post-apartheid era but the realities of contemporary South Africa are such that the spectres of the past still remain financially powerful although not politically or morally. The historical disadvantage which has burdened many sporting communities in South Africa is such that the normalization of sport in South Africa remains a millennium project. It is true that participation and success in international sport have contributed to a sense of nation but the hegemony of apartheid still remains with certain sporting organizations. For most of the twentieth century the realities of apartheid have been such that sport in South Africa has been a story of sport, racism and ethnicity.

Acknowledgements

The material presented in this chapter has been greatly assisted by information provided by Sam Ramsamy. We are grateful for his time and assistance.

References

Allison, L. (ed.) *The Changing Politics of Sport*, Manchester: Manchester University Press.

Apartheid: the facts (1983), London: International Defence and Aid Fund for South Africa.

Archer, R. and Bouillon, B. (1982) *The South African Games*, London: Zed Press.

Biko, S. B. (1979) *The Testimony of Steve Biko*, London: Routledge.

Booth, D. (1995) 'United sport: a united hegemony in South Africa', *International Journal of the History of Sport* (12)3: 105–24.

—— (1997) 'The South African Council on Sport and the political antinomies of the sports boycott', *Journal of African Studies* (23)1: 51–68.

Boshoff, G. B. E. (1997) 'Barefoot sports administrators: laying the foundations of sports development in South Africa', *Journal of Sports Management* 11: 69–79.

Gilimomee, H. and Schlemmer, L. (1993) *From Apartheid to Nation-Building: Contemporary South African Debates*, Oxford: Oxford University Press.

Guardian, various, 1994–7.

Guelke, A. (1993) 'Sport and the end of apartheid', in Allison, L. (ed.) *The Changing Politics of Sport*, Manchester: Manchester University Press, 151–70.

Jarvie, G. (1985) *Class, Race and Sport in South Africa's Political Economy*, London: Routledge.

—— (1989) 'Getting Gatting', *New Statesman and Society* 19 August: 16.

Kellas, J. G. (1991) *The Politics of Nationalism and Ethnicity*, London: Macmillan.

Lapchick, R. (1979) *The Politics of Race and International Sport: the Case of South Africa*, Westport, CT: Greenwood Press.

MacDonald, M. (1996) 'Power politics in the new South Africa', *Journal of African Studies* (22)2: 221–33.

Marks, S. and Trapido, S. (1987) *The Politics of Race, Class and Nationalism in Twentieth Century South Africa*, New York: Longman.

Ramsamy, S. (1982), *Apartheid: The Real Hurdle*, London: International Defence and Aid Fund for South Africa.

Riordan, J. (1986) 'State and Sport in Developing Societies', *International Review for the Sociology of Sport* 21: 287–309.

Scotsman 'South Africa's rand prize', 30 October 1997: 27.

South African Year Book 1985–1995.

Sunday Times (South Africa) 'Sport administrators are letting the side down', 5 October 1997: 3.

The Constitution of the Republic of South Africa (1996).

Zulu, P. and Booth, D. (1988) 'Black participation in South African sport: the case of Natal-KwaZulu, Maurice Webb Race Relations Unit', Working Paper, Durban: University of Natal.

Index

Note: Page numbers in **bold** type refer to Figures and those in *italic* refer to Tables.
Page numbers followed by 'n' refer to footnotes.